The Social Doctrine of the Catholic Church

[DID-uh-kay]

The *Didache* is the first known Christian catechesis. Written in the first century, the *Didache* is the earliest known Christian writing outside of Scripture. The name of the work, *"Didache,"* is indeed appropriate for such a catechesis because it comes from the Greek word for "teaching," and indicates that this writing contains the teaching of the Apostles.

The *Didache* is a catechetical summary of Christian sacraments, practices, and morality. Though written in the first century, its teaching is timeless. The *Didache* was probably written by the disciples of the Twelve Apostles, and it presents the Apostolic Faith as taught by those closest to Jesus Christ. This series of books takes the name of this early catechesis because it shares in the Church's mission of passing on that same Faith, in its rich entirety, to new generations.

Below is an excerpt from the *Didache* in which we see a clear example of its lasting message, a message that speaks to Christians of today as much as it did to the first generations of the Church. The world is different, but the struggle for holiness is the same. In the *Didache*, we are instructed to embrace virtue, to avoid sin, and to live the Beatitudes of our Lord.

> My child, flee from everything that is evil and everything that is like it. Do not be wrathful, for wrath leads to murder, nor jealous nor contentious nor quarrelsome, for from all these murder ensues.
>
> My child, do not be lustful, for lust leads to fornication, nor a filthy-talker nor a lewd-looker, for from all these adulteries ensue.
>
> My child, do not be an interpreter of omens, since it leads to idolatry, nor an enchanter nor an astrologer nor a magical purifier, nor wish to see them, for from all these idolatry arises.
>
> My child, do not be a liar, for lying leads to theft, nor avaricious nor conceited, for from all these thefts are produced.
>
> My child, do not be a complainer, since it leads to blasphemy, nor self-willed nor evil-minded, for from all these blasphemies are produced.
>
> Be meek, for the meek will inherit the earth.
>
> Be long-suffering and merciful and guileless and peaceable and good, and revere always the words you have heard.[1]

The *Didache* is the teaching of the Apostles and, as such, it is the teaching of the Church. Accordingly, this book series makes extensive use of the most recent comprehensive catechesis provided to us, the *Catechism of the Catholic Church*. The *Didache* series also relies heavily on Sacred Scripture, the lives of the saints, the Fathers of the Church, and the teaching of Vatican II as witnessed by the pontificates of St. John Paul II, Benedict XVI, and Francis.

---

1. Swett, Ben H. "The Didache (The Teaching)." ©January 30, 1998. http://bswett.com/1998-01Didache.html

The Social Doctrine of the Catholic Church

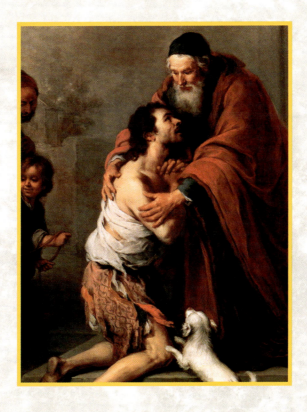

Author: Mike Aquilina
Publisher: Rev. James Socias

MIDWEST THEOLOGICAL FORUM
Downers Grove, Illinois

Published in the United States of America by

Midwest Theological Forum
4340 Cross Street, Suite 1
Downers Grove, IL 60515

Tel: 630-541-8519
Fax: 331-777-5819
mail@mwtf.org
www.theologicalforum.org

Copyright ©2013, 2014 Rev. James Socias
All Rights Reserved
First Edition
ISBN 978-1-936045-96-9

Author: Mike Aquilina
Publisher: Rev. James Socias
Editor in Chief: Jeffrey Cole
Editorial Board: Rev. James Socias, Rev. Peter V. Armenio, Dr. Scott Hahn, Jeffrey Cole
Contributing Editor: Gerald Korson
Design and Production: Marlene Burrell, Jane Heineman of April Graphics, Highland Park, Illinois

Acknowledgements

Excerpts from the English translation of the *Catechism of the Catholic Church* for the United States of America, copyright ©1994, United States Catholic Conference, Inc.—Libreria Editrice Vaticana. Used with permission.

Excerpts from the English translation of the *Catechism of the Catholic Church: Modifications from the Editio Typica*, copyright ©1997, United States Catholic Conference, Inc.—Libreria Editrice Vaticana. Used with permission.

Scripture quotations are adapted from the *Revised Standard Version of the Bible*, copyright ©1946, 1952, 1971, and the *New Revised Standard Version of the Bible*, copyright ©1989, by the Division of Christian Education of the National Council of the Churches of Christ in the United States of America, and are used by permission. All rights reserved.

Excerpts from the *Code of Canon Law, Latin/English Edition*, are used with permission, copyright ©1983 Canon Law Society of America, Washington, DC.

Citations of official Church documents from Neuner, Josef, SJ and Dupuis, Jacques, SJ, eds., *The Christian Faith: Doctrinal Documents of the Catholic Church*, 5th ed. (New York: Alba House, 1992). Used with permission.

Excerpts from *Vatican II: The Conciliar and Post Conciliar Documents, New Revised Edition* edited by Austin Flannery, OP, copyright ©1992, Costello Publishing Company, Inc., Northport, NY, are used with permission of the publisher, all rights reserved. No part of these excerpts may be reproduced, stored in a retrieval system, or transmitted in any form or by any means—electronic, mechanical, photocopying, recording or otherwise, without express written permission of Costello Publishing Company.

Disclaimer: The editor of this book has attempted to give proper credit to all sources used in the text and illustrations. Any miscredit or lack of credit is unintended and will be corrected in the next edition.

Library of Congress Cataloging-in-Publication Data
Aquilina, Mike.
    The social doctrine of the Catholic Church / Mike Aquilina. — First edition.
        pages cm — (The Didache series)
    Includes index.
    ISBN 978-1-936045-96-9
    1. Christian sociology — Catholic Church — Textbooks. 2. Catholic Church — Doctrines — Textbooks. I. Title.
BX1753.A68 2013
261.8088'282 — dc23

                                                                                                                  2013016074

> The Subcommittee on the Catechism, United States Conference of Catholic Bishops, has found that this catechetical high school text, copyright 2013, is in conformity with the *Catechism of the Catholic Church* and that it fulfills the requirements of Course C of the *Doctrinal Elements of a Curriculum Framework for the Development of Catechetical Materials for Young People of High School Age.*

In accordance with c. 824, permission to publish is granted on January 28, 2013 by Rev. Msgr. John F. Canary, Vicar General of the Archdiocese of Chicago. Permission to publish is an official declaration of ecclesiastical authority that the material is free from doctrinal and moral error. No legal responsibility is assumed by the grant of this permission.

Printed in Canada

TABLE OF CONTENTS

viii **Abbreviations used for the Books of the Bible**

viii **General Abbreviations**

ix **Preface**

211 **Art and Photo Credits**

215 **Index**

1 **Introduction: Our Social Nature**
2 Because We Are Social Beings, We Need One Another
5 It Is Not Good to Be Alone
6 *Sidebar:* What the *Catechism* Teaches About Original Sin
7 The Old Testament: Learning to Live as God's Chosen People
8 Social Dimensions of Redemption
9 The New Testament: A Society of Heaven and Earth
10 Conclusion
11 *The Saints: Pillars of the Church* The Twelve Apostles: How to Live Together in Peace
13 *Supplementary Reading*
15 *Vocabulary*
16 *Study Questions*
16 *Practical Exercises*
17 *From the Catechism*

19 **Chapter 1: The Heavenly Model for Earthly Society**
20 Christian Charity Begins in God Himself
22 The Principle of Love
23 *Sidebar:* Bl. Teresa of Calcutta: Her God Is Called Love
24 The Blessed Trinity: Our Origin and Goal
26 The Holy Spirit: Our Bond of Love
27 *Sidebar:* St. Damien of Molokai: A Leper Among the Lepers
28 The Church: The Body of Christ
30 *Sidebar:* Ecumenism: That All May Be One
31 The Blessed Trinity: The Pattern of Social Life
32 Conclusion
33 *The Saints: Pillars of the Church* St. John Paul II: Witnesses to Love
35 *Supplementary Reading*
40 *Vocabulary*
41 *Study Questions*
41 *Practical Exercises*
42 *From the Catechism*

43 **Chapter 2: Justice and Rights: The Foundation of All Order in the World**
44 Justice and Law
45 Defining Justice
46 Justice Is Personal
46 Rights Precede Justice
47 *Sidebar:* John Howard Griffin: Raceless Vision
48 Types of Justice
49 Commutative Justice
49 Legal Justice
49 Distributive Justice
50 What Rights Do We Have?
51 *Sidebar:* Dr. Bernard Nathanson and the Right to Life
53 Justice in the Bible
55 Conclusion
56 *The Saints: Pillars of the Church* St. Thomas Aquinas, On Justice
58 *Supplementary Reading*
62 *Vocabulary*
63 *Study Questions*
64 *Practical Exercises*
65 *From the Catechism*

67 **Chapter 3: The Church Teaches Us How to Live**
68 The Popes and Councils Teach Authoritatively on Social Concerns
69 A Voice of Social Conscience
70 Magisterium

TABLE OF CONTENTS

- 71 The Age of Revolutions
- 72 Responding to Revolutions
- 73 Pope Leo XIII, *Rerum Novarum*
- 74 Building on *Rerum Novarum*: The Social Encyclicals
- 75 *Sidebar:* Cesar Chavez: The Son of *Rerum Novarum*
- 76 Pope Pius XI, *Quadragesimo Anno*
- 77 St. John XXIII, *Mater et Magistra*
- 77 St. John XXIII, *Pacem in Terris*
- 78 Pope Paul VI, *Populorum Progressio*
- 79 St. John Paul II, *Laborem Exercens*
- 80 St. John Paul II, *Sollicitudo Rei Socialis*
- 81 St. John Paul II, *Centesimus Annus*
- 81 St. John Paul II, *Evangelium Vitæ*
- 82 Pope Benedict XVI, *Deus Caritas Est*
- 83 *Sidebar:* Dorothy Day: A Radical Witness
- 84 Pope Benedict XVI, *Caritatis in Veritate*
- 84 Second Vatican Council, *Gaudium et Spes*
- 85 Common Concerns
- 85 Efforts of the U.S. Hierarchy
- 86 Conclusion
- 87 *The Saints: Pillars of the Church* Pope St. Clement I: On Sharing What You Have Been Given
- 88 *Supplementary Reading*
- 93 *Vocabulary*
- 94 *Study Questions*
- 95 *Practical Exercises*
- 95 *From the Catechism*

- 97 **Chapter 4: Principles of Catholic Social Doctrine**
- 98 The Church's Teaching Rests on a Solid Foundation
- 100 Human Dignity
- 101 The Common Good
- 104 Subsidiarity
- 105 Solidarity
- 106 *Sidebar:* Lech Walesa and the Power of Solidarity
- 107 Secondary Principles
- 108 *Sidebar:* Shahbaz Bhatti: Solidarity Among Persecuted Minorities
- 109 Conclusion
- 110 *The Saints: Pillars of the Church* Bl. Juana Maria Condesa Lluch
- 111 *Supplementary Reading*
- 114 *Vocabulary*
- 115 *Study Questions*
- 115 *Practical Exercises*
- 116 *From the Catechism*

- 117 **Chapter 5: Major Themes in Catholic Social Doctrine**
- 118 Clear Messages Delivered with Urgency and Frequency
- 119 The Dignity of Human Life
- 122 The Call to Family, Community, and Participation
- 125 Responsibilities and Rights
- 126 Preferential Option for the Poor
- 128 Private Property and the Universal Destination of Goods
- 129 *The Saints: Pillars of the Church* St. Gregory of Nazianzus, We Are All Poor and Needy
- 131 The Dignity of Work
- 133 *Sidebar:* The Roots of the European Union
- 134 Universal Solidarity
- 137 *Sidebar:* St. Luigi Guanella: Helping People with Disabilities Enjoy Life Abundantly
- 138 Stewardship of God's Creation
- 140 Conclusion
- 141 *The Saints: Pillars of the Church* St. John Chrysostom, A Warning to the Wealthy
- 142 *Supplementary Readings*
- 146 *Vocabulary*
- 147 *Study Questions*
- 147 *Practical Exercises*
- 148 *From the Catechism*

TABLE OF CONTENTS

149 **Chapter 6:**
Law, Love, Sin, and Virtue
150 The Commandments and the Beatitudes: Classic Biblical Expressions of Social Doctrine
151 Personal Sin and Social Sin
154 The Ten Commandments
155 The First Three Commandments
157 The Family: Where Social Order Begins
159 Choose Life
160 *Sidebar:* Baudouin: A King and His Conscience
161   Abortion
161   Euthanasia, Suicide, and Assisted Suicide
162   Self-Defense and Capital Punishment
163   Scandal
163 Just War
164 Holy Purity
165 *Sidebar:* Bl. Franz Jagerstatter: Conscientious Objector and Martyr
167 What Goods Are Good For
169 Trust and Truth
170 *Sidebar:* Giorgio La Pira: The Saintly Statist
172 Abundant Life: The Beatitudes
175 Conclusion
176 *The Saints: Pillars of the Church* St. Thomas Aquinas
177 *Supplementary Readings*
181 *Vocabulary*
182 *Study Questions*
183 *Practical Exercises*
184 *From the Catechism*

185 **Chapter 7:**
Today's Challenges
186 Christ Wants a Civilization of Love; We Must Overcome the Obstacles
189 *Sidebar:* The Blessed Virgin Mary: Solidarity with the World
190 Secularism
191 *Sidebar:* Bl. Salvador Huerta Gutierrez: Martyr and "Wizard of Cars"
192 Materialism
193 Individualism
195 *Sidebar:* St. Gianna Molla: Medic and Mother
197 Conclusion
198 *The Saints: Pillars of the Church* St. Clement of Alexandria
199 *Supplementary Readings*
208 *Vocabulary*
208 *Study Questions*
209 *Practical Exercises*
209 *From the Catechism*

The Good Shepherd by Plockhorst.

ABBREVIATIONS USED FOR THE BOOKS OF THE BIBLE

OLD TESTAMENT

Genesis	Gn	Tobit	Tb	Ezekiel	Ez
Exodus	Ex	Judith	Jdt	Daniel	Dn
Leviticus	Lv	Esther	Est	Hosea	Hos
Numbers	Nm	1 Maccabees	1 Mc	Joel	Jl
Deuteronomy	Dt	2 Maccabees	2 Mc	Amos	Am
Joshua	Jos	Job	Jb	Obadiah	Ob
Judges	Jgs	Psalms	Ps	Jonah	Jon
Ruth	Ru	Proverbs	Prv	Micah	Mi
1 Samuel	1 Sm	Ecclesiastes	Eccl	Nahum	Na
2 Samuel	2 Sm	Song of Songs	Sg	Habakkuk	Hb
1 Kings	1 Kgs	Wisdom	Wis	Zephaniah	Zep
2 Kings	2 Kgs	Sirach	Sir	Haggai	Hg
1 Chronicles	1 Chr	Isaiah	Is	Zechariah	Zec
2 Chronicles	2 Chr	Jeremiah	Jer	Malachi	Mal
Ezra	Ezr	Lamentations	Lam		
Nehemiah	Neh	Baruch	Bar		

NEW TESTAMENT

Matthew	Mt	Ephesians	Eph	Hebrews	Heb
Mark	Mk	Philippians	Phil	James	Jas
Luke	Lk	Colossians	Col	1 Peter	1 Pt
John	Jn	1 Thessalonians	1 Thes	2 Peter	2 Pt
Acts of the Apostles	Acts	2 Thessalonians	2 Thes	1 John	1 Jn
Romans	Rom	1 Timothy	1 Tm	2 John	2 Jn
1 Corinthians	1 Cor	2 Timothy	2 Tm	3 John	3 Jn
2 Corinthians	2 Cor	Titus	Ti	Jude	Jude
Galatians	Gal	Philemon	Phlm	Revelation	Rev

GENERAL ABBREVIATIONS

AG	*Ad Gentes Divinitus* (Decree on the Church's Missionary Activity)
CA	*Centesimus Annus* (On the Hundredth Anniversary)
CCC	*Catechism of the Catholic Church*
CDF	Congregation for the Doctrine of the Faith
CIC	Code of Canon Law (*Codex Iuris Canonici*)
CPG	*Solemn Profession of Faith*: Credo of the People of God
CT	*Catechesi Tradendæ* (On Catechesis in our Time)
DCE	*Deus Caritas Est* (God is Love)
DD	*Dies Domini* (The Lord's Day)
DH	*Dignitatis Humanæ* (Declaration on Religious Freedom)
DoV	*Donum Vitæ* (Respect for Human Life)
DV	*Dei Verbum* (Dogmatic Constitution on Divine Revelation)
DS	Denzinger-Schonmetzer, *Enchiridion Symbolorum, definitionum et declarationum de rebus fidei et morum* (1985)
EV	*Evangelium Vitæ* (The Gospel of Life)
FC	*Familiaris Consortio* (On the Family)
GS	*Gaudium et Spes* (Pastoral Constitution on the Church in the Modern World)
HV	*Humanæ Vitæ* (On Human Life)
IOE	*Iura et Bona* (Declaration on Euthanasia)
LE	*Laborem Exercens* (On Human Work)
LG	*Lumen Gentium* (Dogmatic Constitution on the Church)
MF	*Mysterium Fidei* (The Mystery of Faith)
PH	*Persona Humana* (Declaration on Sexual Ethics)
PL	J.P. Migne, ed., *Patrologia Latina* (Paris: 1841-1855)
PT	*Pacem in Terris* (On Establishing Universal Peace)
QA	*Quadragesimo Anno* (The Fortieth Year)
RP	*Reconciliatio et Pænitentia* (On Reconciliation and Penance)
RH	*Redemptor Hominis* (The Redeemer of Man)
SC	*Sacrosanctum Concilium* (The Constitution on the Sacred Liturgy)
SRS	*Sollicitudo Rei Socialis* (On Social Concerns)
SS	*Spe Salvi* (In Hope We Are Saved)
USCCB	United States Conference of Catholic Bishops
VS	*Veritatis Splendor* (Splendor of the Truth)

Preface

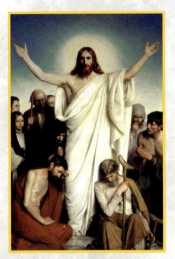

Politics, economics, government, activism—there was a time not long ago when many people kept lively hopes that movements in these fields could bring about a sort of salvation. Poverty and hunger would vanish, wars would cease, people would voluntarily share their possessions, and there would be no more divisions in the human family.

In the eighteenth and nineteenth centuries, great thinkers presented new hypotheses about human fulfillment and social order. Many people placed great hope in various movements that arose to bring about these changes, some even dying for the sake of their movements and their ideals. Others were killed for the sake of a movement or ideal simply because they were perceived to be enemies of the revolution.

It is fair to say that many of the ideals of those centuries have exhausted themselves. The twenty-first century includes a strain of political cynicism, marked by weariness and wariness. After so many bitter disappointments, it has become difficult for many people to be hopeful about politics, economics, government, and activism.

Yet Christians are never without a reason to hope. Some people proffer a caricature of the Christian attitude as "otherworldly" because we believe in an afterlife and a future resurrection of the dead. Those are indeed great and powerful realities—and we are grateful for them—but they are only the bare minimum of the things for which we hope.

Our hope transcends history, most importantly because we believe that God has entered history and dwelt among us. The Almighty and Eternal God took on our human nature and lived a human life in a certain region of the world at a certain historical generation. He came to transform people and peoples. Moreover, he promised to be with his disciples always, until the end of time.

He came to change the way we live our lives, individually and together. He presented a body of social doctrine as "Good News," *not* as a political platform, economic manifesto, or rabble-rouser's pamphlet.

Christianity alone offers a vision of human beings and society that is both transcendent and immanent. It is clear-eyed and realistic about history yet always focused on every human being's ultimate fulfillment and history's final end. Christians do not abandon the world when the current political systems and parties become exhausted and empty. Christians do not abandon the marketplace simply because the economic order is crumbling.

The Christian vision is compelling, increasingly attractive even to people who do not share the fullness of our faith. Not long ago, Justin Welby, the Protestant Anglican archbishop of Canterbury, described Catholic social teaching as "one of the greatest treasures that the churches globally have to offer." Yet, he added, "many Catholics don't know much about it." He told Vatican Radio that Catholic social doctrine presents "a comprehensively thought-through structure of approach to the way we order society…a way that reflects Christian teaching, Christian values: the love, the integrity of Jesus Christ."

The social doctrine of the Catholic Church should be an essential part of our lives for it is up to us to build a just society for our families, friends, communities, country, and world. It is my hope that this text can serve as a useful guide in helping to make the world a more just, more charitable, and more prosperous place for everybody to grow in the love of God.

Mike Aquilina
April 9, 2013

The Eleusa or *Virgin of Tenderness* Icon.

Social Doctrine of the Catholic Church
INTRODUCTION

Our Social Nature

Catholic social doctrine is the application of Christ's teaching to the many problems and opportunities of living in communities.

Social Doctrine of the Catholic Church

INTRODUCTION

Our Social Nature

Charity is at the heart of the Church's social doctrine. Every responsibility and every commitment spelt out by that doctrine is derived from charity which, according to the teaching of Jesus, is the synthesis of the entire Law (cf. Mt 22:36-40). It gives real substance to the personal relationship with God and with neighbor; it is the principle not only of micro-relationships (with friends, with family members or within small groups) but also of macro-relationships (social, economic and political ones). For the Church, instructed by the Gospel, charity is everything because…"God is love" (*Deus Caritas Est*): everything has its origin in God's love, everything is shaped by it, everything is directed towards it. Love is God's greatest gift to humanity, it is his promise and our hope.

—Pope Benedict XVI, *Caritas in Veritate*, 2

IN THIS CHAPTER, WE WILL ADDRESS SEVERAL QUESTIONS:

- What does it mean to be social?
- What does the Genesis creation story teach us about human relationships?
- What does Scripture teach us about living in society?
- How does the Old Testament's social teaching relate to the New Testament's?
- What does the Church say about living in society?
- What is the subject of this book?

BECAUSE WE ARE SOCIAL BEINGS, WE NEED ONE ANOTHER

Our human nature makes us social. From birth, we come to understand the world around us as we share life with others. From other people, we gain knowledge and learn life skills. In the company of others we laugh, share our experiences, and forget our sorrows. They confirm us in what we believe and help us to correct our misconceptions. These interactions help us to grow and sharpen our minds. In short, they form us.

Many of the greatest pleasures in life come from human interaction. For most people, family life is a primary source of happiness and security; and genuine friendship, which requires at least two people, is a source of great joy—and it is healthiest when those two people together seek a widening circle of friends.

OUR SOCIAL NATURE

The People of God gather together to worship in St. Peter's Square.
Catholic social doctrine has the power to change the world for the better, but the change must take place first and fundamentally in the most ordinary human encounters and exchanges.

As human persons, we live not just for our next meal. We live for company and conversation. In fact, we enjoy the next meal much more if it is an occasion for company and conversation with friends and family.

To be human is to live in relationships. As the poet John Donne observed long ago, "No man is an island, entire of itself; every man is a piece of the continent." We can exist apart from relationships with family and friends, but we will not be fulfilled. This is why loneliness, isolation, and rejection are painful to us. They go against our nature, which is social and communal. At the extreme end of isolation, prisoners who have undergone long-term solitary confinement testify that it is more painful than any physical torment they ever had to endure.

Even pursuits that seem asocial or anti-social require social cooperation on a large scale. For example, playing a video game by oneself is only possible because of vast social structures: Someone designed the game, a company paid many other people to manufacture it, and then it was distributed to stores, which are staffed by clerks, managers, and checkout personnel.

Even the legendary shipwrecked traveler, stranded alone on a desert island, could not survive without the bonds of community, even if they were not presently available. How else would it be possible to overcome the many challenges of survival except by using skills learned from others?

The many relationships in our lives vary in complexity. Some, like family relations, are fairly simple and natural, and the role of each family member is learned by custom both within the unique family structure itself and by society in general. But family is only the beginning, the fundamental building block, of human society. People also, and inevitably, organize themselves into neighborhoods, schools, clubs, teams, corporations, towns, and even nation states; and these gatherings require a great deal of formality and governance. People who live together need to agree upon some common values, and they need to obey some common laws.

THE SOCIAL DOCTRINE OF THE CATHOLIC CHURCH

As the *Catechism of the Catholic Church* teaches:

> The human person needs to live in society. Society is not for him an extraneous addition but a requirement of his nature. Through the exchange with others, mutual service and dialogue with his brethren, man develops his potential; he thus responds to his vocation.[1] (CCC 1879)

Because we are social by nature, people need to find ways of living together—of tolerating differences, ensuring justice and fairness, and keeping order. Much of human history is the story of attempts—some successful and some disastrous—to bring order to human relations.

As a result of Original Sin, humans have a fallen nature, and human knowledge (especially self-knowledge) is limited. In fact, without divine guidance, truth itself is subject to dispute and disagreement, and, therefore, attempts to bring order to human relations proceed by trial and error.

God created human nature. God has *revealed* his moral law to humanity and continues to guide human relations through the Catholic Church.

It is a rich body of thought that has had a profound influence on the way the world regards love and family, law and justice, war and peace, wealth and poverty, rights and duties, freedom and obligation. The same body of thought also has much to say about matters of such immediate personal relevance as fairness, friendship, dating and courtship, education, work, and career.

"O God…through the good things which you richly bestow upon all, each human person may be brought to perfection, every division may be removed, and equity and justice may be established."
(Mass "29. For the Progress of Peoples," Collect, *Roman Missal*, Third Edition)

> The Church's social teaching comprises a body of doctrine, which is articulated as the Church interprets events in the course of history, with the assistance of the Holy Spirit, in the light of the whole of what has been revealed by Jesus Christ.[2] This teaching can be more easily accepted by men of good will, the more the faithful let themselves be guided by it. (CCC 2422)

Catholic social doctrine is the subject of this book. We will begin by considering the theological foundations of the teaching. Like all Christian doctrine, Catholic social teaching proceeds from a proper understanding of God. We will then define key terminology and study what saints and scholars have had to say about basic concepts such as justice and rights. Thus equipped, we will be ready to look at how Catholic social thought has developed throughout history, but especially in the centuries since the Industrial Revolution, when social circumstances underwent radical transformation. The Popes and bishops responded to these societal changes with a remarkable series of documents, which we will encounter in an overview. Afterward, we will study the principles of Catholic social teaching and their application in our world and its cultures, nations, and economies, but more particularly in our lives, homes, neighborhoods, and workplaces. As St. John Paul II wrote in *Sollicitudo Rei Socialis*, an encyclical about the Church's concern for the social order:

> The teaching and spreading of her social doctrine are part of the Church's evangelizing mission. And since it is a doctrine aimed at guiding people's behavior, it consequently gives rise to a "commitment to justice," according to each individual's role, vocation and circumstances. (*SRS* 41)

Catholic social doctrine has the power to change the world for the better, but the change must take place *first and fundamentally* in the most ordinary human encounters and exchanges.

IT IS NOT GOOD TO BE ALONE

The first and foundational account of human nature is found in the story of Creation in the Book of Genesis. In this deeply symbolic story, we learn many basic principles that form our understanding of the social order.

- ✛ We learn that God is the origin of all creation. Through his Word, he spoke the universe and all it contains into existence and saw that it was good. Human beings are not an accidental product of random events but rather the summit of God's Creation.
- ✛ We learn that God has given mankind "dominion" over the world and everything in it—all the animals and "every living thing that moves upon the earth," and every plant and natural resource (Gn 1:26-29).
- ✛ We learn that God created our first parents in a state of marriage and that man and woman have roles equal in dignity and characterized by complementarity.
- ✛ We learn that the family is the basic structure or cell of human society, and that God instructed our first parents to "multiply" and "fill the earth" (Gn 1:28).
- ✛ Thus, we learn that God intended that the human creature would not just be *one* person but *many*, and that those many would live not alone in solitude but together in society. The Lord God himself puts this in emphatic terms, saying: "It is not good that the man should be alone" (Gn 2:18).
- ✛ We learn, moreover, that there are fundamental principles for human society. Human nature is not haphazard, but ordered—governed by divinely appointed laws. God instructed the first humans what they were to do to live in harmony with him, with one another, and with creation.

The Expulsion from the Garden of Eden (detail) by Masaccio. Adam and Eve's failure was catastrophic.

The conditions necessary for human fulfillment can only be found in society. For example, family, friendship, companionship, and love cannot be experienced in isolation; they require the participation of more than one person. Within this same society, however, we can also find the preconditions for envy, betrayal, neglect, and even murder. These, too, are possible only when there is more than one person involved. In fact, as the story of the first human family develops in the Book of Genesis, these sins and vices start appearing horribly fast.

In the third chapter of Genesis, we see the demonic serpent invade the Garden of Eden and tempt Eve to sin. God had instructed our first parents not to eat of the fruit of the Tree of the Knowledge of Good and Evil. However, they heeded the deceptions of the Devil and disobeyed God.

Adam and Eve's failure was catastrophic. In Christian tradition, the sin of our first parents is known as "Original Sin," and its consequences are individual, social, and universal. Adam and Eve—and all of their descendants, who inherit the stain of Original Sin (excepting Jesus Christ and the Blessed Virgin Mary)—were alienated from God and in need of salvation. While humanity had been made stewards of all creation, the world now rebelled against human dominion, and work became burdensome. The Apostle Paul summarized the situation:

Sin came into the world through one man and death through sin. (Rom 5:12)

Humans, moreover, grew increasingly alienated from one another as sin increased, one crime of disobedience to God initiating another. Adam and Eve's eldest son, Cain, envied his younger brother, Abel, whose sacrifice found greater favor in the eyes of God, and murdered him. When God came to Cain and asked, "Where is Abel your brother?" (Gn 4:9), Cain responded, "I do not know; am I my brother's keeper?" (Gn 4:9). Cain's question goes unanswered.

Cain's many vices—envy, selfishness, unconcern for others, injustice, and insincerity—are negative qualities made possible only when people are living with others in society. They emerge here, in this primordial story, as hallmarks of sins against others and against the human community.

WHAT THE *CATECHISM* TEACHES ABOUT ORIGINAL SIN

✢ By his sin Adam, as the first man, lost the original holiness and justice he had received from God, not only for himself but for all human beings. (CCC 416)

✢ Adam and Eve transmitted to their descendants a human nature wounded by their own first sin and hence deprived of original holiness and justice; this deprivation is called "original sin." (CCC 417)

✢ As a result of original sin, human nature is weakened in its powers; subject to ignorance, suffering, and the domination of death; and inclined to sin (This inclination is called "concupiscence."). (CCC 418)

✢ The doctrine of original sin, closely connected with that of redemption by Christ, provides lucid discernment of man's situation and activity in the world. By our first parents' sin, the devil has acquired a certain domination over man, even though man remains free. Original sin entails "captivity under the power of him who thenceforth had the power of death, that is, the devil." [3] Ignorance of the fact that man has a wounded nature inclined to evil gives rise to serious errors in the areas of education, politics, social action,[4] and morals. (CCC 407)

✢ The consequences of original sin and of all men's personal sins put the world as a whole in the sinful condition aptly described in St. John's expression, "the sin of the world." [5] This expression can also refer to the negative influence exerted on people by communal situations and social structures that are the fruit of men's sins.[6] (CCC 408)

✢ This dramatic situation of "the whole world [which] is in the power of the evil one" [7] makes man's life a battle:

> The whole of man's history has been the story of dour combat with the powers of evil, stretching, so our Lord tells us, from the very dawn of history until the last day. Finding himself in the midst of the battlefield man has to struggle to do what is right, and it is at great cost to himself, and aided by God's grace, that he succeeds in achieving his own inner integrity.[8] (CCC 409)

The Fall of Man (detail) by Goltzius.

Noah Sacrificing after the Deluge by West.
"'When the bow is in the clouds, I will look upon it and remember the everlasting covenant between God and every living creature of all flesh that is upon the earth.' God said to Noah, 'This is the sign of the covenant which I have established between me and all flesh that is upon the earth.'" (Gn 9:16-17)

THE OLD TESTAMENT: LEARNING TO LIVE AS GOD'S CHOSEN PEOPLE

Following the sin of Adam and Eve, God did not abandon humanity. Rather, he promised a Redeemer who would one day bruise the head of the serpent. In a passage of Scripture known as the *Protoevangelium*, God told Satan:

> I will put enmity between you and the woman, and between your seed and her seed; he shall bruise your head, and you shall bruise his heel. (Gn 3:15)

As Christians, we recognize Mary as the woman whose Son, Jesus Christ, defeated sin and death in his sacrifice of the Cross.

> The Christian tradition sees in this passage an announcement of the "New Adam" who, because he "became obedient unto death, even death on a cross," makes amends superabundantly for the disobedience of Adam.[9] Furthermore many Fathers and Doctors of the Church have seen the woman announced in the *Protoevangelium* as Mary, the mother of Christ, the "new Eve." Mary benefited first of all and uniquely from Christ's victory over sin: she was preserved from all stain of original sin and by a special grace of God committed no sin of any kind during her whole earthly life.[10] (CCC 411)

As seen in the story of Cain and Abel, sin multiplied as people abused their free will to reject God and his plan for creation. As a result, human society became inundated with evil. God permitted them to suffer the consequences of sin—pain and sorrow—in order to lead them to desire the peace and fulfillment that can only be reached in communion with God by "a new participation in grace" made possible by Christ's Paschal Mystery (cf. CCC 654).

Throughout the rest of the Old Testament, we see the history of salvation slowly unfold as God prepared his people for the Incarnation of his Son, Jesus Christ. For example, God chose messengers to teach his people how to live as true children of God.

Thus, God entered into a covenant with Noah to renew a world cleansed of sin (cf. Gn 9) "part by part" by giving "expression to the principle of divine economy toward the 'nations'" (cf. CCC 56). The division of mankind into nations was intended to "limit the pride of a fallen humanity" (cf. CCC 57). The Noahic covenant, which foreshadowed our new life in Baptism (cf. CCC 1094), would remain in effect until the new covenant established by Christ. Generations later, God summoned Abraham from among the idolatrous people in the land of Ur (cf. Gn 12) and created another covenant: God promised that Abraham's descendants, issuing from the Twelve Tribes of Israel, would be as numerous as the stars of the sky. In the time of Moses, God liberated the whole nation of Israel from slavery in the land of Egypt and gave them the Law that was to govern their relationship with him and their neighbors.

Social Dimensions of Redemption

God created humanity with a social nature, and, thus, the sin of Adam and Eve had consequences on the social order. For this reason, God's plan of redemption would also have a social dimension.

With each chosen leader, God revealed more and more of his moral law's application to social relations. To Noah, this law was very basic: It restored dominion over the earth, prohibited murder, and established rules for the use of the earth's resources for food.

As the descendants of Noah proved unwilling to keep these laws, however, sin continued to multiply. Thus, through Moses, God revealed a very detailed and demanding legal code. The Law of Moses governed all relations with God and in human society, prescribing rules for the sharing of meals, for the keeping of a family home, for fair commerce in a tribal setting, and so on. By observing the Law, people could avoid sin. The problem remained, however, that many of the people were not willing to follow God's Law, and so they committed acts that led to injustice, inequity, and widespread social misery.

Following the establishment of Israel as a nation, God sent numerous prophets to urge his people to change their ways and turn from injustice to charity. In addition to calling the people to repent and to worship the one, true God, they called for special care of the most vulnerable members of society:

Old Testament prophets sent by God called for special care of the most vulnerable members of society.

> Thus says the Lord: Do justice and righteousness, and deliver from the hand of the oppressor him who has been robbed. And do no wrong or violence to the alien, the fatherless, and the widow, nor shed innocent blood in this place. (Jer 22:3)

Indeed, God judges wrongdoers harshly:

> I will be a swift witness against…adulterers, against those who swear falsely, against those who oppress the hireling in his wages, the widow and the orphan, against those who thrust aside the sojourner. (Mal 3:5)

The prophets foretold a day when God himself would give his people the power to obey the law. On that day, all the ills of society would be healed—poverty, dissension, division, hunger, homelessness, crime, and war—and God would restore order and prosperity to his people. Isaiah saw such deliverance in terms of a great banquet to which everyone was invited:

> The Lord of hosts will make for all peoples a feast of fat things, a feast of wine on the lees, of fat things full of marrow. (Is 25:6)

In that day, society would enjoy stability, like "an immovable tent, whose stakes will never be plucked up, nor will any of its cords be broken" (Is 33:20). Even the nonhuman aspects of creation would be repaired and returned to man's dominion.

> The wolf and the lamb shall feed together, the lion shall eat straw like the ox...They shall not hurt or destroy in all my holy mountain, says the Lord. (Is 65:25)

These were extravagant promises, and they could only be brought about by God's power. Thus, God's Chosen People awaited the arrival of God's *Anointed One*—in Hebrew, *Messiah* (pronounced *Moshiach*); in Greek, *Christos*. The Messiah, or Christ, would establish a heavenly Kingdom on earth, and he would reign over it in peace as King of Kings.

Since God created the world with a deeply social dimension, sin, too, has had an all-pervading social consequence. Thus, mankind's redemption—salvation—would also include a social dimension.

THE NEW TESTAMENT: A SOCIETY OF HEAVEN AND EARTH

In the fullness of time, God sent his Only-Begotten Son, Jesus Christ, to reconcile humanity to himself and to establish his Kingdom on earth. While the promises made by the prophets might have seemed extravagant, the reality of God made flesh exceeded all expectations. Christ's mission was to bring peace not just to the Chosen People but to all people of all nations and of all times. As an essential part of his plan, Christ founded the Church, his own Mystical Body, which would be universal, transcending nations and borders, and uniting the populations that had been divided by sin and treachery down through the centuries.

The early Church, as seen in the Acts of the Apostles, was a "perfect society" comprising imperfect men and women who strived daily to put the teachings of Christ into practice.

> Now the company of those who believed were of one heart and soul, and no one said that any of the things which he possessed was his own, but they had everything in common (Acts 4:32);... and they sold their possessions and goods and distributed them to all, as any had need. (Acts 2:35)

Pentecost (detail) by Zurbaran.
Christ founded the Church, his own Mystical Body, which would be universal, transcending nations and borders, and uniting the populations that had been divided by sin and treachery down through the centuries.

Baptism of Christ by Navarrete.
God sent his Son, Jesus Christ, to redeem humanity and set people free, restoring unity, peace, and order to the world.

Through Baptism, we are given new life in Christ and are formed into a new people, a new household, a new city, the heavenly Jerusalem. In his Church, Christ unites all people through Baptism and strengthens this communion with God and one another in the Sacrament of the Eucharist (cf. 1 Cor 10:17).

The New Testament presents the Church as a communion of the angels and saints in Heaven, who worship and act harmoniously with believers living on earth (see Heb 12:1, 22-24; Rev 7:9). This Communion of Saints also includes the souls in Purgatory, i.e., those faithful who have died in the grace and love of God and are being purified before entering Heaven because nothing unclean can enter heavenly society (cf. Rev 21:27).

While this Communion of Saints is itself a great thing, Christ's salvation offers still more, even in social terms, because he has restored the communion with God that was lost through Original Sin. In Christ, we are now adopted *children of God*. With sins forgiven and restored to God's friendship, we are called to a life of holiness.

Catholic social doctrine is the application of Christ's teaching to the many problems and opportunities of living in communities, thus making it a supremely important area of theological study. After all, life in these earthly communities is the training ground and proving ground for life in the community of Heaven.

> But if any one has the world's goods and sees his brother in need, yet closes his heart against him, how does God's love abide in him?...For he who does not love his brother whom he has seen, cannot love God whom he has not seen. (1 Jn 3:17, 20)

CONCLUSION

God created men and women to live in harmony as his children. Our first parents gave in to temptation and introduced disorder into the world. Disorder led to enmity, and enmity to murder, theft, and a multitude of other sins. Left to their own devices, the best human efforts to restore order to society failed. Thus, through his Law and through his prophets, God revealed his moral law, teaching his Chosen People how to live as a human community, yet they refused to obey their Father's law.

Therefore, God sent his Son, Jesus Christ, to redeem humanity and set people free, restoring unity, peace, and order to the world, so that all people could live in freedom as God's children. Through the Church, he has revealed a saving doctrine for happiness, not only in Heaven, but even in this world. The Church's social doctrine, based on the Gospels, represents sound guidance for the ordering of society and living in human relationships. In the life of the Church, and in the lives of the saints, we glimpse the beginnings of a fulfillment and happiness that will be perfected for us in Heaven.

THE TWELVE APOSTLES:
How to Live Together in Peace

The oldest Christian document we possess, apart from the Scriptures, is an ancient work called the Didache *(pronounced DID-uh-kay). The Greek title means simply "the teaching." It is a compilation of instructions taken from the Bible and from the traditions handed on by the Apostles of Jesus Christ. The opening chapters lay down simple rules for living together in peace and harmony.*

The Lord's Teaching Through the Twelve Apostles to the Nations.

Chapter 1. The Two Ways and the First Commandment.

There are two ways, one of life and one of death, but a great difference between the two ways. The way of life, then, is this: First, you shall love God who made you; second, love your neighbor as yourself, and do not do to another what you would not want done to you. And of these sayings the teaching is this: Bless those who curse you, and pray for your enemies, and fast for those who persecute you. For what reward is there for loving those who love you? Do not the Gentiles do the same? But love those who hate you, and you shall not have an enemy. Abstain from fleshly and worldly lusts. If someone strikes your right cheek, turn to him the other also, and you shall be perfect. If someone impresses you for one mile, go with him two. If someone takes your cloak, give him also your coat. If someone takes from you what is yours, ask it not back, for indeed you are not able. Give to every one who asks you, and ask it not back; for the Father wills that to all should be given of our own blessings. Happy is he who gives according to the commandment, for he is guiltless. Woe to him who receives; for if one receives who has need, he is guiltless; but anyone who receives needlessly shall pay the penalty — why he received and for what. And coming into confinement, he shall be examined concerning the things he has done, and he shall not escape from there until he pays back the last penny. And also concerning this, it has been said, Let your alms sweat in your hands, until you know to whom you should give.

Chapter 2. The Second Commandment: Grave Sin Forbidden.

And the second commandment of the Teaching; You shall not commit murder, you shall not commit adultery, you shall not commit pederasty, you shall not commit fornication, you shall not steal, you shall not practice magic, you shall not practice witchcraft, you shall not murder a child by abortion nor kill that which is born. You shall not covet the things of your neighbor, you shall not swear, you shall not bear false witness, you shall not speak evil, you shall bear no grudge. You shall not be double-minded nor double-tongued, for to be double-tongued is a snare of death. Your speech shall not be false, nor empty, but fulfilled by deed. You shall not be covetous, nor rapacious, nor a hypocrite, nor to evil disposed, nor haughty. You shall not take evil counsel against your neighbor. You shall not hate any man; but some you shall reprove, and concerning some you shall pray, and some you shall love more than your own life.

Continued

THE TWELVE APOSTLES: How to Live Together in Peace
Continued

Ministry of the Apostles by Zubov.

Chapter 3. Other Sins Forbidden.

My child, flee from every evil thing, and from every likeness of it. Do not be prone to anger, for anger leads to murder. Be neither jealous, nor quarrelsome, nor of hot temper, for out of all these murders are engendered. My child, do not be lustful, for lust leads to fornication. Be neither a filthy talker, nor of lofty eye, for out of all these adulteries are engendered. My child, be not an observer of omens, since it leads to idolatry. Be neither an enchanter, nor an astrologer, nor be willing to look at these things, for out of all these idolatry is engendered. My child, do not be a liar, since a lie leads to theft. Be neither money-loving, nor vainglorious, for out of all these thefts are engendered. My child, do not be a grumbler, since it leads the way to blasphemy. Be neither self-willed nor evil-minded, for out of all these blasphemies are engendered.

Rather, be meek, since the meek shall inherit the earth. Be long-suffering and pitiful and guileless and gentle and good and always trembling at the words that you have heard. You shall not exalt yourself, nor give over-confidence to your soul. Your soul shall not be joined with lofty ones, but with just and lowly ones shall it keep its company. Accept whatever happens to you as good, knowing that apart from God nothing comes to pass.

SUPPLEMENTARY READING

The Creation of Man and Woman

Then God said, "Let us make man in our image, after our likeness; and let them have dominion over the fish of the sea, and over the birds of the air, and over the cattle, and over all the earth, and over every creeping thing that creeps upon the earth." So God created man in his own image, in the image of God he created him; male and female he created them. And God blessed them, and God said to them, "Be fruitful and multiply, and fill the earth and subdue it; and have dominion over the fish of the sea and over the birds of the air and over every living thing that moves upon the earth." And God said, "Behold, I have given you every plant yielding seed which is upon the face of all the earth, and every tree with seed in its fruit; you shall have them for food. And to every beast of the earth, and to every bird of the air, and to everything that creeps on the earth, everything that has the breath of life, I have given every green plant for food." And it was so. And God saw everything that he had made, and behold, it was very good.

— Genesis 1:26-31

The Facts of Human Nature

The pages of the first book of Sacred Scripture, which describe the creation of man and woman in the image and likeness of God (cf. Gen 1:26-27), contain a fundamental teaching with regard to the identity and the vocation of the human person. They tell us that the creation of man and woman is a free and gratuitous act of God; that man and woman, because they are free and intelligent, represent the "thou" created by God and that only in relationship with him can they discover and fulfil the authentic and complete meaning of their personal and social lives; that in their complementarities and reciprocity they are the image of Trinitarian Love in the created universe; that to them, as the culmination of creation, the Creator has entrusted the task of ordering created nature according to his design (cf. Gen 1:28).

— *Compendium of the Social Doctrine of the Church*, 36

The Book of Genesis provides us with certain foundations of Christian anthropology: the inalienable dignity of the human person, the roots and guarantee of which are found in God's design of creation; the constitutive social nature of human beings, the prototype of which is found in the original relationship between man and woman, the union of whom "constitutes the first form of communion between persons"[11]; the meaning of human activity in the world, which is linked to the discovery and respect of the laws of nature that God has inscribed in the created universe, so that humanity may live in it and care for it in accordance with God's will. This vision of the human person, of society and of history is rooted in God and is ever more clearly seen when his plan of salvation becomes a reality.

— *Compendium of the Social Doctrine of the Church*, 37

The Law: What God Requires

God demands proper worship and care for the poor—love of God and love of neighbor is the essence of the Law.

And now, Israel, what does the Lord your God require of you, but to fear the Lord your God, to walk in all his ways, to love him, to serve the Lord your God with all your heart and with all your soul, and to keep the commandments and statutes of the Lord, which I command you this day for your good? Behold, to the Lord your God belong heaven and the heaven of heavens, the earth with all that is in it; yet the Lord set his heart in love upon your fathers and chose their descendants after them, you above all peoples, as at this day…Be no longer stubborn. For the Lord your God is God of gods and Lord of lords, the great, the mighty, and the terrible God, who is not partial and takes no bribe. He executes justice for the fatherless and the widow, and loves the sojourner, giving him food and clothing. Love the sojourner therefore; for you were sojourners in the land of Egypt. You shall fear the Lord your God; you shall serve him and cleave to him, and by his name you shall swear. He is your praise; he is your God, who has done for you these great and terrible things which your eyes have seen. Your fathers went down to Egypt seventy persons; and now the Lord your God has made you as the stars of heaven for multitude.

— Deuteronomy 10:12-22

SUPPLEMENTARY READING continued

The Plan of Redemption Fulfilled

All the earth is restored, renewed, and united in Christ.

Blessed be the God and Father of our Lord Jesus Christ, who has blessed us in Christ with every spiritual blessing in the heavenly places, even as he chose us in him before the foundation of the world, that we should be holy and blameless before him. He destined us in love to be his sons through Jesus Christ, according to the purpose of his will, to the praise of his glorious grace which he freely bestowed on us in the Beloved. In him we have redemption through his blood, the forgiveness of our trespasses, according to the riches of his grace which he lavished upon us. For he has made known to us in all wisdom and insight the mystery of his will, according to his purpose which he set forth in Christ as a plan for the fulness of time, to unite all things in him, things in heaven and things on earth.

— Ephesians 1:3-10

The Grace of the Present Moment

During World War II, the Holy Father reminded Christians of their calling to transform the world.

The hands of the clock of history are now pointing to an hour both grave and decisive for all mankind. An old world lies in fragments. To see arise as quickly as possible from those ruins a new world, healthier, juridically better organized, more in harmony with the exigencies of human nature; such is the longing of its tortured peoples.

— Pope Pius XII, "The Fifth Anniversary of Outbreak of War in Europe," September 1, 1944

It is an entire world which must be rebuilt from its foundations, transformed from savage to human, from human to divine, that is to say, according to the heart of God.

— Pope Pius XII, "To the Faithful of Rome," February 10, 1952

All the Nations of Earth, All the Angels of Heaven

The Communion of Saints encompasses all creation.

After this I saw four angels standing at the four corners of the earth, holding back the four winds of the earth, that no wind might blow on earth or sea or against any tree. Then I saw another angel ascend from the rising of the sun, with the seal of the living God, and he called with a loud voice to the four angels who had been given power to harm earth and sea, saying, "Do not harm the earth or the sea or the trees, till we have sealed the servants of our God upon their foreheads"... After this I looked, and behold, a great multitude which no man could number, from every nation, from all tribes and peoples and tongues, standing before the throne and before the Lamb, clothed in white robes, with palm branches in their hands, and crying out with a loud voice, "Salvation belongs to our God who sits upon the throne, and to the Lamb!" And all the angels stood round the throne and round the elders and the four living creatures, and they fell on their faces before the throne and worshiped God, saying, "Amen! Blessing and glory and wisdom and thanksgiving and honor and power and might be to our God for ever and ever! Amen."

— Revelation 7:1-3, 9-12

The Church Brings Humanity Back to Its Source in Christ

The Church…is mindful that she must bring together the nations for that king to whom they were given as an inheritance (see Psalm 2:8), and to whose city they bring gifts and offerings (see Psalm 72:10; Isaiah 60:4-7; Revelation 21:24). This characteristic of universality which adorns the people of God is a gift from the Lord himself. By reason of it, the Catholic Church strives constantly and with due effect to bring all humanity and all its possessions back to its source in Christ, with him as its head and united in his Spirit.

— *Lumen Gentium* 13

VOCABULARY

ANTHROPOLOGY (THEOLOGICAL ANTHROPOLOGY)
The subset of theology that studies the nature of the race of man (human nature) as it relates to God and Revelation.

ADAM AND EVE
The first human beings; their actions had consequences for their descendants and all history.

CHILDREN OF GOD
The state of those who have been redeemed by Christ and now share in his relationship with God the Father.

CHRIST
Greek for "anointed." This is used in reference to Christ because he accomplished perfectly the divine mission of Priest, Prophet, and King.

COMMUNION OF SAINTS
The unity in Christ of all the redeemed, those on earth and those who have died, especially the unity of faith and charity through the Eucharist.

CREATION
The act by which God gives a beginning to everything other than God himself. Creation can also refer to all that has been created.

DIDACHE
An early Christian writing (mid-first century) of unknown authorship. It summarizes morality as a choice between the path of life and the path of death, liturgical practice, and disciplinary norms.

DOMINION
The authority God gave Adam to rule over creation.

NATURE
The essence of a being considered as the principle of activity and defining its particular characteristics.

ORIGINAL SIN
The act by which Adam and Eve disobeyed the commandment of God. The term is also used to describe the fallen condition that affects all human beings as a result of that transgression.

PROPHET
From the Greek *prophetes*, meaning one who "speaks for"; in this context, one who addresses the people for God.

SIN
A transgression of the Divine Law and an offense against God involving the individual's knowledge and will.

SOCIAL DOCTRINE
Moral teaching of the Church with regard to the dignity of the person, the basic rights of the person, and the requirements of the common good.

Prophet Jeremiah (detail) by Michelangelo.
"'I will give them a heart to know that I am the LORD; and they shall be my people and I will be their God, for they shall return to me with their whole heart.'"
(Jer 24:7)

STUDY QUESTIONS

1. What does it mean to say that human beings are social by nature?

2. In what ways are human beings fulfilled by the company of others?

3. How does God's moral law help human beings to fulfill their nature?

4. What is Catholic social doctrine?

5. What does it mean to say that mankind, starting with Adam, has "dominion" over the earth? What does that suggest about the human race and its place in the world?

6. What are some basic principles of the social order taught in the first chapter of Genesis?

7. What is Original Sin, and what are its effects on individuals and on society?

8. What does the story of Cain and Abel illustrate about human relations in a fallen world?

9. In what ways did God reveal the application of the moral law to social relations in the Old Testament?

10. What teaching did God give Noah's family in order to guide their social relations?

11. What did God give Moses in order to guide Israel's social relations?

12. How does the Law given to Moses differ from the command given to Noah?

13. What was the purpose of Israel's laws?

14. What were the particular concerns of the prophets regarding social relations?

15. In what terms do the prophets envision peace and social order?

16. How does Christ, the Messiah, heal humanity's social relations?

17. How does the Church serve as a sign of fulfilled human society?

18. What are the Church's primary means of promoting reconciliation in the world?

PRACTICAL EXERCISES

1. Research the historical setting of Israel in the time of the prophets Amos and Isaiah. In what ways are the social problems similar to those in your country today? In what ways are they different? How is the message of the prophets relevant to the modern society in which you live?

2. Explain the Bible's images of Eden and of Heaven. In what ways should these influence a Christian's ideas about society?

3. God gave Adam "dominion" over the earth. What does this imply about human stewardship of natural resources? Research what recent Popes have said about matters related to the environment, ecology, and so on. How does proper stewardship affect the common good of humanity?

4. What are the "two ways" of which the *Didache* speaks? Why does the *Didache* describe them in terms of life and death?

5. How does human society make certain virtues possible? How does human society make certain vices possible?

6. Find some examples of people who lived a long time in isolation from other people. (Possible examples: explorers, shipwrecked travelers, prisoners in solitary confinement, voluntary hermits.) How did the experience affect them during their time of isolation? How did it influence the way they lived afterward? What can their experiences teach us about the social nature of human beings?

FROM THE CATECHISM

1878 All men are called to the same end: God himself. There is a certain resemblance between the union of the divine persons and the fraternity that men are to establish among themselves in truth and love.[12] Love of neighbor is inseparable from love for God.

1880 A society is a group of persons bound together organically by a principle of unity that goes beyond each one of them. As an assembly that is at once visible and spiritual, a society endures through time: it gathers up the past and prepares for the future. By means of society, each man is established as an "heir" and receives certain "talents" that enrich his identity and whose fruits he must develop.[13] He rightly owes loyalty to the communities of which he is part and respect to those in authority who have charge of the common good.

1881 Each community is defined by its purpose and consequently obeys specific rules; but "the *human person*…is and ought to be the principle, the subject and the end of all social institutions." [14]

1884 God has not willed to reserve to himself all exercise of power. He entrusts to every creature the functions it is capable of performing, according to the capacities of its own nature. This mode of governance ought to be followed in social life. The way God acts in governing the world, which bears witness to such great regard for human freedom, should inspire the wisdom of those who govern human communities. They should behave as ministers of divine providence.

1885 The principle of subsidiarity is opposed to all forms of collectivism. It sets limits for state intervention. It aims at harmonizing the relationships between individuals and societies. It tends toward the establishment of true international order.

1886 Society is essential to the fulfillment of the human vocation. To attain this aim, respect must be accorded to the just hierarchy of values, which "subordinates physical and instinctual dimensions to interior and spiritual ones:" [15]

> Human society must primarily be considered something pertaining to the spiritual. Through it, in the bright light of truth, men should share their knowledge, be able to exercise their rights and fulfill their obligations, be inspired to seek spiritual values; mutually derive genuine pleasure from the beautiful, of whatever order it be; always be readily disposed to pass on to others the best of their own cultural heritage; and eagerly strive to make their own the spiritual achievements of others. These benefits not only influence, but at the same time give aim and scope to all that has bearing on cultural expressions, economic, and social institutions, political movements and forms, laws, and all other structures by which society is outwardly established and constantly developed.[16]

St. Dominic in Prayer (detail) by El Greco.
Love of neighbor is inseparable from love for God.

FROM THE CATECHISM continued

1887 The inversion of means and ends,[17] which results in giving the value of ultimate end to what is only a means for attaining it, or in viewing persons as mere means to that end, engenders unjust structures which "make Christian conduct in keeping with the commandments of the divine Law-giver difficult and almost impossible."[18]

1888 It is necessary, then, to appeal to the spiritual and moral capacities of the human person and to the permanent need for his *inner conversion*, so as to obtain social changes that will really serve him. The acknowledged priority of the conversion of heart in no way eliminates but on the contrary imposes the obligation of bringing the appropriate remedies to institutions and living conditions when they are an inducement to sin, so that they conform to the norms of justice and advance the good rather than hinder it.[19]

1889 Without the help of grace, men would not know how "to discern the often narrow path between the cowardice which gives in to evil, and the violence which under the illusion of fighting evil only makes it worse."[20] This is the path of charity, that is, of the love of God and of neighbor. Charity is the greatest social commandment. It respects others and their rights. It requires the practice of justice, and it alone makes us capable of it. Charity inspires a life of self-giving: "Whoever seeks to gain his life will lose it, but whoever loses his life will preserve it."[21]

The Charity of St. Elizabeth of Hungary (detail) by Leighton.
"Charity is the greatest social commandment." (CCC 1889)

ENDNOTES – INTRODUCTION

1. Cf. *GS* 25 § 1.
2. Cf. *SRS* 1; 41.
3. Council of Trent (1546): DS 1511; cf. Heb 2:14.
4. Cf. John Paul II, *CA* 25.
5. Jn 1:29.
6. Cf. John Paul II, *RP* 16.
7. 1 Jn 5:19; cf. 1 Pt 5:8.
8. *GS* 37 § 2.
9. Cf. 1 Cor 15:21-22, 45; Phil 2:8; Rom 5:19-20
10. Cf. Pius IX, *Ineffabilis Deus*: DS 2803; Council of Trent: DS 1573.
11. Second Vatican Ecumenical Council, Pastoral Constitution *Gaudium et Spes*, 12: AAS 58 (1966), 1034.
12. Cf. *GS* 24 § 3.
13. Cf. Lk 19:13, 15.
14. *GS* 25 § 1.
15. *CA* 36 § 2.
16. John XXIII, *PT* 36.
17. Cf. *CA* 41.
18. Pius XII, Address at Pentecost, June 1, 1941.
19. Cf. *LG* 36.
20. *CA* 25.
21. Lk 17:33.

Social Doctrine of the Catholic Church
CHAPTER 1

The Heavenly Model for Earthly Society

The Holy Spirit is the bond of love in the Church, as he is the bond of love in the Blessed Trinity.

Social Doctrine of the Catholic Church

CHAPTER ONE

The Heavenly Model for Earthly Society

CHRISTIAN CHARITY BEGINS IN GOD HIMSELF

If you see charity, you see the Trinity.
— St. Augustine, *On the Trinity*

The theological dimension is needed both for interpreting and for solving present day problems in human society.
— St. John Paul II, *Centesimus Annus*

IN THIS CHAPTER, WE WILL ADDRESS SEVERAL QUESTIONS:

- What set early Christianity apart from other religions and philosophies of its day?
- What is Christ's "New Commandment," and what is its place in Christianity?
- What do Christians mean by the term *charity*?
- Who is the Trinity?
- How do Christians come to share in divine love—and love as God loves?
- Who is the Holy Spirit and how does the Spirit form the Church?
- What does it mean to say that the Church is the "Body of Christ"?

Christianity was a relatively new religious movement ca. AD 190 in North Africa. In fact, it was still fairly new on the world scene. It had begun just a few generations before in a remote Roman province called Judea, located at the edge of the Roman Empire, and it was just beginning to reach important African cities like Carthage.

The Christian religion was so unusual that it baffled people and required an explanation. A prominent lawyer named Tertullian, a convert to Christianity from Roman *polytheism*, offered such an explanation in his book entitled *Apologeticum*, which means "The Explanation" or "The Defense." It is from such early Christian works that Christians learned the practice of "apologetics," which is the art of explaining and defending the Christian Faith to nonbelievers.

What non-Christians found so different about Christianity was not its rituals, or its books, or the architecture of its temples, but rather its *kindness.* The most notable feature of Christian life was the *charity* and *unity* of Christian believers. This is how Tertullian explained it:

THE HEAVENLY MODEL FOR EARTHLY SOCIETY

Christ Healing by the Well of Bethesda by Bloch.
"This is my commandment, that you love one another as I have loved you. Greater love has no man than this, that a man lay down his life for his friends." (Jn 15:12-13)

> We have our treasury, but it is not made up of admission fees, as in a religion that may be bought. Once a month, each person puts in a small donation, but only if he wants to, and only if he can. There is no compulsion. Everything is voluntary. These gifts, then,…are not taken and spent on parties, drinking bouts, and restaurants, but to support and bury poor people, to supply the wants of orphans, and elderly people who are homebound, those who have suffered shipwreck, and those who have been condemned to work in the mines, or banished to the islands, or shut up in prisons…It is such deeds of noble love that lead many to put a brand upon us and say, "See how they love one another!"[1]

Charity, peace, unity, kindness: These were the most striking qualities of Christian life, as seen from the outside. The Church's way of life was so distinctive that it was like a brand mark on the Christians.

The citizens of Carthage who worshiped the Roman gods knew little or nothing about the Church's Sacraments and doctrines. They knew little about Christianity's inner life, but they knew the city's Christians by their distinctive way of loving one another, which was evident for all to see. Love is what set Christians apart from their non-Christian neighbors, even as it attracted those same neighbors to Christianity.

This was not a quality unique to the Church in North Africa. We find evidence of it everywhere, especially in the works of the other Christian authors known as the "early Church Fathers." Even before Tertullian, St. Justin Martyr gave the same testimony for the Church in Rome.[2] In yet another document from that time, we find a similar report on the Church in Greece and its "extraordinary kind of life."[3]

It was extraordinary indeed. Social interaction throughout the world was marked by strife, division, conflict, and power struggles. Governors tried unsuccessfully to unite neighboring peoples and ethnic groups in the common cause of the Roman Empire. They often imposed unity by force, and they sometimes brought "peace" by crushing the conflicting parties. They brought order and development by means of taxation, which the people resented.

Yet, as Tertullian emphasized—repeating it more than once—the Christians accomplished peace and mutual support *voluntarily* and freely. Christians obviously observed some social principle that inspired them to deeds of love for other people.

THE PRINCIPLE OF LOVE

Though the principle is not always easy to keep, it is remarkably easy to find. In the New Testament it appears many times, in the writings of many different authors. It is simply this: *Love one another.*

Christ introduced this principle as a commandment, repeating it for emphasis (emphases added):

> A new commandment I give to you, that you love one another; even as I have loved you, that you also love one another. (Jn 13:34)

> This is my commandment, that you love one another as I have loved you...This I command you, to love one another." (Jn 15:12, 17)

The Good Samaritan (detail) by Roque. As Christ loved sacrificially and without discrimination, so Christians must also love others.

Christ's first disciples understood this command to be an essential part of the Gospel. They even held it to be identical with the Gospel. Late in his life, St. John the Apostle wrote of the "New Commandment" as Christ's most original teaching:

> And now I beg you...not as though I were writing you a new commandment, but the one we have had from the beginning, that we love one another. (2 Jn 1:5)

> For this is the message which you have heard from the beginning, that we should love one another...And this is his commandment, that we should believe in the name of his Son Jesus Christ and love one another, just as he has commanded us." (1 Jn 3:11, 23)

The other Apostles echoed the same phrase. St. Peter told Christians to "*love one another* earnestly from the heart" (1 Pt 1:22); and St. Paul said to "*love one another*; for he who loves his neighbor has fulfilled the law" (Rom 13:8; see also Rom 12:10). He assumed that neighborly love is a truth that should be self-evident to Christians, instilled in them by God:

> "But concerning love of the brethren you have no need to have any one write to you, for you yourselves have been taught by God to love one another" (1 Thes 4:9).

It is a simple enough principle. Nevertheless, it is challenging to put it into action. All of Catholic social doctrine is a practical working-out of this simple commandment given by Christ to his followers.

Such love is not mere politeness or courtesy. It's not just getting along with one another. Christ established a different and much higher standard as he issued the command:

> Even as I have loved you...you also love one another. (Jn 13:34)

BL. TERESA OF CALCUTTA:
Her God Is Called Love

She was the most unlikely celebrity. She did nothing to disguise her age. Her face was wizened; she walked with a stoop. Plain-spoken and sometimes blunt, she avoided cleverness in her speech. Her message was simple, and she distilled it into a few set phrases, which she repeated often.

"You know my God," she said. "My God is called Love."

"I'm very happy if you can see Jesus in me, because I can see Jesus in you."

Saying such simple truths—while living a life for others—she became one of the most famous living persons. She won the Nobel Prize and the United States' Presidential Medal of Freedom. The news media made her a sort of spiritual director to the world.

Bl. Teresa of Calcutta. "We can only love one at a time."

She was born in 1910 in what is now the Republic of Macedonia, but was then a part of the Ottoman Empire. She left home at age eighteen to join the missionary Sisters of Loreto. She never saw her family again. After training briefly in Ireland, she arrived in India in 1929 and began teaching in Catholic schools. For almost two decades she taught and served as a school administrator.

In 1946, while she was riding a train across India, God made it clear to her that she was to leave her convent and serve the poor while living among them. She followed all the Church's protocols in order to do this in an orderly and respectful way. When she was granted permission, she replaced her habit (the uniform of a religious sister) with a traditional Indian sari. She cared for dying people who had been abandoned in the street. Soon she was joined by other women, some of them former students from her days as a schoolteacher. Together they themselves lived in extreme poverty, sharing the life of the poor people they served. Mother Teresa and her sisters slept on the floor, ate simple meals, and enjoyed no hot water, air conditioning, or other comforts.

In 1950, Mother Teresa founded the congregation that would become the Missionaries of Charity. She and her sisters committed themselves to serve "the hungry, the naked, the homeless, the crippled, the blind, the lepers, all those people who feel unwanted, unloved, uncared for throughout society, people that have become a burden to the society and are shunned by everyone." The Missionaries of Charity treated all with dignity, and they helped many to make sense of their suffering in light of the Cross of Jesus Christ.

In the course of her lifetime, the Missionaries of Charity grew to include thousands of sisters worldwide, plus an order of priests, an organization of lay coworkers, and a network of suffering intercessors. Mother Teresa worked hard almost to the end of her life, sharing menial tasks in the order's houses for the dying. She smiled constantly, explaining that a smile was the beginning of peace and sometimes the greatest sacrifice a person could make.

"I know there are thousands and thousands of poor," she said, "but I think of only one at a time…We can only love one at a time."

She became a celebrity—according to a Gallup poll, the most admired person of the twentieth century—not because she did big things or undertook projects that were epic in scope, but because she was faithful to small tasks done for the care of people who were unloved and dying in the backstreets of slums of teeming cities. "There are many people who can do big things," she said, "but there are very few people who will do the small things."

She fulfilled small tasks with great love—Christ's love.

Christ loved completely and in a self-giving way. He held nothing back. He gave his life for the sake of his friends, and there is no greater love than this (cf. Jn 15:13). As Christ loved sacrificially and without discrimination, so Christians must also love others. Christian tradition refers to such sacrificial love as *charity*, from the Latin word *caritas* and the Greek word *charis*, which means "gift." The love of charity requires the gift of oneself.

It was abundantly clear, however, in the first century (as it is still today) that such Christlike love does not come naturally to people. As a lasting consequence of Original Sin, people are weakened in their relationship to one another. Adam and Eve's own son, Cain, failed to love his brother and eventually killed him out of envy.

As they preached the Gospel, both Christ and the Apostles returned often to that most basic theme: *Love one another*. But they provided more than just doctrine. Through the Church, they also provided the supernatural means to love in a way that seemed beyond any human being's natural capacities (*see* Rom 5:7-8). Through communion with Jesus Christ, the Church empowers Christians to love as Christ loves, to love with the love of God.

THE BLESSED TRINITY: OUR ORIGIN AND GOAL

Everyone wants to be happy, and everyone wants to live in peace. People cannot have true happiness, however, unless they are living in accordance with the true purpose of their lives. If people cannot agree about life's purpose, then they will inevitably fall into disagreement and conflict over other matters as well.

In his mercy, God has revealed the purpose of human life. He has revealed the origin, nature, and destiny of human beings, and so he has shown the way to happiness. Ultimately, we will know that happiness in its fullness only in Heaven, but we can experience a foretaste, or preview, of this happiness throughout our life on earth. Indeed, we must pursue it here if we wish to possess it fully in Heaven.

The Holy Trinity by Pereda.
Love could not be more perfect, more constant, or more complete than the love shared within the Blessed Trinity.

THE HEAVENLY MODEL FOR EARTHLY SOCIETY

Human beings were created to be social, to interact with each other. Yet, human beings were made for a still greater society and an infinitely higher love.

In the previous chapter, we saw that human beings were created to be social, to interact with each other. Love is the highest degree of human interaction. Yet, human beings were made for a still greater society and an infinitely higher love. St. Augustine, in the fourth century, summed up our origin and destiny in a famous prayer to God:

> You have made us for yourself, O Lord, and our hearts are restless until they rest in you.[4]

God made us for a love that only he can satisfy, for we have been made in his image, and only he is perfect love.

The Catholic Faith teaches us that God is triune: He is three divine Persons, Father, Son, and Holy Spirit, who live coeternally and coequally, each Person truly distinct, yet truly one God. No Person of the Trinity is greater than any other: The Father loves the Son perfectly; the Son returns that love perfectly; and from their love proceeds the Holy Spirit. Love could not be more perfect, more constant, or more complete than the love shared within the Blessed Trinity.

> *The Trinity is One.* We do not confess three Gods, but one God in three persons, the "consubstantial Trinity."[5] The divine persons do not share the one divinity among themselves but each of them is God whole and entire: "The Father is that which the Son is, the Son that which the Father is, the Father and the Son that which the Holy Spirit is, i.e., by nature one God."[6] In the words of the Fourth Lateran Council (1215), "Each of the persons is that supreme reality, viz., the divine substance, essence or nature."[7] (CCC 253)

We do not refer to the triune God as a "society." The Trinity's bond of unity is infinitely greater and closer than any human relationship. Rather, the Trinity's love is so close that St. Augustine called it a *communion*—from the Latin words meaning "one with." When Christ spoke of his relationship with the Father, he said that the Father lived *in* him and he *in* the Father (see, for example, Jn 10:38 and Jn 14:10-11).

Because God's love is a mystery involving a communion of three divine Persons, Christians can say, in the words of the New Testament, "God is love" (1 Jn 4:16). In revealing the Blessed Trinity, "God has revealed his innermost secret: God himself is an eternal exchange of love, Father, Son and Holy Spirit, and he has destined us to share in that exchange" (CCC 221).

This is the love God has shared with the human race through the life, Passion, Death, Resurrection, and Ascension of Jesus Christ. In Christ, the eternal Word "became flesh and dwelt among us" (Jn 1:14). In his life and prayer, Christ revealed the eternal life and relations of the Blessed Trinity. He lived in constant communion with the Father. The Holy Spirit rested upon him at his baptism in the Jordan, and he sent the same Spirit to his disciples at Pentecost.

Christ, however, did more than merely reveal the truth of the Blessed Trinity. Through the Paschal Mystery—through the saving power of the Cross—Christ *shared* that divine life with the human race. He established the Church to dispense the Sacraments of Salvation; and, through these Sacraments, Christians become "partakers of the divine nature" (2 Pt 1:4). Through a holy communion, we come to share the love and life of the Blessed Trinity. As the Son and the Father live *in* one another, so Christians and Christ live in one another:

> In that day you will know that I am in my Father, and you in me, and I in you. (Jn 14:20)

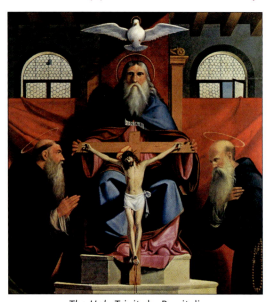

The Holy Trinity by Previtali. The mystery of the Trinity is the central mystery of Christian Faith.

This is the love every human being was made to share. Trinitarian love is the origin and goal of every human person. Everyone since Adam and Eve has been created in the image and likeness of God (cf. Gn 1:26-27), and no one can be truly satisfied in life, i.e., no one can know true happiness or find fulfillment apart from the eternal life of the Blessed Trinity.

From the *Catechism* we learn that the mystery of the Trinity is the central mystery of the Christian Faith, and it is the source of all other mysteries of faith.[8] We can begin to understand the mysteries of faith only when we consider them in light of the Blessed Trinity. Thus, the doctrine of the Trinity, revealed by Jesus Christ and developed in the teaching and preaching of the Church, will have a profound influence on our understanding of Catholic social doctrine.

"As the Father has loved me, so have I loved you," Christ said; "abide in my love" (Jn 15:9). Christian life is an abiding share in the love of the Blessed Trinity. Thus, it is never individualistic. It implies a deeply social life.

THE HOLY SPIRIT: OUR BOND OF LOVE

God created us as individuals, but he created us to live in communion. We are saved individually by Jesus Christ; but we live out our Christian life in the way he commanded us to live, within the communion of his Church.

We are distinct—as individuals, families, cultures, and even nations—yet we are also one. In our unity, we retain great diversity. In our diversity, we enjoy a compact unity. In the Acts of the Apostles, we read that the Gospel was preached to a diversity of peoples: "Parthians and Medes and Elamites and residents of Mesopotamia, Judea and Cappadocia, Pontus and Asia, Phrygia and Pamphylia, Egypt and the parts of Libya belonging to Cyrene, and visitors from Rome, both Jews and proselytes, Cretans and Arabians" (Acts 2:9-11). They were indeed diverse, but "the company of those who believed were of one heart and soul, and no one said that any of the things which he possessed was his own, but they had everything in common" (Acts 4:32).

How was this possible? The narrative makes it clear that the early Church's unity was a work of the Holy Spirit.

As part of his plan of salvation, Christ shared the Holy Spirit with his disciples. Before his Ascension into Heaven, he visited his Apostles and "breathed on them, and said to them, 'Receive the Holy Spirit'" (Jn 20:22).

ST. DAMIEN OF MOLOKAI: A Leper Among the Lepers

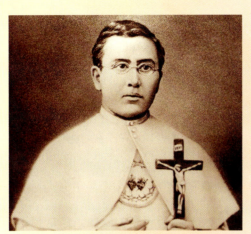

Father Damien as a seminarian in France, ca. 1863.

Jozef De Veuster was born into a large family in Belgium in 1840. When he was a young man, he discerned a call to be a missionary, to bring the Gospel to people who did not know Jesus Christ. He knew that this would likely take him far from the home he loved. Responding to God's call, he followed his older brother Auguste into the Congregation of the Sacred Hearts of Jesus and Mary.

Damien's academic preparation had been mediocre, and he was considered unfit for the advanced studies required for ordination to the priesthood. He worked harder, however, and prayed through the intercession of St. Francis Xavier, the patron of missionaries. His brother tutored him in Latin, and soon he caught up with his peers.

Members of religious orders often take a new name when they profess vows. Jozef received the name Damien.

His brother Auguste was assigned to the missions in the faraway kingdom of Hawaii. When Auguste suddenly fell ill, young Damien was sent in his place. He was ordained a priest in Honolulu in 1864.

At that time, the Hawaiian Islands were emerging as an important center of trade in the Pacific Ocean. More commerce meant more contact between native Hawaiians and foreign visitors. The islands were soon prone to epidemics of new and deadly ailments. The disease most feared was leprosy (now known as Hansen's disease), a chronic, progressive disease that disfigures the skin and damages nerves, limbs, and eyes. Infectious disease was little understood at the time, and people believed (wrongly, it turns out) that leprosy was incurable and highly contagious. Lepers were isolated in remote "colonies" where they could have no contact with healthy people.

Hawaii had several leper colonies, and the bishop of Honolulu knew that these outcasts needed pastoral care. Yet, he did not think it right to command any priest to fulfill an assignment that would be, effectively, a death sentence. So the bishop asked for volunteers, and Father Damien was one of four priests who stepped forward. He was assigned to the main leper colony on the island of Molokai.

He found the people there demoralized. Many had fallen into despair because of their condition. Though the government provided money and supplies for the colony to establish farms, the lepers lacked motivation and hope. They drank heavily and engaged in promiscuous sex.

Father Damien did not keep his parishioners at a distance, but lived among them as a real father. He admonished them, counseled them, forgave their sins, and reminded them of their reasons to live moral and hopeful lives on earth. He wrote: "I make myself a leper among the lepers to gain all for Jesus Christ."

Father Damien reminded the lepers of their basic human dignity that each and every one of them had been created in God's image. He encouraged them to build up respectable houses and keep them clean and in good repair. He built schools, and he himself taught the children on the colony. Though he was free to leave his assignment, he stayed. After sixteen years on Molokai, he contracted leprosy himself, and, in 1889, he died from it. Since Father Damien lived entirely for the love and service of others—even at the cost of his life—he has been called a "martyr of charity."

Father Damien was canonized a saint in 2009. He is honored with a monument in the National Statuary Hall in the United States Capitol. In a recent survey in Belgium, he was chosen the greatest Belgian of all time. His feast day is May 10.

We see the same sign, in greater magnitude, on the first Pentecost, fifty days after Easter Sunday, when there is a great outpouring of the Holy Spirit upon the Church. One of the Spirit's outward signs is "a mighty wind" (Acts 2:2).

Jesus Christ, the Son of God, gave the Holy Spirit as a gift to the Church. The Holy Spirit is the bond of love in the Church, as he is the bond of love in the Blessed Trinity.

Through the Sacraments, especially the Sacraments of Baptism and Confirmation, we receive the Holy Spirit and come to live as children of God in the eternal Son of God:

God has sent the Spirit of his Son into our hearts, crying, "Abba! Father!"
(Gal 4:6; see also Rom 8:15-17)

Because we live in Christ and the Holy Spirit dwells in us, we can call God the Father "Our Father." We can even address him as "Abba," the intimate title Jewish children reserved for their Father, similar to the English word "Daddy."

Pentecost (detail) by Werff.
The Holy Spirit is the bond of love in the Church.

Knowing God as "Our Father" is a special privilege for Christians, and it comes to us from the Holy Spirit's life in each of us and in the Church:

It is the Spirit himself bearing witness with our spirit that we are children of God. (Rom 8:16)

God made the way clear and simple for people to receive the Holy Spirit: He established the Church (cf. Eph 4:5) and made the Holy Spirit abundantly available through the Sacraments. In Baptism and Confirmation we receive the Holy Spirit, and in the Eucharist we share in the Paschal Mystery of Christ and are made one with other believers.

THE CHURCH: THE BODY OF CHRIST

Christians are united to Christ and to one another. "I am the vine," Christ said to his disciples, "you are the branches" (Jn 15:5). In fact, so closely are Christians united to each other in Christ that the New Testament refers to the Church as "Body of Christ."

Now you are the body of Christ and individually members of it. (1 Cor 12:27)

In the Acts of the Apostles, Christ identifies himself with the persecuted Church when he says to Saul, her oppressor, "Why do you persecute me?...I am Jesus, whom you persecute" (Acts 9:4-5).

That very persecutor, once converted to Christianity, came to develop most clearly the doctrine of the Church as Christ's Body. In his First Letter to the Corinthians, St. Paul explains that Christians are "one body" because they share the one bread of the Eucharist (10:16-17)—the Sacrament of which Christ declared, "This is my body" (11:24).

St. Paul's doctrine of the "Body of Christ" accounts for both the unity of the Church and the rich diversity of Christians. It is the Holy Spirit who unifies us and makes us one Body.

By one Spirit we were all baptized into one body—Jews or Greeks, slaves or free—and all were made to drink of one Spirit. For the body does not consist of one member but of many. If the foot should say, "Because I am not a hand, I do not belong to the body," that would not make it any less a part of the body. And if the ear should say, "Because I am not an eye, I do not belong to the body," that would not make it any less a part of the body. If the whole body were an eye, where would be the hearing? If the whole body were an ear, where would be the sense of smell? But

THE HEAVENLY MODEL FOR EARTHLY SOCIETY

> as it is, God arranged the organs in the body, each one of them, as he chose. If all were a single organ, where would the body be? As it is, there are many parts, yet one body. The eye cannot say to the hand, "I have no need of you," nor again the head to the feet, "I have no need of you."
> (1 Cor 12:13-21, emphasis added)

Christians are as dependent upon one another as are the parts of the human body. As believers are the parts of the Body that is the Church, so Christ is the Head. This theme is very important to St. Paul, and he returns to it many times (cf. Rom 12:4, 1 Cor 11:3, Eph 1:22-23, 5:23-30; and Col 1:18).

Since the Church is Christ's Body, her members must care for one another, and each member must respect the special roles of all the others. This implies mutual support, concern, and affection. In practice, it looks a lot like the second-century Church in North Africa described by Tertullian at the beginning of this chapter.

The doctrine bears deep implications for both personal morality and social doctrine—and all the points where these two intersect. Christians are members of Christ's sinless Body, so each and every member must strive to behave according to a very high moral standard. The Apostle asks: "Shall I therefore take the members of Christ and make them members of a prostitute? Never!" (1 Cor 6:15). Whatever choices we make, whatever actions we take, we affect not only our own lives, but also the lives of others, especially our fellow Christians. If we do good things, they benefit. If we do sinful things, people suffer.

The Ointment of the Magdalene by Tissot.
"But Jesus…said to them, 'Why do you trouble the woman? For she has done a beautiful thing to me. For you always have the poor with you, but you will not always have me.'" (Mt 26:10-11)

ECUMENISM: That All May Be One

Jesus Christ established his Church to be a sign and a means of unity in the world. He wanted her to be one, holy, and universal ("catholic"), so that she would be attractive to everyone and draw everyone together in peace. At the Last Supper he prayed:

> Holy Father, keep them in thy name, which thou hast given me, that they may be one, even as we are one…that they may all be one; even as you, Father, are in me, and I in you, that they also may be in us, so that the world may believe that you have sent me. The glory which you have given me I have given to them, that they may be one even as we are one, I in them and you in me, that they may become perfectly one, so that the world may know that you have sent me and hast loved them even as you have loved me. (Jn 17:11, 21-23)

It is contrary to God's will, then, that there are many "churches," divided from catholic unity and from one another by national, ideological, or cultural differences. The fragmentation of Christians is a scandal to nonbelievers. This is especially true when Christians disagree about basic doctrine and present competing claims to the world. These public disputes make Christ seem, to skeptics and inquirers, less knowable and less credible.

Ecumenism is the "promotion of the restoration of unity among all Christians, the unity which is a gift of Christ and to which the Church is called by the Holy Spirit" (CCC Glossary). The Catholic Church, through her work of *ecumenism* (literally, *uniting the whole*), strives actively to heal divisions, so that all Christians "may become perfectly one" and stand united as a powerful sign of Christ's divine mission and the unity of the Trinity.

The Church participates in an ongoing conversation—a dialogue—with most of the bodies of Christians that have departed from Catholic unity. This happens at the highest levels of Church hierarchy, as when the Pope meets with the Orthodox Patriarch of Constantinople or the presiding bishop of the Evangelical Lutheran Church in America. It happens also at the local level, in small-town clergy associations. And it happens in personal, one-on-one conversations between believers, when Catholics listen attentively and strive to help others to understand the truth of their faith. In this dialogue, the Church is called not only to share her experiences but to actively listen to her separated brethren: their history, their spriatual and liturgical life, their religious psychology, and their background. All of this contributes to a better understanding of our separated brethren and a better understanding and explanation of the beliefs of the Church.

In addition to conversation or dialogue, which includes actively listening to our separated brethren, the Church responds to her ecumenical call by a permanent renewal and fidelity to her vocation, conversion of heart among the faithful, prayer in common, and "collaboration among Christians in various areas of service to mankind" (CCC 821).

Christ prayed that "all be one," and Catholics believe his prayer will be answered through the work of the Church in dialogue with separated Christians.

The Church also conducts interfaith dialogue with non-Christian religions, to promote mutual understanding and peace.

Pope Paul VI met with Patriarch Athenagoras I in Jerusalem in 1964. They issued a joint statement withdrawing mutual excommunications that had formalized the Catholic-Orthodox schism in 1054.

THE HEAVENLY MODEL FOR EARTHLY SOCIETY

THE BLESSED TRINITY: THE PATTERN OF SOCIAL LIFE

Every human person has been created to live and love as the Trinity lives and loves. St. John Paul II wrote:

> To be human means to be called to interpersonal communion.[9]

He went on to explain:

> The model for this interpretation of the person is God himself as Trinity, as a communion of Persons. To say that man is created in the image and likeness of God means that man is called to exist "for" others, to become a gift.[10]

Such communion is natural to God but beyond the power of fallen human nature. Yet, it is the essence of the New Commandment that Christ gave his disciples. Since God does not command the impossible, we know that he will provide a way for it to be fulfilled. Indeed, he has. It is our communion with God, our sharing in divine life that makes communion possible, not only in Heaven but even on earth.

St. John wrote: "Beloved, let us love one another; for love is of God, and he who loves is born of God and knows God" (1 Jn 4:7-8). To love like God is a grace from God. Grace is itself a share of divine life that enables us to enjoy *supernaturally* what we cannot possess by nature. No one can, by nature, live divine life as a child of God. Yet God makes it possible through grace.

It may seem too good to be true, but such love is evident in the lives of devout Christians, especially those the Church honors as saints. Bl. Mother Teresa of Calcutta and St. Damien of Molokai gave their lives heroically for love of God and neighbor. They served the poorest of the poor, people who were shunned by the rest of society and left for dead, figuratively as well as literally. As we study Catholic social doctrine more closely, we will meet many others like them.

Bl. Teresa of Calcutta dedicated her life to the poorest of the poor, people who were shunned by the rest of society and left for dead.

Christ summarized all of the Law and all the messages of the prophets in just two commandments: love God and love your neighbor (cf. Mt 22:35-40). In fact, fellowship with neighbor flows from and presupposes communion with God. When we pray as Christ taught us, we say, "Forgive us…as we forgive those who trespass against us." And Christ warned us not to approach the altar if we are living in conflict with others (cf. Mt 5:23-24). We are not living as Christians if we treat others unjustly (cf. Mt 24:48-49). We cannot share divine life, on earth or in Heaven, if we neglect or mistreat our neighbors (Lk 16:19-31).

St. John Paul II wrote, in his *Letter to Families*: "The divine 'We' is the eternal pattern of the human 'we.'" If we want to learn to live together in human society, if we want true and lasting peace and happiness, no lesser model will do. We must look to the Blessed Trinity.

The life of communion that God patterns in the Blessed Trinity, he also empowers through divine grace and the life of the Holy Spirit. Christ promised his disciples:

> You shall receive power when the Holy Spirit has come upon you; and you shall be my witnesses… to the ends of the earth. (Acts 1:7-8)

When we share God's love, through acts of kindness and charity, we become living images of God in the world. Scripture tells us:

> No man has ever seen God; if we love one another, God abides in us and his love is perfected in us. (1 Jn 4:12)

St. Augustine commented: "If you see charity, you see the Trinity."[11] That is indeed the love the pagan citizens of Carthage saw when they said: *See those Christians, how they love one another.*

God willed for such love to be like a fire that consumes the earth. He gave his love as a gift when he sent the Holy Spirit to the Church at Pentecost. The Church remains today the steward of this gift of divine life for the human race. Thus, the Church begins her authoritative *Catechism* with a capsule history:

Jesus and the Little Children by Vogelstein. When we share God's love, through acts of kindness and charity, we become living images of God in the world.

> God, infinitely perfect and blessed in himself, in a plan of sheer goodness freely created man to make him share in his own blessed life. For this reason, at every time and in every place, God draws close to man. He calls man to seek him, to know him, to love him with all his strength. He calls together all men, scattered and divided by sin, into the unity of his family, the Church. To accomplish this, when the fullness of time had come, God sent his Son as Redeemer and Savior. In his Son and through him, he invites men to become, in the Holy Spirit, his adopted children and thus heirs of his blessed life. (CCC 1)

In the Church, we find the family unity that God willed for humankind from the beginning. The Church shows forth this unity in the lives of ordinary Christians, but she also *proclaims* this unity through her social doctrine. The Church teaches by both words and works.

By means of Catholic social teaching, the Church continues the ministry of Christ the divine teacher, showing the world a way to true human fulfillment. Christ himself commissioned his newfound Church for this purpose—to "make disciples of all nations." At the same moment, he gave his Apostles the means to complete their mission by making them teachers of his new law and ministers of his empowering Sacraments:

> Go therefore and make disciples of all nations, baptizing them in the name of the Father and of the Son and of the Holy Spirit, teaching them to observe all that I have commanded you; and lo, I am with you always, to the close of the age. (Mt 28:19-20)

With this divine mandate, the Church has the authority, the competence, the grace—and the obligation—to teach her social doctrine, which, like all Christian doctrine, is saving doctrine and truly the Good News.

CONCLUSION

The Church has always been distinguished by her life of charity. It is evident in her corporate works, such as running schools and hospitals, but also in the lives of the saints—the everyday actions of canonized saints as well as ordinary Christians whose names will never be known to history.

Charity is far greater than mere philanthropy. Good deeds can arise from many different motives—to win recognition or renown, to gain appreciation or praise. To love with charity, however, is to love as God loves, giving sacrificially as Christ gave, giving of one's self and one's substance. When Christians live this way, they manifest God's love to the world. Responding to Christ's New Commandment, they love with God's love, which they have received as grace.

The Saints
PILLARS OF THE CHURCH

ST. JOHN PAUL II: Witnesses to Love

"Love is truly the 'heart' of the Church."

In his Apostolic Letter Novo Millennio Ineunte *("At the Dawn of the New Millennium"), St. John Paul proposed a Trinitarian "spirituality of communion" for the Church and the world.*

42. "By this all will know that you are my disciples, if you have love for one another" (Jn 13:35). If we have truly contemplated the face of Christ, dear Brothers and Sisters, our pastoral planning will necessarily be inspired by the New Commandment which he gave us: "Love one another, as I have loved you" (Jn 13:34).

This is the other important area in which there has to be commitment and planning on the part of the universal Church and the particular Churches: *the domain of communion* (*koinonia*), which embodies and reveals the very essence of the mystery of the Church. Communion is the fruit and demonstration of that love which springs from the heart of the Eternal Father and is poured out upon us through the Spirit which Jesus gives us (cf. Rom 5:5), to make us all "one heart and one soul" (Acts 4:32). It is in building this communion of love that the Church appears as "sacrament," as the "sign and instrument of intimate union with God and of the unity of the human race."[12]

The Lord's words on this point are too precise for us to diminish their import. Many things are necessary for the Church's journey through history, not least in this new century; but without charity (*agape*), all will be in vain. It is again the Apostle Paul who in the hymn to love reminds us: even if we speak the tongues of men and of angels, and if we have faith "to move mountains," but are without love, all will come to "nothing" (cf. 1 Cor 13:2). Love is truly the "heart" of the Church, as was well understood by St. Thérèse of Lisieux, whom I proclaimed a Doctor of the Church precisely because she is an expert in the *scientia amoris*: "I understood that the Church had a Heart and that this Heart was aflame with Love. I understood that Love alone stirred the members of the Church to act… I understood that Love encompassed all vocations, that Love was everything."[13]

A spirituality of communion

43. To make the Church *the home and the school of communion*: that is the great challenge facing us in the millennium which

Continued

POPE ST. JOHN PAUL II: Witnesses to Love
Continued

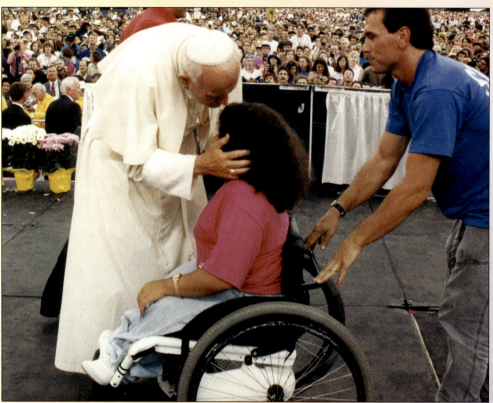

St. John Paul II embraces a woman with disabilities during the eighth World Youth Day in Denver, 1993. "A spirituality of communion implies also the ability to see what is positive in others, to welcome it and prize it as a gift from God."

is now beginning, if we wish to be faithful to God's plan and respond to the world's deepest yearnings.

But what does this mean in practice?…A spirituality of communion indicates above all the heart's contemplation of the mystery of the Trinity dwelling in us, and whose light we must also be able to see shining on the face of the brothers and sisters around us. A spirituality of communion also means an ability to think of our brothers and sisters in faith within the profound unity of the Mystical Body, and therefore as "those who are a part of me." This makes us able to share their joys and sufferings, to sense their desires and attend to their needs, to offer them deep and genuine friendship. A spirituality of communion implies also the ability to see what is positive in others, to welcome it and prize it as a gift from God: not only as a gift for the brother or sister who has received it directly, but also as a "gift for me." A spirituality of communion means, finally, to know how to "make room" for our brothers and sisters, bearing "each other's burdens" (Gal 6:2) and resisting the selfish temptations which constantly beset us and provoke competition, careerism, distrust and jealousy. Let us have no illusions: unless we follow this spiritual path, external structures of communion will serve very little purpose. They would become mechanisms without a soul, "masks" of communion rather than its means of expression and growth.

SUPPLEMENTARY READING

Christ's Legacy: Communion with the Father and the Church

Amid his "farewell discourse," in the fifteenth chapter of St. John's Gospel, Jesus spoke about his family bond in Heaven and on earth: the love of the Holy Spirit.

I am the true vine, and my Father is the vinedresser. Every branch of mine that bears no fruit, he takes away, and every branch that does bear fruit he prunes, that it may bear more fruit. You are already made clean by the word which I have spoken to you. Abide in me, and I in you. As the branch cannot bear fruit by itself, unless it abides in the vine, neither can you, unless you abide in me.

I am the vine, you are the branches. He who abides in me, and I in him, he it is that bears much fruit, for apart from me you can do nothing. If a man does not abide in me, he is cast forth as a branch and withers; and the branches are gathered, thrown into the fire and burned. If you abide in me, and my words abide in you, ask whatever you will, and it shall be done for you.

By this my Father is glorified, that you bear much fruit, and so prove to be my disciples. As the Father has loved me, so have I loved you; abide in my love. If you keep my commandments, you will abide in my love, just as I have kept my Father's commandments and abide in his love. These things I have spoken to you, that my joy may be in you, and that your joy may be full.

This is my commandment, that you love one another as I have loved you. Greater love has no man than this, that a man lay down his life for his friends. You are my friends if you do what I command you. No longer do I call you servants, for the servant does not know what his master is doing; but I have called you friends, for all that I have heard from my Father I have made known to you. You did not choose me, but I chose you and appointed you that you should go and bear fruit and that your fruit should abide; so that whatever you ask the Father in my name, he may give it to you. This I command you, to love one another.

If the world hates you, know that it has hated me before it hated you. If you were of the world, the world would love its own; but because you are not of the world, but I chose you out of the world, therefore the world hates you. Remember the word that I said to you, "A servant is not greater than his master." If they persecuted me, they will persecute you; if they kept my word, they will keep yours also. But all this they will do to you on my account, because they do not know him who sent me. If I had not come and spoken to them, they would not have sin; but now they have no excuse for their sin. He who hates me hates my Father also. If I had not done among them the works which no one else did, they would not have sin; but now they have seen and hated both me and my Father. It is to fulfill the word that is written in their law, "They hated me without a cause." But when the Counselor comes, whom I shall send to you from the Father, even the Spirit of truth, who proceeds from the Father, he will bear witness to me; and you also are witnesses, because you have been with me from the beginning.

—*John 15:1-27*

Trinitarian Love, the Origin and Goal of the Human Person

34. The revelation in Christ of the mystery of God as Trinitarian love is at the same time the revelation of the vocation of the human person to love. This revelation sheds light on every aspect of the personal dignity and freedom of men and women, and on the depths of their social nature. "Being a person in the image and likeness of God…involves existing in a relationship, in relation to the other 'I,'"[14] because God himself, one and triune, is the communion of the Father, of the Son and of the Holy Spirit.

In the communion of love that is God, and in which the Three Divine Persons mutually love one another and are the One God, the human person is called to discover the origin and goal of his existence and of history. The Council Fathers, in the Pastoral Constitution *Gaudium et Spes*, teach that "the Lord Jesus Christ, when praying to the Father 'that they may all be one…as we are one' (Jn 17:21-22), has opened up new horizons closed to human reason by implying that there is a certain parallel between the union existing among the divine Persons and the union of the

SUPPLEMENTARY READING Continued

children of God in truth and love. It follows, then, that if man is the only creature on earth that God has willed for its own sake, man can fully discover his true self only in a sincere giving of himself (cf. Lk 17:33)."

35. *Christian revelation shines a new light on the identity, the vocation and the ultimate destiny of the human person and the human race.* Every person is created by God, loved and saved in Jesus Christ, and fulfils himself by creating a network of multiple relationships of love, justice and solidarity with other persons while he goes about his various activities in the world. Human activity, when it aims at promoting the integral dignity and vocation of the person, the quality of living conditions and the meeting in solidarity of peoples and nations, is in accordance with the plan of God, who does not fail to show his love and providence to his children.

—*Compendium of the Social Doctrine of the Church*

Pope Benedict XVI: The Practice of Love by the Church as a Community of Love

19. "If you see charity, you see the Trinity," [15] wrote St. Augustine. In the foregoing reflections, we have been able to focus our attention on the Pierced one (cf. Jn 19:37, Zech 12:10), recognizing the plan of the Father who, moved by love (cf. Jn 3:16), sent his only-begotten Son into the world to redeem man. By dying on the Cross—as St. John tells us—Jesus "gave up his Spirit" (Jn 19:30), anticipating the gift of the Holy Spirit that he would make after his Resurrection (cf. Jn 20:22). This was to fulfill the promise of "rivers of living water" that would flow out of the hearts of believers, through the outpouring of the Spirit (cf. Jn 7:38-39). The Spirit, in fact, is that interior power which harmonizes their hearts with Christ's heart and moves them to love their brethren as Christ loved them, when he bent down to wash the feet of the disciples (cf. Jn 13:1-13) and above all when he gave his life for us (cf. Jn 13:1, 15:13).

The Spirit is also the energy which transforms the heart of the ecclesial community, so that it becomes a witness before the world to the love of the Father, who wishes to make humanity a single family in his Son. The entire activity of the Church is an expression of a love that seeks the integral good of man: it seeks his evangelization through Word and Sacrament, an undertaking that is often heroic in the way it is acted out in history; and it seeks to promote man in the various arenas of life and human activity. Love is therefore the service that the Church carries out in order to attend constantly to man's sufferings and his needs, including material needs. And this is the aspect, this service of charity, on which I want to focus in the second part of the Encyclical.

Charity as a Responsibility of the Church

20. Love of neighbor, grounded in the love of God, is first and foremost a responsibility for each individual member of the faithful, but it is also a responsibility for the entire ecclesial community at every level: from the local community to the particular Church and to the Church universal in its entirety. As a community, the Church must practice love. Love thus needs to be organized if it is to be an ordered service to the community. The awareness of this responsibility has had a constitutive relevance in the Church from the beginning: "All who believed were together and had all things in common; and they sold their possessions and goods and distributed them to all, as any had need" (Acts 2:44-45). In these words, St. Luke provides a kind of definition of the Church, whose constitutive elements include fidelity to the "teaching of the Apostles," "communion" (*koinonia*), "the breaking of the bread" and "prayer" (cf. Acts 2:42). The element of "communion" (*koinonia*) is not initially defined, but appears concretely in the verses quoted above: it consists in the fact that believers hold all things in common and that among them, there is no longer any distinction between rich and poor (cf. also Acts 4:32-37). As the Church grew, this radical form of material communion could not in fact be preserved. But its essential core remained: within the community of believers there can never be room for a poverty that denies anyone what is needed for a dignified life.

THE HEAVENLY MODEL FOR EARTHLY SOCIETY

SUPPLEMENTARY READING Continued

21. A decisive step in the difficult search for ways of putting this fundamental ecclesial principle into practice is illustrated in the choice of the seven, which marked the origin of the diaconal office (cf. Acts 6:5-6). In the early Church, in fact, with regard to the daily distribution to widows, a disparity had arisen between Hebrew speakers and Greek speakers. The Apostles, who had been entrusted primarily with "prayer" (the Eucharist and the liturgy) and the "ministry of the word," felt overburdened by "serving tables," so they decided to reserve to themselves the principal duty and to designate for the other task, also necessary in the Church, a group of seven persons. Nor was this group to carry out a purely mechanical work of distribution: they were to be men "full of the Spirit and of wisdom" (cf. Acts 6:1-6). In other words, the social service which they were meant to provide was absolutely concrete, yet at the same time it was also a spiritual service; theirs was a truly spiritual office which carried out an essential responsibility of the Church, namely a well-ordered love of neighbor. With the formation of this group of seven, "*diaconia*"—the ministry of charity exercised in a communitarian, orderly way—became part of the fundamental structure of the Church.

22. As the years went by and the Church spread further afield, the exercise of charity became established as one of her essential activities, along with the administration of the Sacraments and the proclamation of the Word: love for widows and orphans, prisoners, and the sick and needy of every kind, is as essential to her as the ministry of the Sacraments and preaching of the Gospel. The Church cannot neglect the service of charity any more than she can neglect the Sacraments and the Word. A few references will suffice to demonstrate this. Justin Martyr († c. 155) in speaking of the Christians' celebration of Sunday, also mentions their charitable activity, linked with the Eucharist as such. Those who are able make offerings in accordance with their means, each as he or she wishes; the bishop in turn makes use of these to support orphans, widows, the sick and those who for other reasons find themselves in need, such as prisoners and foreigners.[16]

The great Christian writer Tertullian († after 220) relates how the pagans were struck by the Christians' concern for the needy of every sort.[17] And when Ignatius of Antioch († c. 117) described the Church of Rome as "presiding in charity (*agape*),"[18] we may assume that with this definition he also intended in some sense to express her concrete charitable activity.

23. Here it might be helpful to allude to the earliest legal structures associated with the service of charity in the Church. Towards the middle of the fourth century we see the development in Egypt of the "*diaconia*": the institution within each monastery responsible for all works of relief, that is to say, for the service of charity. By the sixth century this institution had evolved into a corporation with full juridical standing, which the civil authorities themselves entrusted with part of the grain for public distribution. In Egypt not only each monastery, but each individual Diocese eventually had its own *diaconia*; this institution then developed in both East and West. Pope Gregory the Great († 604) mentions the *diaconia* of Naples, while in Rome the *diaconiae* are documented from the seventh and eighth centuries. But charitable activity on behalf of the poor and suffering was naturally an essential part of the Church of Rome from the very beginning, based on the principles of Christian life given in the Acts of the Apostles. It found a vivid expression in the case of the deacon Lawrence († 258). The dramatic description of Lawrence's martyrdom was known to St. Ambrose († 397) and it provides a fundamentally authentic picture of the saint. As the one responsible for the care of the poor in Rome, Lawrence had been given a period of time, after the capture of the Pope and of Lawrence's fellow deacons, to collect the treasures of the Church and hand them over to the civil authorities. He distributed to the poor whatever funds were available and then presented to the authorities the poor themselves as the real treasure of the Church.[19] Whatever historical reliability one attributes to these details, Lawrence has always remained present in the Church's memory as a great exponent of ecclesial charity.

SUPPLEMENTARY READING Continued

24. A mention of the emperor Julian the Apostate († 363) can also show how essential the early Church considered the organized practice of charity. As a child of six years, Julian witnessed the assassination of his father, brother and other family members by the guards of the imperial palace; rightly or wrongly, he blamed this brutal act on the Emperor Constantius, who passed himself off as an outstanding Christian. The Christian faith was thus definitively discredited in his eyes. Upon becoming emperor, Julian decided to restore paganism, the ancient Roman religion, while reforming it in the hope of making it the driving force behind the empire. In this project he was amply inspired by Christianity. He established a hierarchy of metropolitans and priests who were to foster love of God and neighbor. In one of his letters,[20] he wrote that the sole aspect of Christianity which had impressed him was the Church's charitable activity. He thus considered it essential for his new pagan religion that, alongside the system of the Church's charity, an equivalent activity of its own be established. According to him, this was the reason for the popularity of the "Galileans." They needed now to be imitated and outdone. In this way, then, the Emperor confirmed that charity was a decisive feature of the Christian community, the Church.

25. Thus far, two essential facts have emerged from our reflections:

a) The Church's deepest nature is expressed in her three-fold responsibility: of proclaiming the Word of God (*kerygma-martyria*), celebrating the Sacraments (*leitourgia*), and exercising the ministry of charity (*diakonia*). These duties presuppose each other and are inseparable. For the Church, charity is not a kind of welfare activity which could equally well be left to others, but is a part of her nature, an indispensable expression of her very being.[21]

b) The Church is God's family in the world. In this family no one ought to go without the necessities of life. Yet at the same time *caritas-agape* extends beyond the frontiers of the Church. The parable of the Good Samaritan remains as a standard which imposes universal love towards the needy whom we encounter "by chance" (cf. Lk 10:31), whoever they may be. Without in any way detracting from this commandment of universal love, the Church also has a specific responsibility: within the ecclesial family no member should suffer through being in need. The teaching of the Letter to the Galatians is emphatic: "So then, as we have opportunity, let us do good to all, and especially to those who are of the household of faith" (6:10).

— *Deus Caritas Est*

G.K. Chesterton: The Witness of the Heretics

The great man of letters G.K. Chesterton examines the Church's response to the fourth-century heresy of Arianism. The heretic Arius denied that the Son of God is coeternal and coequal with the Father, and so denied the doctrine of the Trinity. Chesterton shows such errors to be incompatible with love—and bad for society.

The whole great history of the Arian heresy might have been invented to explode this idea [that Christianity's validity—or orthodoxy—is a mere construct, from it having become the official religion of the Roman Empire]. It is a very interesting history often repeated in this connection; and the upshot of it is in so far as there ever was a merely official religion, it actually died because it was merely an official religion; and what destroyed it was the real religion. Arius advanced a version of Christianity which moved, more or less vaguely, in the direction of what we should call Unitarianism; though it was not the same, for it gave to Christ a curious intermediary position between the divine and human. The point is that it seemed to many more reasonable and less fanatical; and among these were many of the educated class in a sort of reaction against the first romance of conversion. Arians were a sort of moderates and a sort of modernists. And it was felt that after the first squabbles this was the final form of rationalized religion into which civilization might well settle down. It was accepted by Divus Caesar himself and became the official orthodoxy; the generals and military princes drawn from the new barbarian powers of the

SUPPLEMENTARY READING Continued

north, full of the future, supported it strongly. But the sequel is still more important. Exactly as a modern man might pass through Unitarianism to complete agnosticism, so the greatest of the Arian emperors ultimately shed the last and thinnest pretense of Christianity; he abandoned even Arius and returned to Apollo. He was a Caesar of the Caesars; a soldier, a scholar, a man of large ambitions and ideals; another of the philosopher kings. It seemed to him as if at his signal the sun rose again. The oracles began to speak like birds beginning to sing at dawn; paganism was itself again; the gods returned. It seemed the end of that strange interlude of an alien superstition. And indeed it was the end of it, so far as there was a mere interlude of mere superstition. It was the end of it, in so far as it was the fad of an emperor or the fashion of a generation. If there really was something that began with Constantine, then it ended with Julian.

But there was something that did not end. There had arisen in that hour of history, defiant above the democratic tumult of the Councils of the Church, Athanasius against the world. We may pause upon the point at issue; because it is relevant to the whole of this religious history, and the modern world seems to miss the whole point of it. We might put it this way. If there is one question which the enlightened and liberal have the habit of deriding and holding up as a dreadful example of barren dogma and senseless sectarian strife, it is this Athanasian question of the co-Eternity of the Divine Son. On the other hand, if there is one thing that the same liberals always offer us as a piece of pure and simple Christianity, untroubled by doctrinal disputes, it is the single sentence, "God is Love!" Yet the two statements are almost identical; at least one is very nearly nonsense without the other. The barren dogma is only the logical way of stating the beautiful sentiment. For if there be a being without beginning, existing before all things, was He loving when there was nothing to be loved? If through that unthinkable eternity He is lonely, what is the meaning of saying He is love? The only justification of such a mystery is the mystical conception that in His own nature there was something analogous to self-expression; something of what begets and beholds what it has begotten. Without some such idea, it is really illogical to complicate the ultimate essence of deity with an idea like love. If the moderns really want a simple religion of love, they must look for it in the Athanasian Creed. The truth is that the trumpet of true Christianity, the challenge of the charities and simplicities of Bethlehem or Christmas Day, never rang out more arrestingly and unmistakably than in the defiance of Athanasius to the cold compromise of the Arians. It was emphatically he who really was fighting for a God of Love against a God of colorless and remote cosmic control; the God of the stoics and the agnostics. It was emphatically he who was fighting for the Holy Child against the grey deity of the Pharisees and the Sadducees. He was fighting for that very balance of beautiful interdependence and intimacy, in the very Trinity of the Divine Nature, that draws our hearts to the Trinity of the Holy Family. His dogma, if the phrase be not misunderstood, turns even God into a Holy Family.

—from *The Everlasting Man* (Part 2, Chapter 4)

Father Damien with the Kalawao Girls Choir, at Kalaupapa, Molokai, ca. 1870.

VOCABULARY

APOLOGIST
One who defends and explains the Christian Faith.

APOLOGETICS
The rhetorical art of defending and explaining the Christian Faith.

BODY OF CHRIST
The New Testament's preeminent image of the Church, which lives in communion with Christ as its Head.

CHARITY
The theological virtue by which a Christian loves God above all things for his own sake, and loves his neighbor as himself for the love of God.

COMMUNION
From the Latin for "mutual participation" or "oneness together," *communion* denotes the most intimate fellowship, a sharing of life; the bond that believers share with Christ and, in Christ, with one another.

FAMILY OF GOD
A description of the fellowship of believers in the Church; the Communion of Saints united to Christ, enjoying the life of the Trinity.

GRACE
The gift of a share in God's life. The state of grace is a stable, supernatural disposition that enables the soul to live in communion with God. God gives actual grace to help us accomplish his will, and special graces (charisms) to help us fulfill our vocation.

HOLY SPIRIT
God, the Third Person of the Blessed Trinity. The Holy Spirit is the personal bond of love between God the Father and God the Son. The Holy Spirit is the gift of the Father and the Son to the Church, to be the Church's bond of loving unity.

NEW COMMANDMENT
The foundational law given by Christ to his disciples: "As I have loved you, so love one another" (Jn 13:34).

PASCHAL MYSTERY
Christ's saving work, accomplished through his dying, rising, and ascension into glory. "Paschal" refers to Passover, or Easter; Christ is the Lamb of the new Passover sacrifice (cf. 1 Cor 5:7).

POLYTHEISM
The idolatrous worship of many gods.

SACRAMENT
An efficacious sign of grace, instituted by Christ and entrusted to the Church, by which divine life is dispensed through the work of the Holy Spirit. There are Seven Sacraments: Baptism, Penance, Eucharist, Confirmation, Matrimony, Holy Orders, and Anointing of the Sick.

TRINITY
The mystery of one God in three Persons: Father, Son, and Holy Spirit; the primary mystery of Christian life and belief.

Bl. Teresa of Calcutta's Home for the Dying, Nirmal Hriday, in Calcutta.

STUDY QUESTIONS

1. Who were the apologists and what role did they play in telling the world about God's love?

2. How does Christ's New Commandment relate to the commandments given to Noah and Moses, as we discussed in the previous chapter?

3. How does the Christian idea of charity differ from common usage of the word?

4. How does the Christian idea of love differ from common usage of that word?

5. What is distinctive about the Christian doctrine of God?

6. What is the Blessed Trinity?

7. Why can we only say "God is love" if God is a communion of three divine Persons?

8. How can the eternal Trinity serve as a model for human relationships?

9. How does Christ share the Trinity's life within the Church?

10. Why do we call the Church the "Body of Christ"? How is the Church like a body? How is it Christ's Body?

11. What is the role of the Holy Spirit in the Church?

12. Why is unity so important for the Church's witness?

13. How is communion with God affected by our relationships with other people?

14. In what sense is the Church a family?

15. What is grace and how do we receive it?

PRACTICAL EXERCISES

1. Use a study Bible or concordance to find all the New Testament references to the Church as Christ's "Body." What do these passages say about the Church's life and gifts? How would the world benefit if all people came to share this life?

2. Think about your faith as a Christian and how it affects the way you think and act. How should the doctrine of the Trinity, and the Christian notion of charity, make you different from people who do not believe?

3. Research the religion of ancient Rome in the time of Christ. In what ways did the practice of Roman religion differ from the practice of Christian religion? How did the Roman gods differ from the God of Israel and from Jesus Christ? What kind of moral standard did the pagan myths set for people? What made Christianity more attractive by comparison? What would have made Christianity intimidating by comparison?

4. Read Matthew 28:18-20 and 2 Corinthians 13:14. What do these brief passages say about the relations among the Three Persons of the Trinity, and the Trinity's love for humanity?

FROM THE CATECHISM

234 The mystery of the Most Holy Trinity is the central mystery of Christian faith and life. It is the mystery of God in himself. It is therefore the source of all the other mysteries of faith, the light that enlightens them. It is the most fundamental and essential teaching in the "hierarchy of the truths of faith."[22] The whole history of salvation is identical with the history of the way and the means by which the one true God, Father, Son and Holy Spirit, reveals himself to men "and reconciles and unites with himself those who turn away from sin."[23]

267 Inseparable in what they are, the divine persons are also inseparable in what they do. But within the single divine operation each shows forth what is proper to him in the Trinity, especially in the divine missions of the Son's Incarnation and the gift of the Holy Spirit.

738 Thus the Church's mission is not an addition to that of Christ and the Holy Spirit, but is its sacrament: in her whole being and in all her members, the Church is sent to announce, bear witness, make present, and spread the mystery of the communion of the Holy Trinity…:

> All of us who have received one and the same Spirit, that is, the Holy Spirit, are in a sense blended together with one another and with God. For if Christ, together with the Father's and his own Spirit, comes to dwell in each of us, though we are many, still the Spirit is one and undivided. He binds together the spirits of each and every one of us,…and makes all appear as one in him. For just as the power of Christ's sacred flesh unites those in whom it dwells into one body, I think that in the same way the one and undivided Spirit of God, who dwells in all, leads all into spiritual unity.[24]

1693 Christ Jesus always did what was pleasing to the *Father*,[25] and always lived in perfect communion with him. Likewise Christ's disciples are invited to live in the sight of the Father "who sees in secret,"[26] in order to become "perfect as your heavenly Father is perfect."[27]

Sermon on the Mount by Olrik.
"As I have loved you, so love one another" (Jn 13:34).

ENDNOTES – CHAPTER ONE

1. *Apologeticum* 39.
2. *First Apology* 67.
3. Anonymous, *Letter to Diognetus* 5.2.
4. *Confessions* 1.1.1.
5. Council of Constantinople II (553): DS 421.
6. Council of Toledo XI (675): DS 530:26.
7. Lateran Council IV (1215): DS 804.
8. Cf. CCC 234.
9. *MD* 7.
10. Ibid.
11. *De Trinitate* ("On the Trinity") 8.8.12.
12. *LG* 1.
13. Manuscript B, *3vo: Oeuvres complètes* (Paris, 1996), 226.
14. John Paul II, Apostolic Letter *Mulieris Dignitatem*, 7: AAS 80 (1988), 1664.
15. *De Trinitate* ("On the Trinity"), VIII, 8, 12: CCL 50, 287.
16. Cf. St. Justin Martyr, *I Apologia*, 67: PG 6, 429.
17. Cf. *Apologeticum*, 39, 7: PL 1, 468
18. *Ep. ad Rom.*, Inscr: PG 5, 801.
19. Cf. St. Ambrose, *De officiis ministrorum*, II, 28, 140: PL 16, 141.
20. Cf. *Ep. 83*: J. Bidez, *L'Empereur Julien, Oeuvres completes* (Paris 1960), v. I, 2a, 145.
21. Cf. Congregation for Bishops, Directory for the Pastoral Ministry of Bishops (*Apostolorum Successores*), (Feb. 22, 2004), 194, Vatican City 2004, 213.
22. *GCD* 43.
23. *GCD* 47.
24. St. Cyril of Alexandria, *In Jo. ev.*, 11, 11: PG 74, 561.
25. Cf. Jn 8:29.
26. Mt 6:6.
27. Mt 5:48.

Social Doctrine of the Catholic Church
CHAPTER 2

Justice and Rights:
The Foundation of All Order in the World

All believers must seek justice, correct oppression, defend the defenseless, and plead for the poor.

Social Doctrine of the Catholic Church

CHAPTER TWO

Justice and Rights: The Foundation of All Order in the World

The Church, therefore, by virtue of the Gospel committed to her, proclaims the rights of man; she acknowledges and greatly esteems the dynamic movements of today by which these rights are everywhere fostered. Yet these movements must be penetrated by the spirit of the Gospel and protected against any kind of false autonomy. For we are tempted to think that our personal rights are fully ensured only when we are exempt from every requirement of divine law. But this way lies not the maintenance of the dignity of the human person, but its annihilation. — Gaudium et Spes, 41

IN THIS CHAPTER, WE WILL ADDRESS SEVERAL QUESTIONS:

✤ What is justice?

✤ What are rights?

✤ What is the foundation of human rights?

✤ What are some major obstacles and threats to human rights?

✤ What are the different types of justice?

✤ What is natural law?

✤ What does the Bible say about justice?

JUSTICE AND LAW

That's not fair....We deserve better....Divide everything evenly—right down the middle....When do I get my share?

People are intensely interested in justice. We want life to be fair. We want good things to be distributed equitably. When deeds must be punished, we want punishments to fit the crimes. We say that murder "cries out for justice," as do lesser crimes such as fraud and theft; and we know that, in an ordered society, such anti-social behavior must have consequences.

We often speak of "rights"—certain goods that are ours by nature and that may not unjustly be taken away from us.

To be concerned about justice is part of being human. And, since human beings are social by nature, we tend to build societies that reflect our innate desire for justice. Every society establishes systems and

JUSTICE AND RIGHTS: THE FOUNDATION OF ALL ORDER IN THE WORLD

Curses Against the Pharisees (detail) by Tissot. "'But woe to you Pharisees! for you tithe mint and rue and every herb, and neglect justice and the love of God; these you ought to have done, without neglecting the others.'" (Lk 11:42)

structures—laws, courts, and law enforcement—to preserve its conception of a just order and to correct and remedy injustices.

From its earliest beginnings, human society has always been concerned with justice. In the ancient world, justice was a primary concern of philosophers as well as the ordinary people. The idea of justice is mentioned more than eight hundred times in the Bible. (The Hebrew and Greek terms for "just" and "justice" are sometimes translated into English as *righteous* and *righteousness*.)

In the Old Testament, the commandment is simple and direct:

> Justice, and only justice, you shall follow, that you may live and inherit the land which the LORD your God gives you. (Dt 16:20)

Justice is therefore at the heart of the law. It is essential to the message of the prophets as well:

> What does the LORD require of you but to do justice, and to love kindness, and to walk humbly with your God? (Mi 6:8)

Christ condemned the religious leaders of his time precisely because they "neglect[ed] justice and the love of God" (Lk 11:42).

Biblical faith is very clear: Justice is a necessary and important characteristic of a godly life.

DEFINING JUSTICE

But what exactly is justice?

Christian theology speaks of justice as a *virtue*—that is, a habitual and firm disposition of the will to do good. Indeed, it was numbered among the four governing virtues, called *cardinal virtues*, the other three being prudence, temperance, and fortitude. Most philosophers considered justice to be the most important of the four.

Yet, even those who placed justice at the pinnacle of human virtue did not agree unanimously on its definition. St. Augustine defined virtue as "nothing else than perfect love of God" and the four cardinal virtues as simply "four forms of love." "Justice," he said, "is love serving God only, and therefore ruling well all else, as subject to man."[1] Thus, he directs our attention to certain facts about justice: It has to do with human dominion over goods—goods that God created in order to sustain and enrich his children.

St. Thomas Aquinas gave a definition that is perhaps more practical, adapting it from ancient Roman law. Justice, he said, is *the steady and lasting willingness to give to others what belongs to them by right*.[2]

Of the four cardinal virtues, only justice is necessarily *social*. Only justice is directed toward other people. Fortitude and temperance are concerned mostly with oneself. Justice is the measure of how well we treat others.

Yet, justice comes into play in the exercise of every other virtue. That is why it is called a *cardinal* virtue. The term "cardinal" comes from the Latin *cardo*, meaning "hinge." While the cardinal virtues are the hinges upon which the door of the moral life opens and closes, it should be remembered that the theological virtue of charity is the superior consideration in every action, and it is charity that completes and perfects justice.

Since most external acts have some social consequences, almost every act of virtue or vice will involve justice or injustice. A small act of temperance—moderation in eating, for example—will leave more food for others to enjoy. An act of fortitude (courage) may save a child from a burning building.

The same principle applies in sinful acts. All sexual sins, for example, are sins against justice, since they involve an abuse or theft of something that belongs to someone else. A person's sexual faculties belong properly to his or her spouse—or, if one is unmarried, to no one—and should not be taken or misused by acts of adultery or fornication. Any unchaste act is social because it involves the unjust use of another person.

Together with charity, justice plays a decisive role in all human relationships. Charity leads us to help others in their need by sharing what we have. Justice teaches us to give others what is rightfully theirs.

All people naturally admire justice and hate injustice. Even criminals—those who commit unjust acts habitually—do not wish to be treated unfairly themselves. When St. Thomas Aquinas spoke of the primacy of justice among the moral virtues, he quoted the pagan Roman statesman and philosopher, Cicero: "Justice is the most resplendent of the virtues, and gives its name to a good person."[3] As it was in pre-Christian Rome, so it is still today: A good person is a just person, and a just person is a good person.

JUSTICE IS PERSONAL

Justice is a social virtue, but it always begins with a personal act. The philosopher Joseph Pieper observed:

> That one man gives to another what belongs to the other is the basis of all just order in the world. In contrast, all injustice means that what belongs to someone is either withheld or taken from him, not indeed by misfortune, bad harvest, fire or earthquake but by man.[4]

Homer and His Guide (detail) by Bouguereau. "Our inviolable rule ought to be never to do anything that wounds our conscience or that makes us ashamed of ourselves."

We will speak often, in this book, of "social justice," but all social justice begins with the personal moral decisions of individual men and women, boys and girls. When we work diligently during all the hours our employer pays us for, we are acting with justice; and, indeed, it is *social* justice. We are giving our employers the time they have bought from us—the time that belongs rightly to them, the time we owe them. When we use the common goods of our household with care, we are preserving them for use by other family members, because they belong to the whole family. Because our family members have a right to the use of appliances that are kept in good repair—the lawnmower kept in good working order, the blender cleaned after making a milkshake—we have a corresponding duty to keep up the maintenance on these things.

Social justice, like charity, may extend to the far reaches of the planet and touch the lives of millions of people, but it must begin at home, in one's own neighborhood, school, playground, or workplace.

RIGHTS PRECEDE JUSTICE

Justice always presumes the existence of *rights*. In fact, the word justice comes from *ius* (or *jus*), the Latin word for "right."

Rights precede justice. If you must pay a bill you owe, it is because someone has a right to collect upon the debt. If you have worked for a full week, you are entitled to payment by your employer. Some portion of the money your employer possesses now *belongs* to you by right. It is your property.

JOHN HOWARD GRIFFIN: Raceless Vision

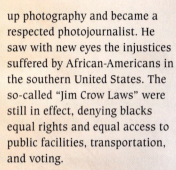

John Howard Griffin was born in Texas in 1920 and grew up in a home filled with music and ideas. His mother was a classical pianist, and he followed after her. But he was also inclined to study medicine to help others. When he was fifteen he sailed to France in pursuit of a classical education. He earned scholarships to study music and medicine at universities in France. He took up both with gusto, studying under great composers and arrangers of his day. Meanwhile, he also assisted at some of the very early research into music therapy for people with mental illness.

His time in France coincided with the beginning of the Nazi occupation of the country. The racist ideology of the Nazis sickened him, and he decided to place his medical training at the service of the French Resistance movement. He also helped Jews escape arrest and certain death.

On leaving France, he entered the United States Army Air Corps, where he served more than three years, the remainder of World War II. Almost all of his time was spent in the South Pacific. He earned medals for bravery—and also pursued research in ethnic studies. Griffin lost his sight in a bombing raid and returned home disabled.

Unable to pursue a career in medicine, he turned to writing, producing five novels. He also gave piano lessons. His study and his suffering led him to the Catholic Faith in 1950. An intense and devout man, he became a Third Order (Lay) Carmelite. In 1953, he married and began a family. He and his wife, Elizabeth, eventually had four children.

In 1957, he miraculously regained his sight. With renewed vigor—and a renewed appreciation for the visual arts—he took up photography and became a respected photojournalist. He saw with new eyes the injustices suffered by African-Americans in the southern United States. The so-called "Jim Crow Laws" were still in effect, denying blacks equal rights and equal access to public facilities, transportation, and voting.

Griffin decided he would suffer everything African-Americans suffered, and he would keep a careful record of it, in words and pictures. In 1959, under a doctor's supervision, he darkened his skin, shaved his head, and set out on a journey through Louisiana, Mississippi, Alabama, South Carolina, and Georgia. He was often denied service in restaurants, motels, and shops. People expressed contempt for him because he appeared to be a black man. Yet, he also recorded instances of genuine kindness. His account of the journey, the book *Black Like Me* (1960), became a bestseller and earned many awards. Its eyewitness testimony roused many people to take up advocacy for civil rights.

For Griffin himself, the journey of 1959 was part of the same struggle for justice that had inspired him to join the French Resistance and then to enter the Catholic Church. He wrote in *Black Like Me*: "The real story is the universal one of men who destroy the souls and bodies of other men (and in the process destroy themselves) for reasons neither really understands. It is the story of the persecuted, the defrauded, the feared and detested. I could have been a Jew in Germany, a Mexican in a number of states, or a member of any 'inferior' group. Only the details would have differed. The story would be the same."

John Howard Griffin died of cancer in 1980.

In justice we receive what is ours and we give others what belongs to them. When we borrow books, we must return them. If we break someone's bicycle, we must pay to have it restored to its former, undamaged condition. If we download music or games that are for sale, we must make sure we have paid the required fees for ownership. We must have the right of ownership over the property we possess, even if it is "intellectual property," such as the nontangible content of books, music, movies, or games.

Certain rights belong to us simply because we are persons created by God. For example:

Dr. Martin Luther King Jr. (1929-1968) dedicated and sacrificed his life for social justice through nonviolent resistance to unjust laws.

✣ We have a right to life. No one is permitted to murder a human being.

✣ We have a right to bodily integrity. No one may legitimately mutilate or physically harm another person. A government may not, for example, force its citizens to undergo surgical sterilization or donate bodily organs against their will.

✣ We have a right to personal and vocational freedom. No one may force us to marry or refrain from marriage. No one may enslave us. We lose our right to personal freedom only if we have forfeited it by committing a crime and subjecting ourselves to the just judgment of a prison sentence.

✣ We have a right to hold property. All the things of the earth were created for the use and benefit of the human race. Everyone has a right to possess the things that are necessary for a good and orderly life.

However, not all rights are absolute and inalienable. The state, for example, may place limitations on the ownership of some property, if those restrictions will benefit society as a whole. In times of severe shortage, a government may ration food or fuel in order to make it available to a greater number of people.

Even the right to life may be abrogated under certain rare circumstances. An individual may legitimately, in self-defense, take the life of an attacker. Military personnel may, if acting under legitimate authority in a just war, kill enemy combatants.

But these are rare exceptions to the general rule. And the state exists in order to protect rights, not take them away.

Such rights to life, limb, liberty, and property are called *natural rights*. We have them by the very *nature* of being human. Natural rights ensure that we have the freedom and the means to fulfill our natural and supernatural destiny as human beings.

TYPES OF JUSTICE

Catholic moral teaching distinguishes different types or dimensions of justice. The *Catechism* summarizes them:

> Contracts are subject to *commutative justice* which regulates exchanges between persons in accordance with a strict respect for their rights. Commutative justice obliges strictly; it requires safeguarding property rights, paying debts, and fulfilling obligations freely contracted. Without commutative justice, no other form of justice is possible.
>
> One distinguishes *commutative* justice from *legal* justice, which concerns what the citizen owes in fairness to the community, and from *distributive* justice which regulates what the community owes its citizens in proportion to their contributions and needs. (CCC 2411)

JUSTICE AND RIGHTS: THE FOUNDATION OF ALL ORDER IN THE WORLD

Commutative justice governs the ordinary mutual transactions of everyday life. Commutative justice directs us to honor our promises and contracts, to do the job we are paid to do, and to pay for the products we have purchased or the services we have engaged. Commutative justice forbids homicide, theft, fraud, exploitation, gossip, and false witness. Why is gossip included here? Our neighbors have a right to their good reputation, and they need it, as they need food and water, in order to live a happy and productive life in society. When commutative justice has been violated, the offending party has an obligation to repair the wrong that has been done.

Legal justice measures the way individuals respond to the obligations of living in society or living under the state. Individuals must not fall into *individualism*, neglecting to obey the law or fulfill their duties to the common good. Legal justice is concerned, not directly with the rights of individuals, but with the common good of society. Legal justice leads us to give generously of ourselves for the sake of the community, placing our time, money, and talents at the service of others.

> The exercise of authority is meant to give outward expression to a just hierarchy of values in order to facilitate the exercise of freedom and responsibility by all. Those in authority should practice distributive justice wisely, taking account of the needs and contribution of each, with a view to harmony and peace. They should take care that the regulations and measures they adopt are not a source of temptation by setting personal interest against that of the community.[5] (CCC 2236)

Abraham Lincoln (1809-1865) as the sixteenth President of the United States preserved the Union and abolished the institution of slavery. "…let every man remember that to violate the law is to trample on the blood of his father, and to tear the charter of his own and his children's liberty."

Distributive justice measures the ways and means by which authority distributes the goods and obligations of social life among the members of society. Distribution is made according to the merits and needs of the different members of society. People should receive in just proportion to what they need and what they contribute. Since needs and accomplishments will vary from person to person, inequality is inevitable and not necessarily unjust. Still, authorities should ensure that inequality does not lead to the exclusion, oppression, or exploitation of some members of society.

In addition to these three classical forms of justice, the Church has paid increasing attention to *social justice*, which considers the cultural, political, and economic aspects of the human community, with particular concern for structural problems and solutions. The *Catechism* explains:

> Society ensures social justice when it provides the conditions that allow associations or individuals to obtain what is their due, according to their nature and their vocation. (CCC 1928)

Thus, true social justice depends upon a proper understanding of human nature:

> Social justice can be obtained only in respecting the transcendent dignity of man. The person represents the ultimate end of society. (CCC 1929)

Social justice is increasingly important in a world united by instantaneous communication, "free" trade, and easy travel. What happens on the stock market in Singapore can affect the disposition of crops in Kenya and the availability of certain products in Kansas. With these new conditions in the world come new responsibilities, duties, obligations, and rights. The world is beginning to discover what they might be; and Christians—and the Church—must take part in that development.

Even so, the morality of justice always comes down to the choices of persons. Peace begins with virtue, which is always personal. Personal virtue leads to individual initiatives, which in turn can attract many others to a cause. This can soon become a movement, which can change the world.

Declaration of Independence by Trumbull.
This famous painting depicts the five-man drafting committee of the Declaration of Independence presenting their work to the Continental Congress on June 28, 1776. The Committee of Five consisted of John Adams of Massachusetts, Benjamin Franklin of Pennsylvania, Thomas Jefferson of Virginia, Robert R. Livingston of New York, and Roger Sherman of Connecticut.

WHAT RIGHTS DO WE HAVE?

Everyone wants justice and fairness. Most people agree that human beings have certain rights by nature. And all sane people want their own rights to be protected.

Many national constitutions guarantee the protection of certain rights. For example, the United States Constitution includes ten amendments known as the "Bill of Rights," and those legally recognized rights include the free exercise of religion, freedom of speech, freedom of the press, freedom of assembly, the right to bear arms, the right to a timely trial by jury, protection from unlawful search and seizure, protection from cruel and unusual punishment, and many others. These rights and guaranteed freedoms have come to define the United States legal system and even the broader culture. They have, moreover, influenced the development of other countries' legal systems, throughout the world.

When St. John Paul II visited the United Nations in 1979, he noted that "the quest for freedom in our time has its basis in those universal rights which human beings enjoy by the very fact of their humanity." In 1995, he argued that nations, too, have rights. In both addresses, he argued from a presumed agreement that human beings possess certain rights by nature. Nevertheless, he acknowledged that, apart from religious faith, it is difficult to determine what those rights are—and who determines what they are.

The Declaration of Independence, written in 1776, addresses these problems directly:

> We hold these truths to be self-evident, that all men are created equal, that they are endowed by their Creator with certain unalienable Rights, that among these are Life, Liberty and the pursuit of Happiness.—That to secure these rights, Governments are instituted among Men, deriving their just powers from the consent of the governed.

According to this account, rights come from the Creator. Government is their custodian, their caretaker, and their guarantor—but not their origin. Government's legitimate task is to recognize and protect the rights that have been given to every human being by God.

DR. BERNARD NATHANSON and the Right to Life

Dr. Bernard Nathanson was once the most vehement advocate for so-called "abortion rights." He was cofounder of the organization that became the National Abortion Rights Action League (now NARAL Pro-Choice America). Until 1973, abortion was illegal or severely restricted in most of the United States. Through the efforts of NARAL, all of the nation's anti-abortion laws were effectively overridden with the U.S. Supreme Court's decision in the case *Roe v. Wade*.

He believed that his ends justified any means, including trickery and deception. Dr. Nathanson later admitted that he was willing to falsify data and lie outright in order to advance the cause. He lied, for example, about the number of women who died from illegal abortions, inflating the figure from hundreds per year to more than ten thousand per year.

Dr. Nathanson knew the abortion business well. He ran the Center for Reproductive and Sexual Health in Manhattan, the largest abortion clinic in the Western world. He personally presided over 75,000 abortions. He even aborted one of his own children.

For all his experience and expertise, however, he did not really understand what happens during an abortion. "I had done many, but abortion is a blind procedure. The doctor does not see what he is doing. He puts an instrument into a uterus and he turns on a motor, and a suction machine goes on and something is vacuumed out; it ends up as a little pile of meat in a gauze bag."

One day, Dr. Nathanson asked a colleague if he would attach an ultrasound to a mother so that they could later watch a tape of the procedure from the perspective of the developing fetus.

He later recalled that he "was shaken to the very roots of my soul by what I saw." He saw a baby, recognizably human, fighting for life, silently screaming in pain, recoiling from the murderous instruments as they approached.

He never performed another abortion. Haunted by the thought of all the suffering he had caused through his years of performing abortions, he felt he had to work as tirelessly as he had worked in advance of *Roe v. Wade*, but now for its undoing. Dr. Nathanson made a documentary film, *The Silent Scream*, which used ultrasound technology to show people the horror of abortion as he himself had seen it on that life-changing day. He wrote a book, *Aborting America*, to make people aware of the effects of abortion on society.

Dr. Nathanson came to realize that every "fetus" was a human being with rights.

When Dr. Nathanson saw abortion as it really was, he realized that every "fetus" he had aborted was a human being with rights—beginning with the right to life. He soon became a tireless advocate of the pro-life cause, producing more books and documentaries, providing expert testimony in court and on television news, and protesting outside abortion clinics.

He sought forgiveness for the acts of homicide he had committed in his years of moral blindness. After years of religious seeking, he asked to be baptized as a Catholic.

Until his death in 2011, Dr. Nathanson continued praying and working for the reversal of laws permitting abortion in America.

Jacques Maritain (1882-1973), a French Catholic philosopher, helped revive St. Thomas Aquinas for modern times. Pope Paul VI, his friend and mentor, presented him with his "Message to Men of Thought and of Science" at the close of Vatican II.

The American founders presumed upon a common notion of God that enabled them to agree upon a shared sense of human rights. Apart from these shared religious beliefs, however, it has become increasingly difficult for people to agree upon which freedoms are guaranteed as rights, and which may be limited, and how much they may be limited. Not all people throughout history have considered it "self-evident" that "all men are created equal" insofar as they are creatures made in the image and likeness of God. Nor do all nations, even today, agree that natural rights may undergird freedom of expression, freedom of the press, public trials, and so on.

In the absence of consensus, it becomes increasingly difficult, and increasingly important, to articulate what we mean by natural rights. St. John Paul II, in his addresses to the United Nations, recognized this difficulty. He was certainly not the first to discuss the problem.

In the years following World War II, world leaders formed the United Nations in order to secure rights universally for the sake of peace. The Catholic philosopher Jacques Maritain was an influential advisor during the drafting of the United Nations' *Universal Declaration of Human Rights*. Years later, he would recall: "During one of the meetings...at which the Rights of Man were being discussed, someone was astonished that certain proponents of violently opposed ideologies had agreed on the draft of a list of rights. Yes, they replied, we agree on these rights, *providing we are not asked why*. With the 'why,' the dispute begins."[6]

The man who prepared the first draft of the *Declaration*, John Humphrey, later recalled that Catholics such as Jacques Maritain provided the theoretical foundation for the document, introducing the notion of the *natural law* that dictates *natural rights*. It was Catholicism's conceptual framework that enabled people from vastly different perspectives to converge and come to an agreement.

The natural law, present in the heart of each man and established by reason, is universal in its precepts and its authority extends to all men. It expresses the dignity of the person and determines the basis for his fundamental rights and duties:

> "For there is a true law: right reason. It is in conformity with nature, is diffused among all men, and is immutable and eternal; its orders summon to duty; its prohibitions turn away from offense....To replace it with a contrary law is a sacrilege; failure to apply even one of its provisions is forbidden; no one can abrogate it entirely."[7] (CCC 1956)

Natural law, in Catholic thought, is an objective order established by God that determines the requirements for people to thrive and reach fulfillment. Natural rights issue from that foundation. But they are also necessarily limited. Freedom of expression may be a natural right, for example, but it does not protect libel, slander, defamation, treason, or pornography. Everyone has a right to ownership of property, but the government cannot tolerate the stockpiling of plutonium or anthrax spores in a suburban home. Freedoms are necessarily limited and restricted. Otherwise, one person's expression of freedom could trample the rights of others. A man who stockpiles plutonium or anthrax is endangering the lives of those around him. A person who uses pornography is supporting an industry that exploits, oppresses, and dehumanizes people; pornography has encouraged the commission of sexual crimes, most heinously against children; and it has destroyed many marriages.

Today, many special-interest groups are advocating "rights" that are destructive to society. It is important that we cultivate a proper understanding of what rights are and where they come from. We must also be able to state articulately our opposition to illusory "freedoms" that actually enslave people—"rights" that destroy the rights of others.

JUSTICE AND RIGHTS: THE FOUNDATION OF ALL ORDER IN THE WORLD

Let us consider the most egregious example. Some people claim that there is a universal "right" to abortion as a matter of "health care." This is absurd for many reasons. Everyone indeed has a right to health care, but abortion is not good for anyone's health. It damages the mother psychologically and often physically as well, resulting in infertility, infections, and other problems; and it always kills the child, who is a human person endowed with the fundamental and inalienable right to life. There can be no justification for this. No authority on earth can give people the freedom to trample the basic rights of others, even to the point of taking innocent life. Thus, abortion is a most abominable injustice.

The right to health care, moreover, is not absolute and unrestricted. If you need a transplant, for example, you cannot demand your neighbor's kidney simply because your neighbor might be a compatible donor. Your right to health care does not require your neighbor to forfeit his right to bodily integrity.

Rights precede justice. Justice, therefore, by definition, requires the protection and preservation of rights.

> *Justice* is the moral virtue that consists in the constant and firm will to give [what is] due to God and neighbor. Justice toward God is called the "virtue of religion." Justice toward men disposes one to respect the rights of each and to establish in human relationships the harmony that promotes equity with regard to persons and to the common good. (CCC 1807)

JUSTICE IN THE BIBLE

In the Old Testament, we see how the prophets sometimes brought God's word of judgment to lands that were enjoying apparent peace and prosperity. Amos and Isaiah tried to awaken the people of Israel from their complacency, so that they could see that their domestic tranquility was bought with the exploitation of poor workers. Their national security came about because of the dire misfortunes of the nations around them. Their wealth stood in horrific contrast to the marginalized and vulnerable people in their own cities, especially orphans and widows. In the marketplaces, merchants were thriving because they routinely cheated their customers. In the courts, judges compromised their office and rendered false decisions, bought by bribes.

Old Testament Prophet Amos, Russian Icon. Amos was not afraid to condemn his countrymen for their injustices.

Amos was not afraid to condemn his countrymen for their injustices. He was particularly horrified when crooked merchants and magistrates took their ill-gotten fortunes and used them to make a show of religious piety.

> They sell the righteous for silver,
>   and the needy for a pair of shoes—
> they that trample the head of the poor into the
>   dust of the earth,
>   and turn aside the way of the afflicted;
> a man and his father go in to the same maiden,
>   so that my holy name is profaned;
> they lay themselves down beside every altar
>   upon garments taken in pledge;
> and in the house of their God they drink
>   the wine of those who have been fined.
> (Am 2:6-8)

He reminds them that they are under judgment. When the Day of the Lord arrived—a day awaited by all the people of Israel—it would be for them a day not of salvation, but of punishment.

The Lord issued similar oracles through the prophet Isaiah. The Book of Isaiah begins with an outright rejection of Israel's prayers of sacrifice. Israel's worship was invalidated by social and personal injustice.

> Bring no more vain offerings;
>   incense is an abomination to me.
> New moon and sabbath and the calling of
>   assemblies—
>   I cannot endure iniquity and solemn assembly.
> Your new moons and your appointed feasts my
>   soul hates;
> they have become a burden to me,
>   I am weary of bearing them.
> When you spread forth your hands,
>   I will hide my eyes from you;
> even though you make many prayers,
>   I will not listen;
>   your hands are full of blood.
> Wash yourselves; make yourselves clean;
>   remove the evil of your doings
>   from before my eyes;
> cease to do evil,
>   learn to do good;
> seek justice,
>   correct oppression;
> defend the fatherless,
>   plead for the widow. (Is 1:13-17)

Old Testament Prophet Isaiah by Michelangelo. "learn to do good; seek justice, correct oppression"

These words, spoken to ancient Israel, remain true today. Justice is an essential component of Christianity. All believers must seek justice, correct oppression, defend the defenseless, and plead for the poor. Justice is, as it ever has been, essential and not optional. Where it is neglected or violated, the people cannot flourish, even if they appear to be prosperous.

In the New Testament, Christ spoke of the Judgment Day in terms that were even more stark for the unjust—and promising for the just.

> Then the King will say to those at his right hand, "Come, O blessed of my Father, inherit the kingdom prepared for you from the foundation of the world; for I was hungry and you gave me food, I was thirsty and you gave me drink, I was a stranger and you welcomed me, I was naked and you clothed me, I was sick and you visited me, I was in prison and you came to me."
>
> Then the righteous will answer him, "Lord, when did we see you hungry and feed you, or thirsty and give you drink? And when did we see you a stranger and welcome you, or naked and clothe you? And when did we see you sick or in prison and visit you?"
>
> And the King will answer them, "Truly, I say to you, as you did it to one of the least of these my brethren, you did it to me."
>
> Then he will say to those at his left hand, "Depart from me, you cursed, into the eternal fire prepared for the devil and his angels; for I was hungry and you gave me no food, I was thirsty and you gave me no drink, I was a stranger and you did not welcome me, naked and you did not clothe me, sick and in prison and you did not visit me."
>
> Then they also will answer, "Lord, when did we see you hungry or thirsty or a stranger or naked or sick or in prison, and did not minister to you?"
>
> Then he will answer them, "Truly, I say to you, as you did it not to one of the least of these, you did it not to me." (Mt 25:34-45)

Whatever we do to the least of our neighbors, we do to God himself. For it is the poor, the widows, the oppressed, whom Christ pronounced "blessed" from the beginning of his ministry, in the Beatitudes of the Sermon on the Mount (cf. Mt 5:1-11). God himself became flesh to share the condition of marginalized people, to suffer their want, and to vindicate them.

JUSTICE AND RIGHTS: THE FOUNDATION OF ALL ORDER IN THE WORLD

Moses Receiving the Tables of the Law (detail) by Tintoretto.
God's laws are the path toward profound personal fulfillment and intense happiness.

CONCLUSION

All human beings possess rights because they have inherent dignity. They are persons, with intelligence and free will, created in the image and likeness of God. It is a matter of justice to give people what is theirs by right.

People have a strong sense of what belongs to them. They want to secure and protect it, whether it is property or freedom or security or livelihood. Thus, rights and justice have always been major preoccupations of individuals and governments.

The modern era has witnessed an increased recognition of the universality of human rights. Yet, this has been undercut by a widespread and radical secularism that forbids the acknowledgment of God in any public accounting of human rights. It is difficult, if not impossible, to make a case for human dignity, human rights, and even human nature, apart from God.

When rights are dependent on mere human decisions, they are easily changed, easily multiplied to the point of meaninglessness, easily put aside, and readily abolished.

Rights come with corresponding duties. We are obliged *always* to do justice, to respect the dignity of others, to contribute to the common good, and to do what is in our power to protect and preserve human rights.

PILLARS OF THE CHURCH

ST. THOMAS AQUINAS: On Justice

Article 1. Whether justice is fittingly defined as being the perpetual and constant will to render to each one his right?

Objection 1. It would seem that lawyers have unfittingly defined justice as being "the perpetual and constant will to render to each one his right" [*Digest*. i, 1; *De Just. et Jure* 10. For, according to the Philosopher (*Ethic*. v, 1), justice is a habit which makes a man "capable of doing what is just, and of being just in action and in intention." Now "will" denotes a power, or also an act. Therefore justice is unfittingly defined as being a will.

Objection 2. Further, rectitude of the will is not the will; else if the will were its own rectitude, it would follow that no will is unrighteous. Yet, according to Anselm (*De Veritate* xii), justice is rectitude. Therefore justice is not the will.

Objection 3. Further, no will is perpetual save God's. If therefore justice is a perpetual will, in God alone will there be justice.

Objection 4. Further, whatever is perpetual is constant, since it is unchangeable. Therefore it is needless in defining justice, to say that it is both "perpetual" and "constant."

Objection 5. Further, it belongs to the sovereign to give each one his right. Therefore, if justice gives each one his right, it follows that it is in none but the sovereign: which is absurd.

Objection 6. Further, Augustine says (*De Moribus Eccl.* xv) that "justice is love serving God alone." Therefore it does not render to each one his right.

I answer that, The aforesaid definition of justice is fitting if understood aright. For since every virtue is a habit that is the principle of a good act, a virtue must needs be defined by means of the good act bearing on the matter proper to that virtue. Now the proper matter of justice consists of those things that belong to our intercourse with other men, as shall be shown further on (2). Hence the act of justice in relation to its proper matter and object is indicated in the words, "Rendering to each one his right," since, as Isidore says (*Etym.* x), "a man is said to be just because he respects the rights [*jus*] of others."

Now in order that an act bearing upon any matter whatever be virtuous, it requires to be voluntary, stable, and firm, because the Philosopher says (*Ethic.* ii, 4) that in order for an act to be virtuous it needs first of all to be done "knowingly," secondly to be done "by choice," and "for a due end," thirdly to be done "immovably." Now the first of these is included in the second, since "what is done through ignorance is involuntary" (*Ethic.* iii, 1). Hence the definition of justice mentions first the "will," in order to show that the act of justice must be voluntary; and mention is made afterwards of its "constancy" and "perpetuity" in order to indicate the firmness of the act.

Accordingly, this is a complete definition of justice; save that the act is mentioned instead of the habit, which takes its species from that act, because habit implies relation to act. And if anyone would reduce it to the proper form of a definition, he might say that "justice is a

Continued

ST. THOMAS AQUINAS: On Justice
Continued

Triumph of St. Thomas Aquinas (detail) by Gozzoli. St. Aquinas is enthroned between Aristotle and Plato.

habit whereby a man renders to each one his due by a constant and perpetual will": and this is about the same definition as that given by the Philosopher (*Ethic.* v, 5) who says that "justice is a habit whereby a man is said to be capable of doing just actions in accordance with his choice."

Reply to Objection 1. Will here denotes the act, not the power: and it is customary among writers to define habits by their acts: thus Augustine says (*Tract. in Joan.* xl) that "faith is to believe what one sees not."

Reply to Objection 2. Justice is the same as rectitude, not essentially but causally; for it is a habit which rectifies the deed and the will.

Reply to Objection 3. The will may be called perpetual in two ways. First on the part of the will's act which endures for ever, and thus God's will alone is perpetual. Secondly on the part of the subject, because, to wit, a man wills to do a certain thing always, and this is a necessary condition of justice. For it does not satisfy the conditions of justice that one wish to observe justice in some particular matter for the time being, because one could scarcely find a man willing to act unjustly in every case; and it is requisite that one should have the will to observe justice at all times and in all cases.

Reply to Objection 4. Since "perpetual" does not imply perpetuity of the act of the will, it is not superfluous to add "constant": for while the "perpetual will" denotes the purpose of observing justice always, "constant" signifies a firm perseverance in this purpose.

Reply to Objection 5. A judge renders to each one what belongs to him, by way of command and direction, because a judge is the "personification of justice," and "the sovereign is its guardian" (*Ethic.* v, 4). On the other hand, the subjects render to each one what belongs to him, by way of execution.

Reply to Objection 6. Just as love of God includes love of our neighbor, as stated above (Question 25, Article 1), so too the service of God includes rendering to each one his due.

— *Summa Theologiæ* 2.2.58.1

SUPPLEMENTARY READING

Compendium of the Social Doctrine of the Church:

The Value of Human Rights

152. The movement towards the identification and proclamation of human rights is one of the most significant attempts to respond effectively to the inescapable demands of human dignity.[8] The Church sees in these rights the extraordinary opportunity that our modern times offer, through the affirmation of these rights, for more effectively recognizing human dignity and universally promoting it as a characteristic inscribed by God the Creator in his creature.[9] The Church's Magisterium has not failed to note the positive value of the *Universal Declaration of Human Rights*, adopted by the United Nations on 10 December 1948, which Pope John Paul II defined as "a true milestone on the path of humanity's moral progress."[10]

153. In fact, the roots of human rights are to be found in the dignity that belongs to each human being.[11] This dignity, inherent in human life and equal in every person, is perceived and understood first of all by reason. The natural foundation of rights appears all the more solid when, in light of the supernatural, it is considered that human dignity, after having been given by God and having been profoundly wounded by sin, was taken on and redeemed by Jesus Christ in his incarnation, death and resurrection.[12]

The ultimate source of human rights is not found in the mere will of human beings,[13] *in the reality of the State, in public powers, but in man himself and in God his Creator.* These rights are "universal, inviolable, inalienable."[14] Universal because they are present in all human beings, without exception of time, place or subject. *Inviolable* insofar as "they are inherent in the human person and in human dignity"[15] and because "it would be vain to proclaim rights, if at the same time everything were not done to ensure the duty of respecting them by all people, everywhere, and for all people."[16] *Inalienable* insofar as "no one can legitimately deprive another person, whoever they may be, of these rights, since this would do violence to their nature."[17]

154. Human rights are to be defended not only individually but also as a whole: protecting them only partially would imply a kind of failure to recognize them. They correspond to the demands of human dignity and entail, in the first place, the fulfilment of the essential needs of the person in the material and spiritual spheres. "These rights apply to every stage of life and to every political, social, economic and cultural situation. Together they form a single whole, directed unambiguously towards the promotion of every aspect of the good of both the person and society ... The integral promotion of every category of human rights is the true guarantee of full respect for each individual right."[18] Universality and indivisibility are distinctive characteristics of human rights: they are "two guiding principles which at the same time demand that human rights be rooted in each culture and that their juridical profile be strengthened so as to ensure that they are fully observed."[19]

St. John XXIII: Rights are the Basis of Order

8. We must devote our attention first of all to that order which should prevail among men.

9. Any well-regulated and productive association of men in society demands the acceptance of one fundamental principle: that each individual man is truly a person. His is a nature, that is, endowed with intelligence and free will. As such he has rights and duties, which together flow as a direct consequence from his nature. These rights and duties are universal and inviolable, and therefore altogether inalienable.[20]

10. When, furthermore, we consider man's personal dignity from the standpoint of divine revelation, inevitably our estimate of it is incomparably increased. Men have been ransomed by the blood of Jesus Christ. Grace has made them sons and friends of God, and heirs to eternal glory.

11. But first we must speak of man's rights. Man has the right to live. He has the right to bodily integrity and to the means necessary for the

SUPPLEMENTARY READING continued

proper development of life, particularly food, clothing, shelter, medical care, rest, and, finally, the necessary social services. In consequence, he has the right to be looked after in the event of ill health; disability stemming from his work; widowhood; old age; enforced unemployment; or whenever through no fault of his own he is deprived of the means of livelihood.[21]

12. Moreover, man has a natural right to be respected. He has a right to his good name. He has a right to freedom in investigating the truth, and—within the limits of the moral order and the common good—to freedom of speech and publication, and to freedom to pursue whatever profession he may choose. He has the right, also, to be accurately informed about public events.

13. He has the natural right to share in the benefits of culture, and hence to receive a good general education, and a technical or professional training consistent with the degree of educational development in his own country. Furthermore, a system must be devised for affording gifted members of society the opportunity of engaging in more advanced studies, with a view to their occupying, as far as possible, positions of responsibility in society in keeping with their natural talent and acquired skill.[22]

14. Also among man's rights is that of being able to worship God in accordance with the right dictates of his own conscience, and to profess his religion both in private and in public. According to the clear teaching of Lactantius, "this is the very condition of our birth, that we render to the God who made us that just homage which is His due; that we acknowledge Him alone as God, and follow Him. It is from this ligature of piety, which binds us and joins us to God, that religion derives its name."[23]

Hence, too, Pope Leo XIII declared that "true freedom, freedom worthy of the sons of God, is that freedom which most truly safeguards the dignity of the human person. It is stronger than any violence or injustice. Such is the freedom which has always been desired by the Church, and which she holds most dear. It is the sort of freedom which the Apostles resolutely claimed for themselves. The apologists defended it in their writings; thousands of martyrs consecrated it with their blood."[24]

15. Human beings have also the right to choose for themselves the kind of life which appeals to them: whether it is to found a family—in the founding of which both the man and the woman enjoy equal rights and duties—or to embrace the priesthood or the religious life.[25]

16. The family, founded upon marriage freely contracted, one and indissoluble, must be regarded as the natural, primary cell of human society. The interests of the family, therefore, must be taken very specially into consideration in social and economic affairs, as well as in the spheres of faith and morals. For all of these have to do with strengthening the family and assisting it in the fulfilment of its mission.

17. Of course, the support and education of children is a right which belongs primarily to the parents.[26]

18. In the economic sphere, it is evident that a man has the inherent right not only to be given the opportunity to work, but also to be allowed the exercise of personal initiative in the work he does.[27]

19. The conditions in which a man works form a necessary corollary to these rights. They must not be such as to weaken his physical or moral fiber, or militate against the proper development of adolescents to manhood. Women must be accorded such conditions of work as are consistent with their needs and responsibilities as wives and mothers.[28]

20. A further consequence of man's personal dignity is his right to engage in economic activities suited to his degree of responsibility.[29] The worker is likewise entitled to a wage that is determined in accordance with the precepts of justice. This needs stressing. The amount a worker receives must be sufficient, in proportion to available funds, to allow him

SUPPLEMENTARY READING Continued

and his family a standard of living consistent with human dignity. Pope Pius XII expressed it in these terms: "Nature imposes work upon man as a duty, and man has the corresponding natural right to demand that the work he does shall provide him with the means of livelihood for himself and his children. Such is nature's categorical imperative for the preservation of man."[30]

21. As a further consequence of man's nature, he has the right to the private ownership of property, including that of productive goods. This, as we have said elsewhere, is "a right which constitutes so efficacious a means of asserting one's personality and exercising responsibility in every field, and an element of solidity and security for family life, and of greater peace and prosperity in the State."[31]

22. Finally, it is opportune to point out that the right to own private property entails a social obligation as well.[32]

23. Men are by nature social, and consequently they have the right to meet together and to form associations with their fellows. They have the right to confer on such associations the type of organization which they consider best calculated to achieve their objectives. They have also the right to exercise their own initiative and act on their own responsibility within these associations for the attainment of the desired results.[33]

24. As we insisted in our encyclical *Mater et Magistra*, the founding of a great many such intermediate groups or societies for the pursuit of aims which it is not within the competence of the individual to achieve efficiently, is a matter of great urgency. Such groups and societies must be considered absolutely essential for the safeguarding of man's personal freedom and dignity, while leaving intact a sense of responsibility.[34]

25. Again, every human being has the right to freedom of movement and of residence within the confines of his own State. When there are just reasons in favor of it, he must be permitted to emigrate to other countries and take up residence there.[35] The fact that he is a citizen of a particular State does not deprive him of membership in the human family, nor of citizenship in that universal society, the common, world-wide fellowship of men.

26. Finally, man's personal dignity involves his right to take an active part in public life, and to make his own contribution to the common welfare of his fellow citizens. As Pope Pius XII said, "man as such, far from being an object or, as it were, an inert element in society, is rather its subject, its basis and its purpose; and so must he be esteemed."[36]

27. As a human person he is entitled to the legal protection of his rights, and such protection must be effective, unbiased, and strictly just. To quote again Pope Pius XII: "In consequence of that juridical order willed by God, man has his own inalienable right to juridical security. To him is assigned a certain, well-defined sphere of law, immune from arbitrary attack."[37]

28. The natural rights of which we have so far been speaking are inextricably bound up with as many duties, all applying to one and the same person. These rights and duties derive their origin, their sustenance, and their indestructibility from the natural law, which in conferring the one imposes the other.

29. Thus, for example, the right to live involves the duty to preserve one's life; the right to a decent standard of living, the duty to live in a becoming fashion; the right to be free to seek out the truth, the duty to devote oneself to an ever deeper and wider search for it.

SUPPLEMENTARY READING continued

30. Once this is admitted, it follows that in human society one man's natural right gives rise to a corresponding duty in other men; the duty, that is, of recognizing and respecting that right. Every basic human right draws its authoritative force from the natural law, which confers it and attaches to it its respective duty. Hence, to claim one's rights and ignore one's duties, or only half fulfill them, is like building a house with one hand and tearing it down with the other.

31. Since men are social by nature, they must live together and consult each other's interests. That men should recognize and perform their respective rights and duties is imperative to a well ordered society. But the result will be that each individual will make his whole-hearted contribution to the creation of a civic order in which rights and duties are ever more diligently and more effectively observed.

32. For example, it is useless to admit that a man has a right to the necessities of life, unless we also do all in our power to supply him with means sufficient for his livelihood.

33. Hence society must not only be well ordered, it must also provide men with abundant resources. This postulates not only the mutual recognition and fulfillment of rights and duties, but also the involvement and collaboration of all men in the many enterprises which our present civilization makes possible, encourages or indeed demands.

Pope Leo XIII, ca. 1878.
Pope Leo XIII's influential encyclical on social justice *Rerum Novarum* (*On Capital and Labor*) outlined, for the first time, the principles of Catholic Social Teaching.

VOCABULARY

ABORTION
The destruction of a child after conception but before birth. Direct abortion or cooperation in it is forbidden by the Fifth Commandment; it is a violation of the child's fundamental right to life.

CARDINAL VIRTUES
Prudence, justice, fortitude, and temperance. Because they are pivotal, these virtues are called "cardinal" (from the Latin *cardo*, "hinge"). They are stable dispositions of the intellect and will that govern actions, order passions, and guide conduct in accordance with reason and faith.

COMMUTATIVE JUSTICE
The form of justice that governs the ordinary transactions of everyday life, directing us to honor promises, contracts, and commitments.

DISTRIBUTIVE JUSTICE
The form of justice that governs the ways and means by which authority distributes the goods and obligations of social life among the members of society.

JUSTICE
One of the four cardinal virtues; this virtue refers to the steady and lasting willingness to give to God and to others what belongs to them by right.

LEGAL JUSTICE
The form of justice that governs the way individuals respond to the obligations of living in society or living under the state.

NATURAL LAW
An objective order established by God that determines the requirements for people to thrive and reach fulfillment.

RESPONSIBILITY (OR DUTY)
The demand for an account of one's acts; it includes accepting the consequences of those acts.

RIGHTS (ALSO, NATURAL RIGHTS)
The goods that are owed to a person by nature. Natural rights are inviolable and belong to every human being because of his or her inherent dignity as a person, possessing a rational intellect and free will.

SOCIAL JUSTICE
The form of justice that governs the cultural, political, and economic aspects of human community, with particular concern for structural problems and solutions.

PROPERTY
What belongs to someone; what someone owns. Persons have the right to private ownership of property, but that right is not absolute, and it may be limited.

VIRTUE
A habitual and firm disposition to do good.

STUDY QUESTIONS

1. What makes justice a virtue?
2. What is justice?
3. Why is justice always a social virtue?
4. How does justice apply in daily events in school and family life?
5. Why is justice a cardinal virtue? What other virtues depend upon it and why?
6. What are rights?
7. Why must rights precede justice?
8. What are natural rights, and which rights belong to human beings by nature?
9. Why do human beings have natural rights?
10. Which rights may be limited by the state?
11. What is commutative justice? Give an example of it in action.
12. What is distributive justice? Give an example of it in action.
13. What is legal justice? Give an example of it in action.
14. What is social justice? Give an example of it in action.
15. What is the origin of rights? Why does the origin of rights present a problem for modern societies?
16. How did the United Nations enlist Catholic social thought as it prepared its *Universal Declaration of Human Rights*?
17. Name two twentieth-century Catholic philosophers known for their work on justice and rights.
18. What is natural law and how does it relate to human rights?
19. Why is abortion a particularly egregious violation of human rights?
20. What injustices did the biblical prophets identify in their own lands and times? What solutions did they offer?

Christ and the Children (detail) by Bloch.
"Whoever humbles himself like this child, he is the greatest in the kingdom of heaven." (Mt 18:4)

THE SOCIAL DOCTRINE OF THE CATHOLIC CHURCH

PRACTICAL EXERCISES

1. Read the United Nations' *Universal Declaration of Human Rights*, the United States' Bill of Rights, and another country's charter or constitution of basic rights. Compare and contrast the way they account for the origin of rights; which rights they guarantee; and which rights they limit. Evaluate these efforts in light of the Supplemental Readings from St. John XXIII and the *Compendium of the Social Doctrine of the Church*.

2. In the course of a single day, keep a journal of instances when your friends, family members, teachers, or others make appeals to justice (or fairness, rights, restitution, payback, revenge, and so on). What do your findings tell you about the importance of justice? How would you analyze these ordinary appeals in light of Christian teaching and tradition?

3. What are the most important human-rights issues today? Write an essay arguing your case in light of Catholic teaching, biblical witness, and natural law.

4. Find an example, in world history of the twentieth century, of a regime suspending, limiting, or abolishing a human right for some or all of its citizens (e.g., freedom of the press, freedom of religion, or the right to life for preborn children). Explain the circumstances leading to this action, with the response from the populace. Was the right restored over time? If so, how? If not, why not?

Parable of the Man Who Hoards by Tissot.
Charity leads us to help others in their need by sharing what we have. *Justice* teaches us to give others what is rightfully theirs.

JUSTICE AND RIGHTS: THE FOUNDATION OF ALL ORDER IN THE WORLD

FROM THE CATECHISM

1807 *Justice* is the moral virtue that consists in the constant and firm will to give their due to God and neighbor. Justice toward God is called the "virtue of religion." Justice toward men disposes one to respect the rights of each and to establish in human relationships the harmony that promotes equity with regard to persons and to the common good. The just man, often mentioned in the Sacred Scriptures, is distinguished by habitual right thinking and the uprightness of his conduct toward his neighbor. "You shall not be partial to the poor or defer to the great, but in righteousness shall you judge your neighbor."[38] "Masters, treat your slaves justly and fairly, knowing that you also have a Master in heaven."[39]

1928 Society ensures social justice when it provides the conditions that allow associations or individuals to obtain what is their due, according to their nature and their vocation. Social justice is linked to the common good and the exercise of authority.

2238 Those subject to authority should regard those in authority as representatives of God, who has made them stewards of his gifts:[40] "Be subject for the Lord's sake to every human institution….Live as free men, yet without using your freedom as a pretext for evil; but live as servants of God."[41] Their loyal collaboration includes the right, and at times the duty, to voice their just criticisms of that which seems harmful to the dignity of persons and to the good of the community.

2239 It is the *duty of citizens* to contribute along with the civil authorities to the good of society in a spirit of truth, justice, solidarity, and freedom. The love and service of *one's country* follow from the duty of gratitude and belong to the order of charity. Submission to legitimate authorities and service of the common good require citizens to fulfill their roles in the life of the political community.

2240 Submission to authority and co-responsibility for the common good make it morally obligatory to pay taxes, to exercise the right to vote, and to defend one's country:

> Pay to all of them their dues, taxes to whom taxes are due, revenue to whom revenue is due, respect to whom respect is due, honor to whom honor is due.[42]

> [Christians] reside in their own nations, but as resident aliens. They participate in all things as citizens and endure all things as foreigners….They obey the established laws and their way of life surpasses the laws…. So noble is the position to which God has assigned them that they are not allowed to desert it.[43]

The Apostle exhorts us to offer prayers and thanksgiving for kings and all who exercise authority, "that we may lead a quiet and peaceable life, godly and respectful in every way."[44]

2412 In virtue of commutative justice, *reparation for injustice* committed requires the restitution of stolen goods to their owner:

Jesus blesses Zacchaeus for his pledge: "If I have defrauded anyone of anything, I restore it fourfold."[45] Those who, directly or indirectly, have taken possession of the goods of another, are obliged to make restitution of them, or to return the equivalent in kind or in money, if the goods have disappeared, as well as the profit or advantages their owner would have legitimately obtained from them. Likewise, all who in some manner have taken part in a theft or who have knowingly benefited from it—for example, those who ordered it, assisted in it, or received the stolen goods—are obliged to make restitution in proportion to their responsibility and to their share of what was stolen.

St. John Paul II stated clearly the gravity of the sin of abortion in *Evangelium Vitæ*. "*I declare that…abortion willed as an end or as a means, always constitutes a grave moral disorder*, since it is the deliberate killing of an innocent human being." (*EV* 60)

ENDNOTES – CHAPTER TWO

1. *Morals of the Catholic Church* 25.
2. *Summa Theologiæ* 2.2.58a1c.
3. Cicero, *On Duties* 1.7.
4. Joseph Pieper, *A Brief Reader on the Virtues of the Human Heart* (San Francisco: Ignatius Press, 1991), 22.
5. Cf. *CA* 25.
6. Jacques Maritain, *Man and the State* (Washington DC: Catholic University of America Press, 1998), 77.
7. Cicero, *Rep.* III, 22, 33.
8. Cf. *DH* 1.
9. Cf. *GS* 41; Congregation for Catholic Education, *Guidelines for the Study and Teaching of the Church's Social Doctrine in the Formation of Priests*, 32 (Rome: Vatican Polyglot Press, 1988), 36-37.
10. John Paul II, *Address to the 34th General Assembly of the United Nations* (October 2, 1979), 7: AAS 71 (1979), 1147-1148; for John Paul II, this Declaration "remains one of the highest expressions of the human conscience of our time": *Address to the Fiftieth General Assembly of the United Nations* (October 5, 1995), 2: *L'Osservatore Romano*, English edition, October 11, 1995, 8.
11. Cf. *GS* 27; CCC 1930.
12. Cf. *PT*; *GS* 22.
13. Cf. *PT*.
14. Cf. *PT*.
15. John Paul II, *Message for the 1999 World Day of Peace*, 3: AAS 91 (1999), 379.
16. Paul VI, *Message to the International Conference on Human Rights*, Teheran (April 15, 1968): L'Osservatore Romano, English edition, May 2, 1968, 4.
17. John Paul II, *Message for the 1999 World Day of Peace*, 3: AAS 91 (1999), 379.
18. John Paul II, *Message for the 1999 World Day of Peace*, 3: AAS 91 (1999), 379.
19. John Paul II, *Message for the 1998 World Day of Peace*, 2: AAS 90 (1998), 149.
20. Cf. Pius XII's broadcast message, Christmas 1942, AAS 35 (1943) 9-24; and John XXIII's sermon, Jan. 4, 1963, AAS 55 (1963) 89-91.
21. Cf. Pius XI's encyclical *Divini Redemptoris*, AAS 29 (1931) 78; and Pius XII's broadcast message, Pentecost, June 1, 1941, AAS 33 (1941) 195-205.
22. Cf. Pius XII's broadcast message, Christmas 1942, AAS 35 (1943) 9-24.
23. *Divinæ Institutiones*, lib. IV, c.28.2; PL 6.535.
24. Pope Leo XIII's encyclical *Libertas praestantissimum*.
25. Cf. Pius XII's broadcast message, Christmas 1942, AAS 35 (1943) 9-24.
26. Cf. Pius XI's encyclical *Casti connubii*, and Pius XII's broadcast message, Christmas 1942, AAS 35 (1943) 9-24.
27. Cf. Pius XII's broadcast message, Pentecost, June 1, 1941, AAS 33 (1941) 201.
28. Cf. *RN* 128-129.
29. Cf. *MM*.
30. Cf. Pius XII's broadcast message, Pentecost, June 1, 1941, AAS 33 (1941) 201.
31. *MM*.
32. Cf. ibid., p. 430; TPS v. 7, no. 4, 318.
33. Cf. *RN* 134-142; *QA*; and *SL*.
34. Cf. AAS 53 (1961) 430.
35. Cf. Pius XII's broadcast message, Christmas 1952, AAS 45 (1953) 36-46.
36. Cf. Pius XII's broadcast message, Christmas 1944, AAS 37 (1945) 12.
37. Cf. Pius XII's broadcast message, Christmas 1942, AAS 35 (1943) 21.
38. Lev 19:15.
39. Col 4:1.
40. Cf. Rom 13:1-2.
41. 1 Pt 2:13, 16.
42. Rom 13:7.
43. *Ad Diognetum* 5, 5 and 10; 6, 10: PG 2, 1173 and 1176.
44. 1 Tm 2:2.
45. Lk 19:8.

Social Doctrine of the Catholic Church
CHAPTER 3

The Church Teaches Us How to Live
Catholics are called to accept the teaching of the Church's Magisterium as they accept the teachings of Christ himself.

Social Doctrine of the Catholic Church

CHAPTER THREE

The Church Teaches Us How to Live

THE POPES AND COUNCILS TEACH AUTHORITATIVELY ON SOCIAL CONCERNS

At the beginning of industrialized society, it was "a yoke little better than that of slavery itself" which led my predecessor to speak out in defense of man. Over the past hundred years the Church has remained faithful to this duty. Indeed, she intervened in the turbulent period of class struggle after the First World War in order to defend man from economic exploitation and from the tyranny of the totalitarian systems. After the Second World War, she put the dignity of the person at the center of her social messages, insisting that material goods were meant for all, and that the social order ought to be free of oppression and based on a spirit of cooperation and solidarity. The Church has constantly repeated that the person and society need not only material goods but spiritual and religious values as well. Furthermore, as she has become more aware of the fact that too many people live, not in the prosperity of the Western world, but in the poverty of the developing countries amid conditions which are still "a yoke little better than that of slavery itself," she has felt and continues to feel obliged to denounce this fact with absolute clarity and frankness, although she knows that her call will not always win favor with everyone.

—St. John Paul II, *Centesimus Annus*

IN THIS CHAPTER, WE WILL ADDRESS SEVERAL QUESTIONS:

✤ What historical circumstances required the Church to develop her social doctrine in the modern era?

✤ What is the Church's Magisterium?

✤ How did the Magisterium respond to "new situations" in society?

✤ Which Church documents reflected, influenced, and articulated modern developments in Catholic social doctrine?

✤ What were the "social encyclicals"?

He Did No Miracles but He Healed Them (detail) by Tissot.
Christ's love for the poor is an essential dimension of Christian charity. We are Christ's disciples, and if we imitate our Lord's love for the poor, we will indeed use our possessions well and advance the cause of social justice.

A VOICE OF SOCIAL CONSCIENCE

Through works of justice and charity, Catholics in every age have presented Christ to the world. By their lives they have demonstrated the doctrine of Christ as it is found, implicit and explicit, in Scripture and Sacred Tradition. In every age and in every place, therefore, Christians must respond to different historical circumstances and different needs.

Consider one classic example. In the middle of the fourth century, the city of Caesarea in Cappadocia (in modern Turkey) welcomed a new bishop named Basil. He came from a distinguished family, and he had received the best education available in his time. Yet, nothing could quite have prepared Basil for the job he was given. Christianity had been legal in the Roman Empire for only a short time, and so the religion's role in society was not clearly defined.

It was, moreover, a time of turmoil. While there were wars at the empire's borders, Basil's own city had seen an explosion of prosperity and growth for which it was unprepared. Then, in AD 368, a series of natural disasters—including hailstorms, floods, and earthquakes—destroyed crops and brought famine to the lands of Cappadocia. Many families were reduced to poverty. Many children were left without family or home.

Basil mobilized his congregation to serve everyone hurt by these afflictions, regardless of rank or station. He identified needs, and then he sought donors and laborers who would meet those needs with acts of self-giving charity. In time he constructed a campus of facilities to serve the needy. There was a soup kitchen to fulfill the basic need for food. There was a homeless shelter. There was a trade school to train beggars to work for a living. There was a hostel for poor travelers—a most vulnerable group of people in those centuries before motorized transportation, when journeys could last for weeks or months. There was a hospital for the sick and hospices for the dying.

So vast was this complex of buildings that the citizens of Caesarea called it "The New City" or simply the *Basileidas*, "Basil's Place."

THE SOCIAL DOCTRINE OF THE CATHOLIC CHURCH

Looking back over the course of centuries, we recognize Basil's projects as common works of Catholic charity, the sort of programs that are routinely undertaken by Catholic institutions throughout the world. In Basil's time, however, they were a new phenomenon. Christians had always striven to act with charity toward their neighbors. And congregations had regularly taken up collections for the poor. But only recently had the Church, as an institution, won the freedom to sponsor massive public works. Basil was working out the theory and practice in direct response to rapidly changing social circumstances and the shifting role of the Church in relation to the state.

The doctrine was implicit in the works. But Basil went further than that and made it explicit in his teaching, preaching, and admonitions "Neither can the supply of the needy fail, nor is it possible for us to refuse them the favor."[1] Basil spoke out against traders who grew wealthy by inflating food prices during times of famine. Like St. John Chrysostom after him, he condemned this as an unconscionable sin. But he was more inclined to urge the wealthy to grow in virtue by acts of justice and charity in public life. It will go well for such people, he explained, when they stand before Christ in judgment.

As a bishop, St. Basil the Great was not simply a man of action. He was also, and perhaps primarily, a teacher. As a bishop, he taught with the authority bestowed by Jesus Christ on the Apostles and passed on to the bishops in legitimate succession. As a bishop, Basil shared the Church's Magisterium.

MAGISTERIUM

Magisterium is the name given to the Church's living teaching office, which authentically interprets Scripture and Tradition. This special authority ensures the Church's fidelity to the Apostles' teaching in matters of faith and morals. The *Catechism* explains:

Christ in Majesty, Book of Gospels Illumination. The Magisterium introduces no new revelation, but rather interprets Revelation, which ended with the Apostles.

> "The task of giving an authentic interpretation of the Word of God, whether in its written form or in the form of Tradition, has been entrusted to the living, teaching office of the Church alone. Its authority in this matter is exercised in the name of Jesus Christ."[2] This means that the task of interpretation has been entrusted to the bishops in communion with the successor of Peter, the Bishop of Rome. (CCC 85)

Catholics are called to accept the teaching of the Church's Magisterium as they accept the teachings of Christ himself. In speaking of the proper disposition that the faithful should have toward the teachings of the Magisterium, the *Catechism* uses the term "docility," which literally means "teachability." Catholics are to be open to the Church's teaching, i.e., willing to be taught.

> Mindful of Christ's words to his apostles: "He who hears you, hears me,"[3] the faithful receive with docility the teachings and directives that their pastors give them in different forms. (CCC 87)

In its teaching, the Magisterium introduces no new revelation, but rather interprets Revelation, which ended with the Apostles, as it applies to changing circumstances in the world, and illumines the emerging circumstances with the light of God's Revelation. The *Catechism* makes clear:

> "Yet this Magisterium is not superior to the Word of God, but is its servant. It teaches only what has been handed on to it. At the divine command and with the help of the Holy Spirit, it listens to this devotedly, guards it with dedication and expounds it faithfully. All that it proposes for belief as being divinely revealed is drawn from this single deposit of faith."[4] (CCC 86)

Over the course of centuries, Catholic social doctrine, which is implicit in the Scriptures, has been worked out theologically and practically by the Church's Magisterium—by the Popes, bishops, and councils of the Church. Until recently, this took place in a gradual and diffuse way. In the last century and a half, however, social doctrine has occupied an increasingly prominent place in the Church's public teaching. This renewed emphasis came about as a response to historically unprecedented upheavals in the world order accompanied by radical changes in the living conditions of most of the people on earth.

As St. Basil's activity and preaching had once addressed similar upheavals in the ancient world, so the Church must address anew the revolutions of the modern.

THE AGE OF REVOLUTIONS

The Protestant Reformation shredded Europe's Christian unity and divided people not only by nation but also by religion. Medieval Christians could all appeal to common bonds of religion and a common court of authority, but the Reformation ended all that. This weakened the bonds within societies as well, and in the centuries that followed the old monarchies and aristocracies began to crumble as people revolted against established authority.

Coalbrookdale by Night by Loutherbourg.
Coalbrookdale, England was the birthplace of the Industrial Revolution. Here in 1709, Abraham Darby developed a blast furnace fired by coke (a clean-burning fuel derived from coal) to smelt iron.

More far-reaching, however, were the effects of the Industrial Revolution. This was not a violent uprising with battles in the streets, but rather a comprehensive change in social economy and industry brought about by advances in technology.

It began with improved efficiency in the methods of mining, which in turn made metals and energy sources (like coal) more abundantly available. These led to powered machinery, which could then be harnessed for mass production. Changes came rapidly as entire professions became obsolete, replaced by automated means of production. Populations shifted from farmlands to the cities, where factories were located, and the character of cities also underwent drastic changes. Not only men, but also women and children went to work outside the home. Their workdays could run twelve hours or more. These conditions radically reconfigured not only the most common ideas about work, but also long-cherished notions of "home" and "family."

In the mid-nineteenth century, more than twenty percent of employees in textile mills and coal mines were under the age of ten. Child wages were the lowest and injury and loss of life was frequent.

Philosophers and activists cried out against the injustices of the new systems and called for change. As the French and American revolutions had overthrown monarchs and aristocrats, so new generations were proposing more far-reaching changes—revolutionary ideologies that would coalesce under various names: socialism, communism, and anarchism, among others. In the name of justice for workers, some activists promoted revolution by violent means—"class warfare"—resulting in civil unrest, terroristic acts, and further acts of repression by frightened governments and industrialists.

Meanwhile, democracy in national government was a relatively new experiment, and by the late nineteenth century some observers feared it was failing, and that its failure would result in anarchy or mob rule.

The philosopher Karl Marx (1818-1883) was pessimistic about the ability of ordinary people—or democracy—to bring about a just order in society. He believed that, in American-style democracy, the owner classes simply manipulated the uneducated masses to do their bidding anyway. Marx advocated violent uprising as a solution to the struggles between social classes; bloody revolution, he believed, would give way at first to a society where the state controlled the means of production and distributed the fruits of industry, and later to a stateless and voluntary workers' paradise. This constellation of ideas—known as "communism" or "Marxism"—was to become increasingly influential in the twentieth century, with devastating consequences for many people throughout the world. Communist regimes, brought about by riot and war, recklessly destroyed economies and ruthlessly killed off critics and dissidents. In the name of "revolution," they claimed the authority to deny human rights. Fundamentally atheistic, communist regimes brutally suppressed religion, freedom of conscience, and wreaked havoc on the institution of the family.

RESPONDING TO REVOLUTIONS

By the late nineteenth century, there were many "new things" in the world, and the world was experiencing the exhilaration and anxiety that always accompany great change. There were new opportunities for personal and social advancement; but there were just as many opportunities for exploitation and abuse.

There remained only one universal body with the authority, conferred by God, to discern the times and to teach in a manner that was reliably true. Such authority—transcending nations and ideologies—belongs only to the Catholic Church.

The Church responded to the social revolutions in many ways: through the witness of the saints, institutional charities (especially in the newly teeming cities), and the founding of religious orders that served the poor. But the Church also responded through its Magisterium. In response to the novelties of history, the Church spoke up, clearly and forcefully, and spelled out a coherent and compelling social doctrine.

As St. Basil had preached and taught in the fourth century, so many bishops preached and taught in the nineteenth. In Germany, for example, Bishop Wilhelm Emmanuel von Ketteler (1811-1877) resisted the statist, secularist, and militarist ideology of Chancellor Otto von Bismarck, a Protestant. He was a pioneer of ecumenism, promoting the reconciliation of Catholics and Protestants. And he established many Church-run charities, including orphanages and homeless shelters. (For more than a century, the people of Mainz have celebrated an annual "Workers' Day" in his honor.)

Bishop von Ketteler's action was not a solitary witness. In the United States, Cardinal James Gibbons defended the Knights of Labor, a union, when some churchmen denounced them before the Pope. A similar figure in the Italian Church was Bishop Vincenzo Pecci of Perugia. These bishops were typical of a movement that was taking place throughout the world. It led to the organization of societies of lay Catholic intellectuals such as the Fribourg Union, founded in 1885. The historical movement manifested itself most authoritatively after Bishop Pecci was elected Pope in 1878. He took the name Leo XIII.

POPE LEO XIII, *RERUM NOVARUM*

Pope Leo reigned from 1878 to 1903. His was one of the longest pontificates in history, and it holds an important place in history. Pope Leo was an industrious teacher with a lively intellect and holy ambitions. An encyclical letter is one of the Pope's most effective and authoritative means of teaching, and Pope Leo issued eighty-five encyclicals in his twenty-five years as Pope. He used his letters to catechize and to promote devotions. He used them to direct the course of education and philosophy. He found teachable moments in all the breaking events on the world scene. Often, his encyclicals focused on particular social issues. *In Plurimis*, in 1888, sought the worldwide abolition of slavery. *Quam Aerumnosa*, the same year, examined the plight of Italian immigrants. *Sapientiæ Christianæ*, in 1890, examined the rights and duties of Christians as citizens. Other encyclicals analyzed marriage and family, the power of the state, religious freedom, the emerging phenomenon of socialism, education, and the nature of human liberty (among other social issues).

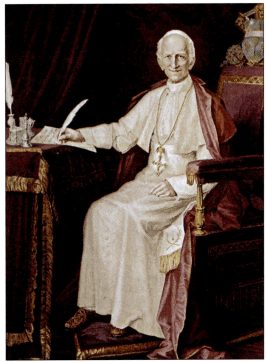

Pope Leo XIII issued eighty-five encyclicals in his twenty-five years as Pope. *Rerum Novarum* was a watershed moment in Catholic thought.

His most comprehensive effort by far, however, was his 1891 encyclical *Rerum Novarum*. Though it was not Pope Leo's first encyclical to address questions of social order, it is often named as the first of the great documents of modern Catholic social doctrine. Pope Benedict XVI, in his social encyclical *Deus Caritas Est*, begins a summary history of the field with the publication of *Rerum Novarum*.

Pope Leo wrote this groundbreaking and systematic treatment of the subject at the behest of many bishops, especially those in the countries most affected by the Industrial Revolution.

The title means, literally, "Of New Things," and Pope Leo does address the complex social problems that had arisen along with new forms of production, new forms of government, new distribution of wealth, and the new configuration of cities.

It is a carefully considered and nuanced response to each of the "new things." Pope Leo acknowledged the "misery and wretchedness pressing so unjustly on the majority of the working class," and he expressed alarm at the growing disparity between the wealth of a tiny minority of industrialists and the poverty of their laborers. He decried the effects of poverty on family life and morals. He supported the right of workers to organize in labor unions for the protection of their interests. He rejected *laissez-faire* capitalism, yet condemned communism as an unacceptable alternative. He affirmed the right to private property. He detailed the rights and the duties of workers and employers, as well as the role of the state as guarantor and custodian of those rights and duties.

Rerum Novarum was a watershed moment in Catholic thought. Some commentators speak of it as "the big bang" of the Church's social doctrine, as if it were a creation out of nothing. That is a bit of an exaggeration. A later Pope, Pius XI, offered a more precise metaphor when he called it a "foundation" to be built upon. As in a building, this foundation was constructed from sturdy materials quarried from the Scriptures and the writings of the saints and great theologians of the past, but cut, shaped, and put together in a new way for the sake of the modern era's "new things."

Pius XI also called *Rerum Novarum* the "Magna Carta" of Catholic social teaching. That, too, is a useful metaphor; *Rerum Novarum* did serve as a constitution of sorts, a charter of principles that would inform and guide all future Catholic social doctrine.

BUILDING ON *RERUM NOVARUM*: THE SOCIAL ENCYCLICALS

A textbook treatment of the Church's "social encyclicals" will be necessarily brief. But brevity can give the wrong impression. The Catholic Church's major social encyclicals were important moments in the development of Catholic doctrine. They were not, however, isolated events. A complete list of papal documents on social issues would be fairly extensive and overwhelming for an introductory course in Catholic social doctrine. And papal documents, while the most refined and authoritative statements, are representative of so much more intellectual activity and human effort.

What this book seeks to present is an examination of a few significant milestones. Between one milestone and the next, a careful student of history can find the footsteps of a multitude of faithful Catholics who influenced the course of intellectual history. They were workers and union organizers. They were activists for many different causes. They were professors and theologians. They were politicians and economists. They were journalists and broadcasters. They were preachers and schoolteachers.

Scholars differ on the question of which documents belong on the "short list" of major social encyclicals. There is a general consensus, though, about the historical importance of the following letters. They marked critical moments in the development of Catholic social doctrine because of their fresh insights, because of their influence on later teaching, or simply because of their timing.

POPE	TITLE OF ENCYCLICAL	DATE
Pius XI	*Quadragesimo Anno*	1931
St. John XXIII	*Mater et Magistra*	1961
	Pacem in Terris	1963
Paul VI	*Populorum Progressio*	1967
St. John Paul II	*Laborem Exercens*	1981
	Sollicitudo Rei Socialis	1987
	Centesimus Annus	1991
	Evangelium Vitæ	1995
Benedict XVI	*Deus Caritas Est*	2005
	Caritas in Veritate	2009

Any list will be partial. Most textbooks on social doctrine omit (as we do) *Mit Brennender Sorge* ("With Burning Concern"), Pope Pius XI's 1937 encyclical condemning racism and criticizing the ideology of Nazism. Its effect on history was certainly important, but its ideas are covered more thoroughly elsewhere.

A list of encyclicals does not even take into consideration the vast body of papal statements. The list above provides no place for a discussion of Pope Benedict XV's efforts to mediate peace before and during World War I. Nor can it take into account Pope Paul VI's deeply influential apostolic letter *Octogesima Adveniens*.

CESAR CHAVEZ: The Son of *Rerum Novarum*

Cesar Chavez (1927-1993) was born to a hard-working Mexican-American family in the western United States. With his parents and siblings, he harvested fruits and vegetables, moving about from season to season. They tried to help their fellow laborers by sharing rides and finding them medical care when it was needed. He dropped out of school in eighth grade, so that he could be more available for work. During World War II, he enlisted in the U.S. Navy, where he found that Mexican-Americans were consigned to low-level duties in wretched conditions. Returning home, he married and started a family. With his wife, Helen, he eventually had seven children.

Returning to civilian life meant returning to work in the fields, the only opportunity open to him as a Mexican-American. He continued working as he had before the War. In 1952, however, his life was changed when he met Fr. Donald McDonnell. In conversation, the priest introduced Chavez to Catholic social doctrine and explained the principles of *Rerum Novarum*, Pope Leo XIII's 1891 encyclical on the conditions of labor. Chavez saw immediately how these should translate into the lives of his fellow migrant farm workers. Chavez later recalled how he would pepper Father McDonnell with questions, keeping him up past midnight. He began to accompany the priest on prison and hospital visits. Gradually, he saw how these teachings would shape his life.

Chavez helped workers to organize so that they could have greater bargaining power, to negotiate safer working conditions and a living wage. He organized many peaceful strikes and work stoppages in order to demonstrate the true value of America's underpaid farm labor. Through the 1960s and 1970s he drew attention to the difficulties migrants endured so that Americans could have fresh produce on their tables at low prices. His 1970 "Salad Bowl Strike" was the largest farm-labor strike in U.S. history.

He openly acknowledged his dependence on Catholic social teaching. "I don't think

Chavez' life bears witness to the power and influence of Catholic social doctrine.

that I could base my will to struggle on cold economics or on some political doctrine," he once said. "I don't think there would be enough to sustain me. For me, the base must be faith!" He would quote from *Rerum Novarum* when he met with the press. He would gather protesters and strikers around a banner of Our Lady of Guadalupe and pray publicly for her protection and intercession.

Some farm owners were willing to listen to Chavez and work with him. Others feared the movement and accused Chavez of communism. Some enlisted criminals to oppose the strikers with violence. Chavez stood his ground and promoted a positive attitude. His slogan was "*Sí, se puede*"— "Yes, it can be done!"

Never in robust health, Chavez pressed on even as he suffered from discomfort and illness. In 1988, he staged a 36-day "Fast for Life" to draw attention to the dangers farm workers and their children faced from exposure to pesticides.

He died in 1993, by then revered as a major figure in American history. He was awarded the Pacem in Terris Peace and Freedom Award as well as the Presidential Medal of Freedom. Cesar Chavez Day is celebrated in several states. His portrait hangs in the National Gallery in Washington, D.C.

His life bears witness to the power and influence of Catholic social doctrine, especially as it was expressed in papal encyclicals.

Besides papal statements, furthermore, there are also the documents produced by synods of bishops as well as by various congregations, councils, offices, and commissions in the Vatican. The literature of Catholic social teaching in the last century and a half is vast, and in the course of a semester we can afford only a swift sampling of it.

POPE PIUS XI, *QUADRAGESIMO ANNO*

The encyclical *Quadragesimo Anno* appeared exactly forty years after *Rerum Novarum*, a fact reflected in its Latin title, which means "In the Fortieth Year." The letter appeared in the midst of a worldwide economic depression. For Pope Leo XIII, communism was still a theoretical proposition to be condemned on theoretical grounds. Pope Pius XI, on the other hand, had already witnessed more than a decade of large-scale application of communist theory in Russia—a world power that aspired to be a communist empire. Other countries were well into their own experiments with totalitarian government. Italy was ruled by the fascist Benito Mussolini, and, in Germany, the National Socialist (Nazi) party was marching to power.

Pius XI reviewed and reaffirmed the doctrine of *Rerum Novarum* and surveyed the influence Leo XIII had in the decades that followed, in fields as diverse as law and government, labor, and the social sciences.

He noted that the socialism (or attenuated form of communism) spoken of theoretically by Leo XIII had evolved with the changing economic situations and, at that time, had effectively split into two branches. One branch had devolved into communism, which advocated violent class warfare and the absolute abolition of all private property. The other branch, which retained the name socialism, rejected violence but still viewed the world's economic systems as a struggle between classes and advocated, at least to some extent, the abolition of private ownership of industry.

Pius XI echoed and amplified Leo's critique of communism and unrestrained capitalism. He was most concerned to address the communist notion of "class struggle," which had already caused so much enmity and bloodshed in the first decades of the twentieth century. He issued a strong condemnation of socialism:

Pope Pius XI (1922-1937) issued a strong condemnation of socialism, but condemned *laissez-faire* states that stood by while industrialists abused and exploited poor workers.

"No one can be at the same time a sincere Catholic and a true socialist." While socialism recognizes humanity's social nature, he said, it reduces the meaning of life to "material advantage alone." He called upon the proponents of socialism to reject the idea of class struggle and the abolition of private ownership of industry and to enter into peaceful dialogue with and to seek peaceful cooperation with industries and professions.

Quadragesimo Anno differed from *Rerum Novarum* in that it proposed guiding moral principles not only for individuals—owners and laborers—but also for governments. Pope Pius was critical of statist solutions to social problems—legislation and regulation that imposed a high degree of control on trades, investors, and labor. On the other hand, he condemned those *laissez-faire* states that stood by while industrialists abused and exploited poor workers.

Seeing the people of Europe torn apart by perverse ideologies, the Holy Father called on social reformers to continue seeking justice—yet not justice alone, but justice based on charity.

ST. JOHN XXIII, *MATER ET MAGISTRA*

St. John XXIII published his encyclical *Mater et Magistra* (Latin for "Mother and Teacher") in 1961, to mark the seventieth anniversary of *Rerum Novarum*. He revisited the teachings of that encyclical and considering many newer "new things" that had appeared in the intervening years: advances in technology, for example, that enabled space exploration, but also weapons of mass destruction. The world map had significantly changed after the demise of the old empires. Now nations were emerging into independence as communism promised them a "worker's paradise." The encyclical took issue with such vain promises.

The encyclical also decried the imbalance of wealth in the world, calling upon developed nations to share methods and means of production with those whose farming, for example, was still relatively primitive. John XXIII, who had grown up in a rural area, devoted a significant portion of the letter to issues related to agriculture. This sets his letter apart from those of his predecessors, which focused more on factories and urban centers.

He also addressed the pseudo-scientific claims of his contemporaries who were sounding alarms about impending "overpopulation." He affirmed the place of the family in society and economy. He praised marriage and called all people to respect its indissolubility.

St. John XXIII was a man of traditional faith and piety whose friendly manner won him fame as "Good Pope John."

If anyone had doubted the binding character of Catholic social doctrine, *Mater et Magistra* settled the matter, stating that "the permanent validity of the Catholic Church's social teaching admits of no doubt." That statement irritated some proponents of *laissez-faire* capitalism, who said that they would accept the Church as mother, but not as teacher. Their slogan became "*Mater* si, *Magistra* no."

In the decades that followed, dissidents would extend such selective adherence to matters far beyond social doctrine, indeed to all areas of faith. It is absurd to say that one's mother is not also a teacher. Parents are, by nature, every child's primary educators. The Church could not be a "mother" if she were not also the primary educator of humanity under God.

ST. JOHN XXIII, *PACEM IN TERRIS*

His second social encyclical, *Pacem in Terris* ("Peace on Earth"), arrived in 1963 in the midst of the so-called "Cold War" between the United States and the Soviet Union. In the aftermath of the Second World War, smaller countries were weakened and found themselves pulled to one or another ideological pole. The two "superpowers" dominated the world scene. Their philosophical differences were profound, and their conflict acrimonious—rhetorically supercharged, yet usually stopping short of armed warfare except through proxies. For good reasons, both sides feared an escalation of hostility. With the atomic bomb, first dropped in 1945 upon the populous Japanese cities of Hiroshima and Nagasaki, weaponry had reached new levels of deadliness. The stakes of world conflict were now much higher, and many people lived in fear that nuclear warfare would destroy the world.

This encyclical spoke to that growing enmity and fear. John XXIII argued that lasting peace could be achieved only through obedience to the natural law, which must not be reduced to material concerns. Truth, justice, and dignity require a sense of spirituality and cannot be attained apart from God. *Pacem in Terris* includes an extensive discussion of natural human rights and duties.

THE SOCIAL DOCTRINE OF THE CATHOLIC CHURCH

St. John XXIII signing *Pacem in Terris* (Peace on Earth). This encyclical appeared less than six months after the Cuban Missile Crisis which had brought two superpowers to the brink of war.

The Pope explained that God, not the state, provides the meaning of life for every human person as well as collective humanity. Civil authority exists to serve the human person and the common good.

Since God is the ultimate end of human life, the authority of conscience ranks higher than the power of the state. Like Sts. Augustine and Thomas Aquinas, and following Scripture (Acts 5:29), the Holy Father taught that unjust or immoral laws were not binding. "A law which is at variance with reason is to that extent unjust and has no longer the rationale of law. It is rather an act of violence."

He made clear that the principles of peace and justice apply not only to relationships within a nation—between governors and the governed, for example—but also to relationships between nations. The Pope taught that just as persons are created equal, so are nations; and thus strong nations should not exploit or coerce weaker nations.

Pacem in Terris was the first papal encyclical to be addressed not only to Catholics, but to all people of good will.

POPE PAUL VI, *POPULORUM PROGRESSIO*

Populorum Progressio ("On the Development of People"), promulgated in 1967, was the only encyclical of Pope Paul VI exclusively dedicated to social doctrine. It focused almost entirely on relations among nations, rich and poor. Like his predecessor's encyclical *Pacem in Terris*, *Populorum Progressio* was addressed not only to Catholics, but to all people of good will. The tone, however, is much more urgent. The Pope was anxious about the increasing disparity between rich and poor nations. He saw that this situation was destabilizing the world, with devastation sure to follow unless governments worked to remedy the situation.

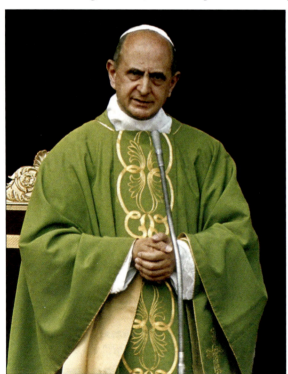

Pope Paul VI became the first pope to visit all five continents earning him the nickname "the Pilgrim Pope." He was committed to Christian unity and met with many leaders of other churches and religious bodies.

"Human society," he said, "is sorely ill. The cause is not so much the depletion of natural resources, nor their monopolistic control by a privileged few; it is rather the weakening of brotherly ties between individuals and nations" (no. 66). Thus, he ruled out any notion of "class struggle," as members of all classes were created to share a common human bond.

Pope Paul VI called upon the wealthy to assist the poor. If they will not do this, he said, states have a right to expropriate property for just distribution.

"Development," he said, "is the new name for peace" (no. 76). He urged nations to see beyond nationalistic pride and profit motive, and rather take on a sense of universal brotherhood, responsibly sharing wealth and providing opportunities for education and economic advancement in the human family.

THE CHURCH TEACHES US HOW TO LIVE

St. John Paul II believed that God had called him to lead the Church into the third millennium of the Christian era. Human dignity and rights, the challenge of the third millennium, and renewal of the Church as prescribed by the Second Vatican Council would remain central to his pontificate.

ST. JOHN PAUL II, *LABOREM EXERCENS*

Over a very long pontificate (1978-2006), St. John Paul II wrote many encyclical letters, including four that were entirely (or mostly) devoted to Catholic social doctrine.

In 1981, on the ninetieth anniversary of *Rerum Novarum*, he promulgated *Laborem Exercens* ("On Human Work"). The encyclical summarizes the development of social doctrine since *Rerum Novarum*.

Laborem Exercens is an extended meditation on the nature and dignity of human labor. Work, according to St. John Paul II, is intrinsic to human nature. It is distinctively human, because God's first commandment to Adam was to "subdue the earth" (Gn 1:28). Work, then, is also a response to humanity's divine vocation. Human beings work because they are made in the image of God, the Creator, and so they also make things in imitation of their heavenly model.

Modern ideologies such as communism and economic liberalism (*laissez-faire* capitalism) do not grasp the original meaning of work, and so they frustrate workers, impeding their response to God's call, thwarting their desire to fulfill their human nature. Both capitalism and communism tend to reduce labor to something less than it is. They value it exclusively in material and economic terms—efficiency, utility, and productivity.

Laborem Exercens considers work in its objective and subjective dimensions. On the one hand, work is valuable for its products. On the other hand, work is valuable because it is activity that fulfills a divine vocation. Thus, someone can find fulfillment even if they seem to have failed in their professional efforts. Bl. Mother Teresa of Calcutta often said that we are called not to be successful, only faithful. We owe God our best human efforts, but we cannot control whether our works will succeed with the market or the critics.

The encyclical ends with a profound consideration of Christ as a laborer—a carpenter in the workshop of his foster-father, Joseph, in Nazareth. The Holy Father urged workers to consider that they imitate Christ as they labor; and, more than that, they participate in his work of redemption.

> Sweat and toil, which work necessarily involves the present condition of the human race, present the Christian and everyone who is called to follow Christ with the possibility of sharing lovingly in the work that Christ came to do (see John 17:4). This work of salvation came about through

St. John Paul II saw two fundamental threats to Christianity in the modern world: the secular humanism of Marxist Communism in the Soviet Union and the secular humanism of the consumer societies in Europe and the U.S.

suffering and death on a Cross. By enduring the toil of work in union with Christ crucified for us, man in a way collaborates with the Son of God for the redemption of humanity. He shows himself a true disciple of Christ by carrying the cross in his turn every day (see Luke 9:23) in the activity that he is called upon to perform.

Christ, "undergoing death itself for all of us sinners, taught us by example that we too must shoulder that cross which the world and the flesh inflict upon those who pursue peace and justice"; but also, at the same time, "appointed Lord by his Resurrection and given all authority in heaven and on earth, Christ is now at work in people's hearts through the power of his Spirit…He animates, purifies, and strengthens those noble longings too, by which the human family strives to make its life more human and to render the whole earth submissive to this goal" (Second Vatican Council, *Gaudium et Spes* 38)

The Christian finds in human work a small part of the Cross of Christ and accepts it in the same spirit of redemption in which Christ accepted his Cross for us. In work, thanks to the light that penetrates us from the Resurrection of Christ, we always find a glimmer of new life, of the new good, as if it were an announcement of "the new heavens and the new earth" (*see* 2 Peter 3:13; Revelation 21:1) in which man and the world participate precisely through the toil that goes with work. Through toil—and never without it. On the one hand this confirms the indispensability of the Cross in the spirituality of human work; on the other hand the Cross which this toil constitutes reveals a new good springing from work itself, from work understood in depth and in all its aspects and never apart from work.

ST. JOHN PAUL II, *SOLLICITUDO REI SOCIALIS*

St. John Paul II wrote *Sollicitudo Rei Socialis* ("On Social Concerns") in 1987 to mark the twentieth anniversary of Pope Paul VI's encyclical *Populorum Progressio*. John Paul II restated the themes of the earlier letter, responding to critics who claimed that Paul VI's prescriptions had strayed far beyond the competence of the Church's Magisterium, into the fields of social science and advocacy. John Paul II disagreed, noting that Pope Paul VI "emphasized the ethical and cultural character of the problems connected with development." He concluded that Paul VI's intervention was not only legitimate, but necessary: "When the Church concerns herself with the 'development of peoples,' she cannot be accused of going outside her own specific field of competence and, still less, outside the mandate received from the Lord."

In *Populorum Progressio*, said John Paul II, Catholic social doctrine "once more demonstrated its character as an application of the word of God to people's lives and the life of society, as well as to the earthly realities connected with them." It offers "principles for reflection," "criteria of judgment," and "directives for action."

Yet, the Holy Father was severe in his judgment of society's actual "progress" in the preceding twenty years. Many people throughout the world were still mired in poverty, with few opportunities for advancement, improvement, or education. He placed the responsibility with the "developed" nations that had withdrawn themselves into the two armed camps of the Cold War: capitalist versus communist. Small, poor countries were victims in the larger power struggle, exploited for their resources or strategic military value—or virtually enslaved by massive national debt. He worried, too, that the so-called "first world" powers were forcing a racist and eugenic program of abortion and contraception upon the poorer nations in order to "control" their population growth.

Though his tone is somber and he paints a dire picture, the Holy Father insisted that his message was not one of pessimism or despair. He was, rather, calling members of the Church—especially those in affluent nations—to work for peace, human dignity, and the development of people. He emphasized the virtue of solidarity, in contrast to the divisiveness (based on class, nationality, or ideology) promoted by the world's two dominant powers.

ST. JOHN PAUL II, *CENTESIMUS ANNUS*

Centesimus Annus was promulgated in 1991, the centennial of *Rerum Novarum*. It was a year to celebrate, for many reasons. Just two years earlier, the Soviet empire had crumbled, peacefully; and the Holy Father, who had lived for many years in communist Poland, a Soviet satellite, performed a postmortem analysis of sorts in this encyclical.

History seemed to vindicate the critique of Popes Leo XIII, Pius XI, John XXIII, and Paul VI. Communism was a destructive ideology that could not sustain itself without bloodshed and repression. St. John Paul II did not, however, award the victory to economic liberalism. He acknowledged that some regimes had visited horrors upon their people, using opposition to Marxism as a justification or pretext. He restated his predecessors' cautions about consumerism and *laissez-faire* capitalism; and he called for a universal commitment to human dignity and human rights.

Centesimus Annus was a celebration of a century of Catholic social doctrine. It also celebrated the downfall of a cruel and despotic ideology. That downfall was itself a vindication of a century of prophetic teaching.

ST. JOHN PAUL II, *EVANGELIUM VITÆ*

In his 1995 encyclical *Evangelium Vitæ* ("The Gospel of Life"), St. John Paul II identified a vast international "conspiracy against life"—a conspiracy that "involves not only individuals in their personal, family or group relationships, but goes far beyond, to the point of damaging and distorting, at the international level, relations between peoples and States." He condemned the resulting "culture of death" that promotes abortion, euthanasia, assisted suicide, contraception, sterilization, and the death penalty.

St. John Paul II identified a "conspiracy against life" in *Evangelium Vitæ*.

The Holy Father issued absolute condemnations of abortion and euthanasia, calling them sins and violations of the most fundamental laws of human nature. He reviewed the Church's consistent condemnation of these practices since the beginning of Christianity. He spoke also against the death penalty, though with significant qualifications, noting "a growing tendency, both in the Church and in civil society, to demand that it be applied in a very limited way or even that it be abolished completely." Throughout his pontificate, he wrote frequently to beg clemency for convicted criminals on death row.

Throughout the encyclical, he issued a passionate summons for Christians to replace the culture of death with a "civilization of love":

> To all the members of the Church, the people of life and for life, I make this most urgent appeal, that together we may offer this world of ours new signs of hope, and work to ensure that justice and solidarity will increase and that a new culture of human life will be affirmed, for the building of an authentic civilization of truth and love.

"God is love."
Deus Caritas Est provides the Magisterium's most thorough exposition of the theological foundations for the exercise of charity in society.

POPE BENEDICT XVI, *DEUS CARITAS EST*

Pope Benedict XVI promulgated his first encyclical, *Deus Caritas Est* ("God Is Love"), during the first year of his pontificate in 2005. This document was the fruit of his years of collaboration with his predecessor. The second half of the encyclical was said to be assembled from notes and fragments left behind by St. John Paul II.

It is not, strictly speaking, a social encyclical, but it provides the Magisterium's most thorough exposition, by far, of the theological foundations for the exercise of charity in society.

The Holy Father examined the different forms of love and identified charity with the highest form. He spoke of charity as part of the Church's threefold mission, along with the Sacraments and the proclamation of the Gospel. He urged Christians to form their consciences and take an active part in the political process, always seeking social justice. But he gave a still more exalted position to charity. He invoked the exemplary lives of many canonized saints and figures from recent history. He spoke of Christian charity as "a manifestation of Trinitarian love" and quoted St. Augustine, who said, "If you see charity, you see the Trinity."

DOROTHY DAY: A Radical Witness

Dorothy Day grew up in a Protestant family. Her father was a journalist, and his work took the family from city to city. The Days lived in San Francisco during the great earthquake of 1906, a disaster that left the family jobless and many others homeless. Just eight years old, Dorothy witnessed tremendous suffering, but she also saw many people coming to the assistance of those in need. It made a deep impression on her. Throughout her youth, she was consumed by religious questions (though her family rarely attended church) and by concern for the poor. She was moved by the suffering she saw in the cities where she lived.

Dorothy Day with Mother Teresa, two women who devoted their lives to help the poor.

Young Dorothy was drawn to socialist, communist, and anarchist movements. Like her father, she worked as a journalist for prestigious newspapers, though her employers were more politically oriented. She drifted from her youthful religious concerns and lived an unmoored life, having sexual affairs, conceiving a child out of wedlock, and even procuring an abortion. She suffered from the residual guilt of that abortion for the rest of her life.

She achieved a measure of success in publishing. She wrote a novel and sold the movie rights to Hollywood, earning enough to buy herself a small cottage retreat. But she was still unsettled. Her religious questions came back again, this time with greater intensity. She was living with a man, whom she loved, but he was an atheist who had no sympathy for her search after God. She became pregnant, and this provoked a crisis. He had no desire to raise a child, yet he was also infuriated by Dorothy's desire to have the child baptized. Even though she loved the man, Dorothy knew that the relationship would have to end.

She became a Catholic in 1927 and moved to New York City. She no longer felt at home among the socialists, communists, and anarchists, who tended also to be atheists and sometimes anti-Christian. Yet, she still felt a strong desire to help the poor workers in America's cities, especially with the onset of the Great Depression in 1929. She was unaware of Catholic social doctrine.

Then, in 1931, she met Peter Maurin, an immigrant from France and itinerant poet. He opened Dorothy's eyes to "the prophets of Israel and the Fathers of the Church" and St. Francis of Assisi. Those lives showed the way, he said, but the Church had also provided a road map, a plan, and it was called "the social encyclicals."

Inspired by the encyclicals, Day and Maurin founded the Catholic Worker movement, which published its own newspaper, *The Catholic Worker*, modeled after the radical papers for which Dorothy had written when she was young. The movement, loosely organized and even anarchic, opened "Houses of Hospitality," where homeless people could find a bed and hungry people could have a decent meal. They bought cemetery plots, where the bodies of the indigent dead could be buried.

Though she founded a movement, Dorothy Day followed a largely solitary way. Obedient to the Church, she also practiced a radical and voluntary separation from the market economy, with its banks and advertising and military. She opposed all war, seeing it as incompatible with Catholic universality and the witness of Christ's own passion. She was suspicious of governmental solutions to social problems, and believed that the poor were better served by neighborhood efforts. Charity and justice, she said, must be matters of personal initiative.

She became a Benedictine Oblate in 1955. True to her way, she continued a life of writing, speaking, and service, inspiring but never directing the movement she founded and which she wanted always to be spontaneous and voluntary. She died in 1980. The Archdiocese of New York introduced her cause for canonization in 2000. Cardinal John O'Connor praised her as "a model for all in the third millennium, but especially for women who have had or are considering abortions." She is an inspiration also for single parents who seek holiness.

POPE BENEDICT XVI, *CARITAS IN VERITATE*

"Love in truth."
Caritas in Veritate poignantly contrasts the suffering of the hungry with the blessings of those who enjoy abundance.

Pope Benedict XVI began drafting his encyclical *Caritas in Veritate* ("Love in Truth") as an appreciation and renewed application of Pope Paul VI's encyclical *Populorum Progressio*. He finished a draft in 2007, in time for the fortieth anniversary of Pope Paul's encyclical, but undertook revisions as the global economy sank deeper into recession. He promulgated the document finally in 2009.

Praising the letter of Pope Paul VI, Pope Benedict adapted its arguments for changes in geopolitics and technology in the intervening forty years. He clarified, too, that the Magisterium does not claim competence in economics, sociology, or government; Benedict hoped, rather, to equip competent professionals in those fields with solid moral principles, thereby helping them to make good decisions as they pursued technical solutions to social problems. At various points in the encyclical, he addressed himself to leaders in business and industry, in government, in finance, and in aid agencies.

His treatment of hunger is especially poignant, contrasting the suffering of the hungry with the blessings of those who enjoy abundance. He dedicates portions of the letter to other problems related to the global economy, e.g., the plight of migrants, the horrors of sex tourism, and the abuse of biotechnology.

The encyclical is significant also for its ecological concern, a hallmark of Pope Benedict's pontificate. In *Caritas in Veritate*, the Holy Father spoke against the "unregulated exploitation of the earth's resources."

SECOND VATICAN COUNCIL, *GAUDIUM ET SPES*

The Church held only one general council in the twentieth century, the Second Vatican Council (1962-1965), and social doctrine came to the fore throughout its deliberations and in many of its documents. The Council Fathers dedicated an entire document to the subject of religious liberty (the declaration *Dignitatis Humanæ*, "On Human Dignity") and another to social communications (the decree *Inter Mirifica*).

But by far the most comprehensive statement of social concern was the Pastoral Constitution on the Church in the Modern World: *Gaudium et Spes*. The Latin title means "Joy and Hope," and the Council did indeed present a positive response to the challenges of the day. It called upon Catholics to read the "signs of the times" in light of the Gospel. Those signs included rapid and far-reaching technological and social changes, and the results of these were mixed. In many cases they enhanced health and culture, but they also disrupted long-established patterns of family and community life. With such changes had also come new strains of thought, including an increasingly antagonistic atheism.

Gaudium et Spes presents the Church's social doctrine as a way to respect human dignity and guarantee human rights amid new circumstances. Starting from Christianity's doctrine of human nature, the document offers a coherent framework for understanding freedom, justice, and peace. The Council Fathers emphasized that the Church is not committed to any ideology, political or economic. Technical solutions in those fields are always beyond its competence and outside its authority. But all human activity includes a moral dimension, and decisions made in government, industry, and media can affect multitudes of people, for better or worse. With *Gaudium et Spes*, the Church staked its place with the people of the modern world.

The Second Vatican Council formally opened under the pontificate of Pope John XXIII on October 11, 1962 and closed under Pope Paul VI on December 8, 1965.
"The joys and hopes, the grief and anguish of the people of our time, especially of those who are poor or afflicted, are the joys and hopes, the grief and anguish of the followers of Christ as well." (*Gaudium et Spes*, 1)

COMMON CONCERNS

In the chapters that follow, we will examine the principles and major themes of Catholic social teaching in greater detail. In all the major social encyclicals, as well as the lesser-known papal statements and the Council documents, certain concerns remain consistently in the foreground:

✠ The need for the moral law because it provides the foundation for all social teaching by accounting for man's duties and consequent rights (cf. CCC 1959, 2070, 2242).

✠ God is the source of all civil authority: Man does not confer authority upon himself, but authority flows from God to all just governments and laws (cf. CCC 1899).

✠ The common good helps perfect individuals: Man is perfected not only by private goods such as food and shelter but by "common goods" such as peace and truth that come about through his life with others in community (cf. CCC 1905-1912, 1925-1927).

✠ Promotion of the fundamental rights of the person.

✠ Prosperity, or the development of the spiritual and temporal goods of society.

✠ The peace and security of society and its members.

EFFORTS OF THE U.S. HIERARCHY

In the early twentieth century, Catholics around the world found new ways to disseminate the Church's social doctrine and put it to work. In 1917, the United States bishops established the National Catholic War Council as an emergency measure to deal with "all Catholic activities" related to World War I. When the War ended, the organization became the National Catholic Welfare Council (NCWC), with a broader range of interests. The Council received guidance from the bishops, who met annually. An executive committee oversaw departments that promoted the interests of Catholics in five areas: education,

Immigrants arriving at Ellis Island, New York, 1902. Many immigrants were Catholic and were assisted by the NCWC to acclimate to life in America.

legislation, social action, lay initiatives, and press and publicity.

It was a time of great growth in the fields of Catholic education and health care. The NCWC advocated for these interests in the national capital and the state capitals. It was also a time when throngs of immigrants came to American shores for the abundant jobs in mines, mills, and factories. Many of these came from countries that were predominantly Catholic, and they faced misunderstanding—and sometimes outright bigotry—in their new country. The NCWC assisted these new immigrants by meeting them at the ports, helping them complete the necessary paperwork, directing them to employment opportunities, and even giving them loans.

Over time, the NCWC changed its name—first to the National Catholic Welfare *Conference*, which later divided into the National Conference of Catholic Bishops and its administrative-lobbying arm, the United States Catholic Conference. Eventually, the two entities were rejoined as the United States Conference of Catholic Bishops. The Conference continues its work today.

The United States bishops meet annually and regularly issue pastoral letters and policy statements that apply Catholic social doctrine to specific circumstances. Some examples are *Brothers and Sisters to Us* (on racism, 1979); *The Challenge of Peace: God's Promise and Our Response* (1983) and *Sowing Weapons of War* (1995); *Economic Justice for All: A Pastoral Letter on Catholic Social Teaching and the U.S. Economy* (1986); and *A Good Friday Appeal to End the Death Penalty* (1999) and *A Culture of Life and the Penalty of Death* (2005).

CONCLUSION

Since *Rerum Novarum* the Church has addressed the "social question" with increasing clarity, frequency, and volume. The *Catechism of the Catholic Church*, in 1993, brought together the authoritative teachings in an abbreviated, but orderly way. The *Compendium of the Social Doctrine of the Church*, published in 2004 by the Pontifical Council for Justice and Peace, is a more complete account of the Church's teaching. The *Compendium* is not a magisterial document in itself, but is largely composed of selections from the official teachings of the Popes and the Councils, arranged in a more complete and systematic way.

St. John Paul II began his encyclical *Sollicitudo Rei Socialis* with a remarkable summary of the material covered in this chapter: Catholic social doctrine as it has been taught by the Church's Magisterium.

> The social concern of the Church, directed towards an authentic development of man and society which would respect and promote all the dimensions of the human person, has always expressed itself in the most varied ways. In recent years, one of the special means of intervention has been the Magisterium of the Roman Pontiffs which, beginning with the Encyclical *Rerum Novarum* of Leo XIII as a point of reference, has frequently dealt with the question…
>
> The Popes have not failed to throw fresh light by means of those messages upon new aspects of the social doctrine of the Church. As a result, this doctrine, beginning with the outstanding contribution of Leo XIII and enriched by the successive contributions of the Magisterium, has now become an updated doctrinal "corpus." It builds up gradually, as the Church, in the fullness of the word revealed by Christ Jesus[5] and with the assistance of the Holy Spirit (cf. Jn 14:16, 26; 16:13-15), reads events as they unfold in the course of history. She thus seeks to lead people to respond, with the support also of rational reflection and of the human sciences, to their vocation as responsible builders of earthly society.

The Saints
PILLARS OF THE CHURCH

POPE ST. CLEMENT I:
On Sharing What You Have Been Given

A disciple of the Apostles Peter and Paul, Pope St. Clement wrote a letter of admonition and discipline to the Church of Corinth. He counseled members of the first-century Church, as the Pope today still teaches, to share the goods they have received.

Let our whole body, then, be preserved in Christ Jesus; and let every one be subject to his neighbor, according to the special gift bestowed upon him. Let the strong not despise the weak, and let the weak show respect to the strong. Let the rich man provide for the wants of the poor; and let the poor man bless God, because God has given him one by whom his need may be supplied. Let the wise man display his wisdom, not by words, but through good deeds. Let the humble not bear testimony to himself, but leave witness to be borne to him by another.

Let him who is celibate not grow proud of it and boast. He should know that it was Another who gave him the gift of continence.

Let us consider, then, brethren, of what stuff we were made—who we are and how we came into the world, as if out of a tomb and out of utter darkness. He who made us and fashioned us, having prepared his bountiful gifts for us before we were born, introduced us into his world. Since, therefore, we receive all these things from him, we ought for everything to give him thanks. To him be glory forever and ever. Amen.

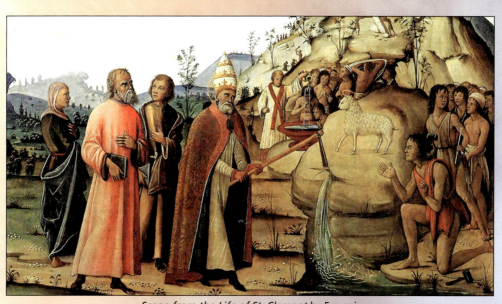

Scene from the Life of St. Clement by Fungai.
"Let the wise man display his wisdom, not by words, but through good deeds."

SUPPLEMENTARY READING

Compendium of the Social Doctrine of the Church

On the Authoritative Documents

b. From *Rerum Novarum* to our own day

89. *In response to the first great social question, Pope Leo XIII promulgated the first social encyclical, Rerum Novarum.*[6] This Encyclical examines the condition of salaried workers, which was particularly distressing for industrial labourers who languished in inhuman misery. The *labour question* is dealt with according to its true dimensions. It is explored in all its social and political expressions so that a proper evaluation may be made in the light of the doctrinal principles founded on Revelation and on natural law and morality.

Rerum Novarum lists errors that give rise to social ills, excludes socialism as a remedy and expounds with precision and in contemporary terms "the Catholic doctrine on work, the right to property, the principle of collaboration instead of class struggle as the fundamental means for social change, the rights of the weak, the dignity of the poor and the obligations of the rich, the perfecting of justice through charity, on the right to form professional associations."[7]

Rerum Novarum became the document inspiring Christian activity in the social sphere and the point of reference for this activity.[8] The Encyclical's central theme is the just ordering of society, in view of which there is the obligation to identify criteria of judgment that will help to evaluate existing socio-political systems and to suggest lines of action for their appropriate transformation.

90. *Rerum Novarum* dealt with the *labour question* using a methodology that would become *"a lasting paradigm"*[9] for successive developments in the Church's social doctrine. The principles affirmed by Pope Leo XIII would be taken up again and studied more deeply in successive social encyclicals. The whole of the Church's social doctrine can be seen as an updating, a deeper analysis and an expansion of the original nucleus of principles presented in *Rerum Novarum*. With this courageous and farsighted text, Pope Leo XIII "gave the Church 'citizenship status' as it were, amid the changing realities of public life"[10] and made an "incisive statement"[11] which became "a permanent element of the Church's social teaching."[12] He affirmed that serious social problems "could be solved only by cooperation between all forces"[13] and added that, "in regard to the Church, her cooperation will never be found lacking."[14]

91. At the beginning of the 1930s, following the grave economic crisis of 1929, Pope Pius XI published the Encyclical *Quadragesimo Anno*,[15] commemorating the fortieth anniversary of *Rerum Novarum*. The Pope reread the past in the light of the economic and social situation in which the expansion of the influence of financial groups, both nationally and internationally, was added to the effects of industrialization. It was the post-war period, during which totalitarian regimes were being imposed in Europe even as the class struggle was becoming more bitter. The Encyclical warns about the failure to respect the freedom to form associations and stresses the principles of solidarity and cooperation in order to overcome social contradictions. The relationships between capital and labour must be characterized by cooperation.[16]

Quadragesimo Anno confirms the principle that salaries should be proportional not only to the needs of the worker but also to those of the worker's family. The State, in its relations with the private sector, should apply the *principle of subsidiarity*, a principle that will become a permanent element of the Church's social doctrine. The Encyclical rejects liberalism, understood as unlimited competition between economic forces, and reconfirms the value of private property, recalling its social function....

94. The 1960s bring promising prospects: recovery after the devastation of the war, the beginning of decolonization, and the first timid signs of a *thaw* in the relations between the American and Soviet blocs. This is the context within which St. John XXIII reads deeply into

SUPPLEMENTARY READING Continued

the "signs of the times."[17] *The social question is becoming universal and involves all countries:* together with the labour question and the Industrial Revolution, there come to the fore problems of agriculture, of developing regions, of increasing populations, and those concerning the need for global economic cooperation. Inequalities that in the past were experienced within nations are now becoming international and make the dramatic situation of the Third World ever more evident....

95. With the Encyclical *Pacem in Terris*,[18] Blessed Pope John XXIII brings to the forefront the problem of peace in an era marked by nuclear proliferation. Moreover, *Pacem in Terris* contains one of the first in-depth reflections on rights on the part of the Church; it is the Encyclical of peace and human dignity. It continues and completes the discussion presented in *Mater et Magistra*, and, continuing in the direction indicated by Pope Leo XIII, it emphasizes the importance of the cooperation of all men and women. It is the first time that a Church document is addressed also to "all men of good will,"[19] who are called to a great task: "to establish with truth, justice, love and freedom new methods of relationships in human society."[20] *Pacem in Terris* dwells on the public authority of the world community, called to "tackle and solve problems of an economic, social, political or cultural character which are posed by the universal common good."[21] On the tenth anniversary of *Pacem in Terris*, Cardinal Maurice Roy, the President of the Pontifical Commission for Justice and Peace, sent Pope Paul VI a letter together with a document with a series of reflections on the different possibilities afforded by the teaching contained in Pope John XXIII's Encyclical for shedding light on the new problems connected with the promotion of peace.[22]

96. The Pastoral Constitution *Gaudium et Spes*[23] of the Second Vatican Council is a significant response of the Church to the expectations of the contemporary world. In this Constitution, "in harmony with the ecclesiological renewal, a new concept of how to be a community of believers and people of God are reflected. It aroused new interest regarding the doctrine contained in the preceding documents on the witness and life of Christians, as authentic ways of making the presence of God in the world visible."[24] *Gaudium et Spes* presents the face of a Church that "cherishes a feeling of deep solidarity with the human race and its history,"[25] that travels the same journey as all mankind and shares the same earthly lot with the world, but which at the same time "is to be a leaven and, as it were, the soul of human society in its renewal by Christ and transformation into the family of God."[26]...

97. Another very important document of the Second Vatican Council in the corpus of the Church's social doctrine is the Declaration *Dignitatis Humanæ*,[27] in which the *right to religious freedom* is clearly proclaimed. The document presents the theme in two chapters. The first, of a general character, affirms that religious freedom is based on the dignity of the human person and that it must be sanctioned as a civil right in the legal order of society. The second chapter deals with the theme in the light of Revelation and clarifies its pastoral implications, pointing out that it is a right that concerns not only people as individuals but also the different communities of people.

98. "Development is the new name for peace,"[28] Pope Paul VI solemnly proclaims in his Encyclical *Populorum Progressio*,[29] which may be considered a development of the chapter on economic and social life in *Gaudium et Spes*, even while it introduces some significant new elements. In particular, it presents the outlines of an integral development of man and of a development in solidarity with all humanity: "These two topics are to be considered the axes around which the Encyclical is structured. In wishing to convince its receivers of the urgent need for action in solidarity, the Pope presents development as 'the transition from less humane conditions to those which are more humane' and indicates its characteristics."[30] This *transition* is not limited to merely economic or technological

SUPPLEMENTARY READING Continued

dimensions, but implies for each person the acquisition of culture, the respect of the dignity of others, the acknowledgment of "the highest good, the recognition of God Himself, the author and end of these blessings."[31] Development that benefits everyone responds to the demands of justice on a global scale that guarantees worldwide peace and makes it possible to achieve a "complete humanism"[32] guided by spiritual values.

101. Ninety years after *Rerum Novarum*, Pope John Paul II devoted the Encyclical *Laborem Exercens*[33] to *work*, the fundamental good of the human person, the primary element of economic activity and the key to the entire social question. *Laborem Exercens* outlines a spirituality and ethic of work in the context of a profound theological and philosophical reflection. Work must not be understood only in the objective and material sense, but one must keep in mind its subjective dimension, insofar as it is always an expression of the person. Besides being a decisive paradigm for social life, work has all the dignity of being a context in which the person's natural and supernatural vocation must find fulfilment.

102. With the Encyclical *Sollicitudo Rei Socialis*,[34] Pope John Paul II commemorates the twentieth anniversary of *Populorum Progressio* and deals once more with the theme of development along two fundamental lines: "on one hand, the dramatic situation of the modern world, under the aspect of the failed development of the Third World, and on the other, the meaning of, conditions and requirements for a development worthy of man."[35] The Encyclical presents differences between progress and development, and insists that "true development cannot be limited to the multiplication of goods and service—to what one possesses—but must contribute to the fullness of the 'being' of man. In this way the moral nature of real development is meant to be shown clearly."[36] Pope John Paul II, alluding to the motto of the pontificate of Pope Pius XII, "*opus iustitiæ pax*" (peace is the fruit of justice), comments: "Today, one could say, with the same exactness and the same power of biblical inspiration (cf. Is 32:17; Jas 3:18), *opus solidaritatis pax* (peace is the fruit of solidarity)."[37]

103. On the hundredth anniversary of *Rerum Novarum*, Pope John Paul II promulgates his third social encyclical, *Centesimus Annus*,[38] whence emerges the doctrinal continuity of a hundred years of the Church's social Magisterium. Taking up anew one of the fundamental principles of the Christian view of social and political organization, which had been the central theme of the previous Encyclical, the Pope writes: "What we nowadays call the principle of solidarity…is frequently stated by Pope Leo XIII, who uses the term 'friendship'… Pope Pius XI refers to it with the equally meaningful term 'social charity.' Pope Paul VI, expanding the concept to cover the many modern aspects of the social question, speaks of a 'civilization of love.'"[39] Pope John Paul II demonstrates how the Church's social teaching moves along the axis of reciprocity between God and man: recognizing God in every person and every person in God is the condition of authentic human development. The articulate and in-depth analysis of the "new things," and particularly of the great breakthrough of 1989 with the collapse of the Soviet system, shows appreciation for democracy and the free economy, in the context of an indispensable solidarity.

Brothers and Sisters to Us (1979): United States Conference of Catholic Bishops

Racism is a sin: a sin that divides the human family, blots out the image of God among specific members of the family, and violates the fundamental human dignity of those called to be children of the same Father. Racism is the sin that says some human beings are inherently superior and others essentially inferior because of race. It is the sin that makes racial characteristics the determining factor for the exercise of human rights.…racism is more than a disregard for the words of Jesus; it is a denial of the truth of the dignity of each human being revealed by the mystery of the Incarnation.

SUPPLEMENTARY READING Continued

Sowing Weapons of War: A Pastoral Reflection on the Arms Trade and Landmines (June 16 1995): National Conference of Catholic Bishops

The arms trade is a scandal.[40] That weapons of war are bought and sold almost as if they were simply another commodity like appliances or industrial machinery is a serious moral disorder in today's world.[41] The predominant role of our own country in sustaining and even promoting the arms trade, sometimes for economic reasons, is a moral challenge for our nation. Jobs at home cannot justify exporting the means of war abroad.

In too many cases, the global arms trade has brought not security, but aggression, repression and long-term instability. Starving Somali children, destroyed Angolan villages, Cambodian lands rendered uninhabitable by landmines, and seemingly endless conflict in Afghanistan are the fruits of this deadly trade. "By their fruits you will know them" (Mt 7:20).

These attacks on life led the Holy Father, in his recent encyclical, to condemn "the violence inherent not only in wars as such but in the scandalous arms trade, which spawns the many armed conflicts which stain our world with blood." [42] These realities moved the African bishops last year to appeal to those in the North to "stop arms sales to groups locked in conflict in Africa." [43] This suffering impelled Cardinal Vinko Puljic of Sarajevo to tell Americans that more weapons will lead to "more destruction, to complete cataclysm" in Bosnia-Herzegovina.[44] Our own relief workers and missionaries, whose lives are often at risk, can recite an endless litany of horrors brought about by this deadly trade.

In response to these appeals and the recent Vatican reflection on the arms trade,[45] we renew our call for our nation and the international community to undertake more serious efforts to control and radically reduce the trade in arms. The arms trade is an integral part of "the culture of violence" we deplored a year ago.[46] Just as we seek to stop the proliferation of arms in our streets, we, too, must stop the proliferation of arms around the world. Curbing the arms trade is now an essential part of the peacemaking vocation we outlined in "The Challenge of Peace" more than a decade ago.

A nuclear weapon test by the United States at Bikini Atoll, Micronesia, July 1946. The water released by the explosion was highly radioactive.

SUPPLEMENTARY READING Continued

Economic Justice For All: Pastoral Letter on Catholic Social Teaching and the U.S. Economy (1986): United States Catholic Bishops

66. The virtues of citizenship are an expression of Christian love more crucial in today's interdependent world than ever before. These virtues grow out of a lively sense of one's dependence on the commonweal and obligations to it. This civic commitment must also guide the economic institutions of society. In the absence of a vital sense of citizenship among the businesses, corporations, labor unions, and other groups that shape economic life, society as a whole is endangered. Solidarity is another name for this social friendship and civic commitment that make human moral and economic life possible.

67. The Christian tradition recognizes, of course, that the fullness of love and community will be achieved only when God's work in Christ comes to completion in the kingdom of God. This kingdom has been inaugurated among us, but God's redeeming and transforming work is not yet complete. Within history, knowledge of how to achieve the goal of social unity is limited. Human sin continues to wound the lives of both individuals and larger social bodies and places obstacles in the path toward greater social solidarity. If efforts to protect human dignity are to be effective, they must take these limits on knowledge and love into account. Nevertheless, sober realism should not be confused with resigned or cynical pessimism. It is a challenge to develop a courageous hope that can sustain efforts that will sometimes be arduous and protracted.

A Culture of Life and the Penalty of Death: A Statement of the United States Conference of Catholic Bishops Calling For an End to the Use of the Death Penalty (2005)

Twenty-five years ago, our Conference of bishops first called for an end to the death penalty.

We renew this call to seize a new moment and new momentum. This is a time to teach clearly, encourage reflection, and call for common action in the Catholic community to bring about an end to the use of the death penalty in our land.

In these reflections, we join together to share clearly and apply faithfully Catholic teaching on the death penalty. We reaffirm our common judgment that the use of the death penalty is unnecessary and unjustified in our time and circumstances.

Our nation should forgo the use of the death penalty because

- The sanction of death, when it is not necessary to protect society, violates respect for human life and dignity.
- State-sanctioned killing in our names diminishes all of us.
- Its application is deeply flawed and can be irreversibly wrong, is prone to errors, and is biased by factors such as race, the quality of legal representation, and where the crime was committed.
- We have other ways to punish criminals and protect society.

VOCABULARY

ATHEISM
Rejection of the existence of God, founded often on a false conception of human autonomy. This is forbidden by the First Commandment.

CLASS STRUGGLE
In Marxist ideology, the never-ending conflict between the ownership and working classes, based on their opposing interests. The Church has opposed the idea as contrary to fraternal charity.

COLD WAR
A state of tense political and military rivalry between two powers; usually applied to the hostility between the United States and the Soviet Union through much of the twentieth century.

COMMUNISM
A political theory based on the writings of Karl Marx, promoting violent class struggle and the abolition of private property.

ENCYCLICAL
An authoritative papal letter, usually addressed to all the bishops of the world and treating a matter of great importance.

FASCISM
An extremely nationalistic form of socialism, advocating state control or ownership of key industries, with government overseen by extremely authoritarian leadership.

GENERAL COUNCIL
A major, authoritative assembly of bishops representative of the Church throughout the world.

IDEOLOGY
A body of doctrine, usually political or economic, that makes grand systematic truth claims.

INDUSTRIAL REVOLUTION
The rapid development of industry in the eighteenth and nineteenth centuries, brought on by advances in technology for mass production and automation.

LAISSEZ-FAIRE CAPITALISM
An economic approach that opposes governmental interference in business and industry.

LIBERALISM (ECONOMIC)
See *Laissez-Faire* Capitalism.

MAGISTERIUM
The Church's teaching authority.

MARXISM
See communism.

NAZISM (NATIONAL SOCIALISM)
The statist, racist, nationalist ideology behind the National Socialist German Workers Party, which reigned under Adolf Hitler in the 1930s and 1940s. Nazi racism was condemned by Pope Pius XI in his encyclical addressed to the German people, *Mit Brennender Sorge* ("With Burning Concern"), and by Pope Pius XII in his radio and other addresses.

SOCIALISM
A variety of political and economic theories that advocate a high degree of government control over—or outright ownership of—the means of production, distribution, and exchange. Though most forms of socialism reject violence as a means of achieving their ends, many of its forms espouse the idea of class struggle.

SOVIET UNION
A former federation of communist republics that extended over the northern half of Asia and much of Eastern Europe. Established in 1922, it expanded especially after World War II. Its capital was Moscow.

STATISM
The tendency, in politics or economics, to concentrate control in the state at the cost of individual liberty.

STUDY QUESTIONS

1. How did the political and industrial revolutions change life for individuals, families, and societies?

2. What specific actions did bishops take to address the social problems emerging in the nineteenth century?

3. Who were the pioneering figures in the Church's active and doctrinal response to society's problems?

4. How did Pope Leo XIII approach the social problems of his day?

5. What influence did *Rerum Novarum* have over the next century? In what ways was it vindicated by history?

6. How does the Church critique socialist and statist ideologies? How does the Church critique *laissez-faire* capitalism?

7. What circumstances prompted Pope Pius XI to write *Quadragesimo Anno*? How had the world scene changed in the years since *Rerum Novarum*?

8. What circumstances prompted St. John XXIII to write his two social doctrine encyclicals? How had the world scene changed in the years since *Quadragesimo Anno*?

9. What dire conditions preoccupied Pope Paul VI and led him to write so passionately in *Populorum Progressio*?

10. What is distinctive about St. John Paul II's approach to human labor?

11. What world event took place just before the centenary of *Rerum Novarum*? How did that event affect St. John Paul II's celebration of the anniversary?

12. What forces conspire, according to St. John Paul II, to promote anti-life policies and practices in the world?

13. What are the themes and concerns common to the Church's magisterial documents?

14. What structures did the United States bishops establish in order to respond to social crises in the early twentieth century? What were the most pressing issues at the time?

Poverty in Serbia.
It is a grievous neglect of basic human rights to ignore groups of people suffering misery and destitution while other nations have a surplus of riches.

THE CHURCH TEACHES US HOW TO LIVE

PRACTICAL EXERCISES

1. Find a theme that recurs in most of the social documents discussed in this chapter (the role of the state, for example, or inequity of wealth). Trace that theme through the documents, noting its development over time.

2. Identify a current trend—in the world economy, for example, or in the conduct of war—that you think would be a timely topic for a new social encyclical. Outline such a document, basing your argument on established Catholic teaching. Follow the form of an encyclical letter as found in the actual documents.

3. Research the life of Pope Leo XIII, St. John XXIII, or St. John Paul II (choose one). Discuss the major events of his life and how they might have influenced the emphases in his social teaching.

4. Read *Quadragesimo Anno* and *Gaudium et Spes*. Note any differences you find in the tone and intellectual approach of the documents. Discuss the historical and other factors that might account for these differences.

FROM THE CATECHISM

2421 The social doctrine of the Church developed in the nineteenth century when the Gospel encountered modern industrial society with its new structures for the production of consumer goods, its new concept of society, the state and authority, and its new forms of labor and ownership. The development of the doctrine of the Church on economic and social matters attests the permanent value of the Church's teaching at the same time as it attests the true meaning of her Tradition, always living and active.[47]

2423 The Church's social teaching proposes principles for reflection; it provides criteria for judgment; it gives guidelines for action:

Any system in which social relationships are determined entirely by economic factors is contrary to the nature of the human person and his acts.[48]

2424 A theory that makes profit the exclusive norm and ultimate end of economic activity is morally unacceptable. The disordered desire for money cannot but produce perverse effects. It is one of the causes of the many conflicts which disturb the social order.[49]

A system that "subordinates the basic rights of individuals and of groups to the collective organization of production" is contrary to human dignity.[50] Every practice that reduces persons to nothing more than a means of profit enslaves man, leads to idolizing money, and contributes to the spread of atheism. "You cannot serve God and mammon."[51]

2425 The Church has rejected the totalitarian and atheistic ideologies associated in modern times with "communism" or "socialism." She has likewise refused to accept, in the practice of "capitalism," individualism and the absolute primacy of the law of the marketplace over human labor.[52] Regulating the economy solely by centralized planning perverts the basis of social bonds; regulating it solely by the law of the marketplace fails social justice, for "there are many human needs which cannot be satisfied by the market."[53] Reasonable regulation of the marketplace and economic initiatives, in keeping with a just hierarchy of values and a view to the common good, is to be commended.

THE SOCIAL DOCTRINE OF THE CATHOLIC CHURCH

Poverty in South Africa.
The overarching premise of Catholic social teaching is that no people should suffer in squalor while others are able to live in comfort.

ENDNOTES – CHAPTER THREE

1. *Letters* 35.
2. *DV* 10 § 2.
3. Lk 10:16; cf. *LG* 20.
4. *DV* 10 § 2.
5. Cf. Dogmatic Constitution on Divine Revelation, *Dei Verbum*, 4.
6. Cf. Leo XIII, Encyclical Letter *Rerum Novarum: Acta Leonis XIII*, 11 (1892), 97-144.
7. Congregation for Catholic Education, *Guidelines for the Study and Teaching of the Church's Social Doctrine in the Formation of Priests*, 20, (Rome: Vatican Polyglot Press, 1988), 24.
8. Cf. *QA* 39; Pius XII, Radio Message for the fiftieth anniversary of *Rerum Novarum: AAS* 33 (1941), 198.
9. *CA* 5.
10. Ibid.
11. *CA* 56.
12. *CA* 60.
13. Ibid.
14. *RN* 63; cf. *CA* 56.
15. Cf. *QA* 177-228.
16. Cf. *QA* 186-189.
17. Cf. PT.
18. Cf. John XXIII, Encyclical Letter *Pacem in Terris: AAS* 55 (1963), 257-304.
19. John XXIII, Encyclical Letter *Pacem in Terris*, Title: *AAS* 55 (1963), 257.
20. John XXIII, Encyclical Letter *Pacem in Terris: AAS* 55 (1963), 301.
21. Cf. *PT: AAS* 55 (1963), 294.
22. Cf. Cardinal Maurice Roy, Letter to Paul VI and Document on the occasion of the tenth anniversary of *Pacem in Terris*, L'Osservatore Romano, English edition, April 19, 1973, 1-8.
23. Cf. Second Vatican Ecumenical Council, Pastoral Constitution *Gaudium et Spes: AAS* 58 (1966), 1025-1120.
24. Congregation for Catholic Education, *Guidelines for the Study and Teaching of the Church's Social Doctrine in the Formation of Priests*, 24 (Rome: Vatican Polyglot Press 1988), 28.
25. *GS* 1.
26. *GS* 40.
27. Cf. Second Vatican Ecumenical Council, Declaration *Dignitatis Humanæ: AAS* 58 (1966), 929-946.
28. *PP* 76-80.
29. Cf. *PP* 257-299.
30. Congregation for Catholic Education, *Guidelines for the Study and Teaching of the Church's Social Doctrine in the Formation of Priests*, 25, (Rome: Vatican Polyglot Press, 1988), 29.
31. *PP* 21.
32. *PP* 42.
33. Cf. *LE*.
34. Cf. *SRS* 39.
35. Congregation for *Catholic Education, Guidelines for the Study and Teaching of the Church's Social Doctrine in the Formation of Priests*, 26, (Rome: Vatican Polyglot Press, 1988), 32.
36. Ibid.
37. *SRS* 39.
38. Cf. John Paul II, Encyclical Letter *Centesimus Annus: AAS* 83 (1991), 793-867.
39. *CA* 10.
40. Pope John Paul II, *The Gospel of Life* (1995): no. 10.
41. Pope John Paul II, *On Social Concern*, no. 24.
42. *The Gospel of Life*, no. 10.
43. "Final Message of the Special Synod for Africa," May 6, 1994, in *Origins* 24:1 (May 19, 1994): p. 8.
44. Cardinal Vinko Puljic, address at the Center for Strategic and International Studies, March 30, 1995, in Catholic News Service, April 3, 1995, p. 7.
45. Pontifical Council for Justice and Peace, "The International Arms Trade: An Ethical Reflection," in *Origins* 24:8 (July 7, 1994).
46. NCCB, "Confronting a Culture of Violence" (Washington: USCCB Office of Publishing and Promotion Service, 1994).
47. Cf. *CA* 3.
48. Cf. *CA* 24.
49. Cf. *GS* 63 § 3; *LE* 7; 20; *CA* 35.
50. *GS* 65 § 2.
51. Mt 6:24; Lk 16:13.
52. Cf. *CA* 10; 13; 44.
53. *CA* 34.

Social Doctrine of the Catholic Church
CHAPTER 4

Principles of Catholic Social Doctrine

These principles represent the reflection of the great Popes, saints, and theologians, over the course of centuries, upon the fundamental teachings of Christ.

Social Doctrine of the Catholic Church

CHAPTER FOUR

Principles of Catholic Social Doctrine

THE CHURCH'S TEACHING RESTS ON A SOLID FOUNDATION

The permanent principles of the Church's social doctrine[1] constitute the very heart of Catholic social teaching. These are the principles of: *the dignity of the human person*, which has already been dealt with in the preceding chapter, and which is the foundation of all the other principles and content of the Church's social doctrine;[2] *the common good*; *subsidiarity*; and *solidarity*. These principles, the expression of the whole truth about man known by reason and faith, are born of "the encounter of the Gospel message and of its demands summarized in the supreme commandment of love of God and neighbor in justice with the problems emanating from the life of society."[3] In the course of history and with the light of the Spirit, the Church has wisely reflected within her own tradition of faith and has been able to provide an ever more accurate foundation and shape to these principles, progressively explaining them in the attempt to respond coherently to the demands of the times and to the continuous developments of social life.

—*Compendium of the Social Doctrine of the Church*, 160

IN THIS CHAPTER, WE WILL ADDRESS SEVERAL QUESTIONS:

✛ What are the four basic principles of Catholic social doctrine?
✛ What gives human beings their inherent dignity?
✛ What is the common good? How can it be misunderstood?
✛ What is the principle of subsidiarity?
✛ What is the principle of solidarity?
✛ What is the universal destination of goods and how does it relate to the right to private property?
✛ What values are presupposed in Catholic social teaching?

PRINCIPLES OF CATHOLIC SOCIAL DOCTRINE

Sermon on the Mount by Rosselli.
The God who created the human race has revealed the means by which the human race can live in peace.

In even a brief survey of the Church's social teaching, we see that certain principles and themes come up again and again. The Popes and councils develop the Church's understanding of these basic matters, but the principles remain firm. Based surely on divine law, they are permanent; and they form the foundation for all the other principles and content in the Church's social doctrine.

Human nature does not change, and human behavior follows the same patterns today as it did millennia ago. Circumstances change. Technology changes. The economy has its ups and downs. But the way of living peacefully in community has not changed and will not change. The God who created the human race has revealed the means by which the human race can live in peace. Each person, however, remains free to accept or reject Divine Revelation. In the last century and a half, the Church has developed its social doctrine in order to proclaim the matter clearly and persuasively for new generations.

Christian doctrine develops over time. It becomes gradually more explicit and detailed, though later statements of doctrine remain consistent with earlier statements. Terminology may change in order to address new circumstances; but authoritative teaching in one generation will never contradict authoritative teaching from another generation. All that changes is the way the facts are expressed—the degree to which the truth is elaborated.

Now that we have briefly considered the Church's key documents in this area, we will focus on the principles they hold in common. The four most basic are: *the dignity of the human person*; *the common good*; *subsidiarity*; and *solidarity*.

These principles are particularly important because they apply in all social relationships, from the most immediate and local, like family and friendship, to the most complex and global, like peacemaking and international trade. They are moral principles, and therefore are binding on our consciences; for the Catholic Church teaches infallibly in matters of faith and morals. One commentator recently described Catholic social thinking as "nothing less than the Beatitudes of the gospel refined for action in the world." These principles represent the reflection of the great Popes, saints, and theologians, over the course of centuries, upon the fundamental teachings of Christ.

Thus, it is important for us to become familiar with—and even expert in—the basic terms of the Church's doctrine. These are the terms that should define our social relationships—our business dealings, our friendships and romantic interests, our civic involvement, and our family life.

In the encyclicals and other Catholic documents, however, the Church's principles are often presented in a specialized and somewhat technical vocabulary that is often misconstrued, exploited, and misunderstood. The terms are sometimes presented as the sole possession of one faction or another, but they are not. They transcend politics and economics—and are, in fact, the measure by which we judge the proposals and platforms of political parties and economic policies themselves. Practical applications in particular circumstances are beyond the expertise of the Church. Individual citizens are called to apply these moral principles in countless different ways, based on their own professional expertise.

HUMAN DIGNITY

The most fundamental principle of Catholic social thought is human dignity. We must honor every person, from the moment of conception until natural death, because that person is made in the image and likeness of God (cf. CCC 1700). Personal dignity does not depend upon one's job, possessions, accomplishments, career potential, physical strength, or even particular virtues. The divine image can be obscured by sin, but it can never be taken away; it is essential to every human being. Thus, everyone—even the most hardened and unrepentant criminal—deserves to be treated with dignity.

Every person—man, woman, or child—is radically equal in the sight of God. All people have the same nature and the same origin. All are called to enjoy the same destiny: to be children of God, blessed forever in Heaven. Jesus Christ shed his Blood and died for the sake of "all" (cf. 2 Cor 5:14-15). God desires the salvation of everyone indiscriminately (cf. 1 Tm 2:3-6).

Christians strive to "have the mind of Christ" (1 Cor 2:16). To think as Christ, we must always recognize human dignity and equality. God "shows no partiality" (Acts 10:34), and neither should human laws and institutions. Quoting the Second Vatican Council, the *Catechism* (CCC 1935) condemns as "incompatible with God's design" every form of social or cultural discrimination regarding human rights, on the grounds of sex, race, color, social conditions, language, or religion.

Human beings do differ from one another. Some are younger, some older. Some are more intelligent, some less. Some are stronger, some weaker. Yet, all possess the same dignity because of the divine image. God creates everyone with different gifts to ensure our interdependence. We need one another's help. We need to help one another. Our differences give us the conditions for mutual enrichment.

The Poor Lazarus at the Rich Man's Door by Tissot. "There was a rich man, who was clothed in purple and fine linen and who feasted sumptuously every day. And at his gate lay a poor man named Lazarus, full of sores, who desired to be fed with what fell from the rich man's table; moreover the dogs came and licked his sores." (Lk 16:19-21)

When babies are born or adopted, they are dependent upon their parents for everything—food, clothing, hygiene, even survival. The parents give sacrificially for the care of their children. They spend a lot of money. They go without sleep. They give up leisure time and surrender some of their freedom. Yet, the parents receive as much as they give, if not more. In rearing children, parents can grow in maturity, wisdom, and many virtues. They also can build a more loving relationship. The same dynamic is at work, to varying degrees, in other social relationships.

Interdependence is mutually beneficial. We grow through the practice of charity, justice, and mercy. Thus, we experience the providential purpose of material inequalities. In giving, the giver receives as much or

Everyone on earth is capable of giving *something*. Even the most impoverished people can bless others with their prayers and kind words.

more than the people who have accepted his charitable gift. Christ said: "It is more blessed to give than to receive" (Acts 20:35). And everyone on earth is capable of giving *something*. Even the most impoverished people can bless others with their prayers, their kind words and sincere compliments, and their forgiveness.

The Catholic tradition, however, distinguishes natural differences from *"sinful inequalities"* (CCC 1938). In many places, a small elite class lives in lavish luxury while the majority of people around them struggle in squalid conditions, with few or no opportunities for social advancement or material improvement. Many are also, in effect, denied access to spiritual goods because the conditions of their poverty make it difficult or dangerous to sustain pastoral care.

Such conditions are widespread in the world, affecting millions of people. They are scandalous, in a world in which the Gospel has been preached for two millennia, and they are clearly contrary to Christ's teachings. The Church, in the Second Vatican Council, noted that the conditions of so many poor people should cause their wealthier neighbors to strive more earnestly to narrow the gap in income and living conditions.

> "Their equal dignity as persons demands that we strive for fairer and more humane conditions. Excessive economic and social disparity between individuals and peoples of the one human race is a source of scandal and militates against social justice, equity, human dignity, as well as social and international peace."[4] (CCC 1938)

Material inequality does not deprive the poor of the divine image. Nor does it deprive them of their inherent dignity. These are inalienable and inviolable. But that dignity means that they do deserve better. They deserve to have access to basic goods and to the means of social advancement and active participation. They deserve the chance to fulfill their divine vocation, and so fulfill their human nature, by working, having a family, and enjoying peace and security.

Neglect of the poor is most detrimental not to the poor themselves, but to the negligent rich, who obscure the divine image in themselves by hoarding their wealth and possessions. Selfish lives do not reflect God's generosity.

THE COMMON GOOD

As we noted in the first chapter, no one can live a healthy life in isolation. "No man is an island." Human beings are social by nature. We are created in the image and likeness of God, and we cannot be fulfilled apart from our relationships with other persons. Our relationships, to be godlike, must be marked by love—specifically, by the self-giving love called *charity*, whose perfect expression is found in Christ. We are impelled to seek not only our own individual or personal good, but the common good.

One of the most ancient Christian documents outside the Scriptures, the first-century *Letter of Barnabas*, puts the matter succinctly: "Do not live entirely isolated, having retreated into yourselves, as if you were already justified, but gather instead to seek the common good together."[5]

The common good has always been the centerpiece of Christian social ethics. St. Thomas Aquinas, in his *Summa Theologicæ*, returns to the theme repeatedly. He identifies the "common good of all citizens" as the purpose of all law. He says that vices are *vicious* precisely because they are "repugnant to the common good." He equates the common good with social justice. He says that "the common good of many is more godlike than the good of an individual."

What, exactly, is the common good? The *Catechism* provides a useful definition.

> By common good is to be understood "the sum total of social conditions which allow people, either as groups or as individuals, to reach their fulfillment more fully and more easily."[6] The common good concerns the life of all. It calls for prudence from each, and even more from those who exercise the office of authority. (CCC 1906)

The *Catechism* goes on to specify "three essential elements" of the common good.

First, the common good presupposes human dignity and respect for each person. Authorities may not claim the common good as a justification for suppressing the rights of individuals—rights such as privacy, religious liberty, freedom to act according to conscience, and freedom to pursue one's vocation. A government may not, for example, outlaw or restrict the practice of celibacy because the national population is in decline. Nor can a state forbid marriage or childbearing because its cities are already overcrowded. The common good is held in common, but it is for the sake of *persons* (cf. CCC 1907).

Second, authorities should see to it that all people have access to the basic goods necessary to lead a truly human life. The *Catechism* mentions just a few examples: "food, clothing, health, work, education and culture, suitable information, and the right to have a family"[7] (CCC 1908).

Finally, the common good requires peace. St. Augustine defined peace as "tranquility in order," and the *Catechism* recognizes that such order requires the personal ability to defend oneself, as well as the community's need to maintain security forces for its collective protection (cf. CCC 1909).

Sacred Heart of Jesus by Chambers. "And he took a cup, and when he had given thanks he gave it to them, and they all drank of it. And he said to them, 'This is my blood of the covenant, which is poured out for many.'" (Mk 14:23-23)

To act in the interest of the common good is to imitate Jesus Christ, who identified his own vocation with fulfilling the common good: "I came that they may have life, and have it abundantly" (Jn 10:10). Christ "gave himself as a ransom for all" (1 Tm 2:6). He "died for all" (2 Cor 5:14-15). His one "act of righteousness" led to "acquittal and life for all" (Rom 5:18). His blood was poured out not for a few, but "for many" (Mk 14:24). It should be clear, then, why St. Thomas Aquinas said: "The common good of many is more godlike than the good of an individual."

The common good is not the same as the collective will of the people. It does not necessarily correspond to the most popular desires or beliefs. Majorities, like individuals, can make bad choices and have misdirected desires. Mobs do not rule more wisely than dictators. Indeed, it was perhaps a majority that sought the death of Christ. Neither his own people nor their Roman overlords recognized his desire to save them. They saw him as a threat to their religious, social, economic, and political concerns.

It was not a unique event. People who seek justice selflessly are often misjudged and even condemned harshly for doing so. The playwright Henrik Ibsen dramatized this in perhaps his most famous work, *An Enemy of the People*. In that play, a coastal town is caught up in the construction of a spa and resort. The citizens look forward to an increase in tourism and wealth. Shortly after the grand opening, however, a local physician, Dr. Peter Stockmann, discovers that the supposedly curative waters are actually contaminated—and present a health hazard to anyone who bathes in them. Though he presents a solution to the problem, it is costly and will cut deeply into the profits of the spa. The local people reject his proposal, vilify him for telling the truth, ostracize him, and declare him to be their enemy.

PRINCIPLES OF CATHOLIC SOCIAL DOCTRINE

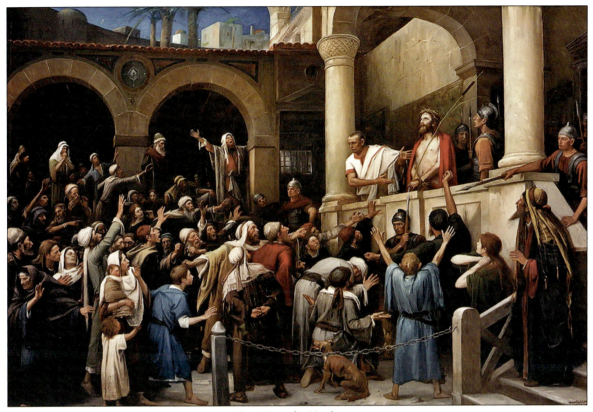

Ecce Homo by Munkacsy.
We should always keep in mind that the common good is for the sake of *persons*, not the state.
Motivated by greed, bigotry, and ignorance, majorities sometimes advocate for causes that are foolish,
morally askew, or outright evil.

The play is still performed, more than a hundred years after it was written, because it speaks a certain truth. Democratic process is no guarantee of the best outcome. The common good is not always identical with the common will or majority opinion. Motivated by greed, bigotry, and ignorance, majorities sometimes advocate for causes that are foolish, morally askew, or outright evil.

For example, if a majority of citizens favored a war of conquest—a blatantly unjust war—their numbers would not make them right. Their advocacy should be opposed. Or, if a majority of citizens favored harsher and more frequent application of the death penalty, that would not mean that Catholics in general—or Catholic politicians in particular—should support such a policy. In fact, Catholics may discern an obligation to oppose it (cf. CCC 2266-2267).

If a majority of citizens favored the legalization of abortion, a Catholic must nevertheless oppose such license as inimical to the common good and a violation of human dignity and individual rights.

We should always keep in mind that the common good is for the sake of *persons*, not the state. The state, with its laws and institutions, exists for the sake of the common good of *persons*. As much as possible, the common good should also be more the responsibility of persons than of the state; and it should be expressed by individual acts of prudence, justice, and fortitude. The common good is everyone's concern, everyone's duty, everyone's business.

While the common good concerns itself with material social conditions, it is not limited to them. In fact, the primary goods are spiritual: salvation, for example, and righteousness. The *Compendium of the Social Doctrine of the Church* (170) makes a pointed observation: "A purely historical and materialistic vision would end up transforming the common good into a simple *socio-economic well-being*, without any transcendental goal, that is, without its most intimate reason for existing."

If people lack God, they lack the most fundamental good, the ultimate good common to all humanity. Without God, people cannot be fulfilled.

SUBSIDIARITY

Subsidiarity is an organizing principle in society. It means that matters should be handled by the smallest and most local competent authority possible, rather than by a central authority. Central authority should perform only tasks that cannot be done well on the local level.

We can see the principle of subsidiarity at work in Christ's counsel:

> If your brother sins against you, go and tell him his fault, between you and him alone. If he listens to you, you have gained your brother. But if he does not listen, take one or two others along with you, that every word may be confirmed by the evidence of two or three witnesses. If he refuses to listen to them, tell it to the church; and if he refuses to listen even to the church, let him be to you as a Gentile and a tax collector. (Mt 18:15-17)

Berlin Wall Victims Memorial. From 1961-1989, over 600 people died attempting to cross from communist East Germany to the freedom and democracy of West Germany. The Berlin Wall (torn down in 1989) was a symbol of the "Iron Curtain" and the tyranny that can overcome a country without respect for subsidiarity.

Christ instructs his disciples to resolve problems using the most immediate authority and escalate matters only when necessary.

As social doctrine, the idea appeared in the first social encyclical, Pope Leo XIII's *Rerum Novarum*. But it was Pope Pius XI, in his encyclical *Quadragesimo Anno*, who introduced the word *subsidiarity* into the Church's teaching. His times demanded a more precise treatment of the subject. He was speaking out specifically against the concentration of wealth and power among an elite few—or in an almighty state. In 1931, many countries were pursuing statist or collectivist solutions to the problems of modern life. Some had begun a disastrous, dehumanizing experiment with Marxist communism. Others were sliding toward a technocratic (fascist) socialism that was just as degrading. The principle of subsidiarity emerged as a powerful competing force in social thought.

Indeed, Pius XI voiced the matter in very strong terms:

> Just as it is gravely wrong to take from individuals what they can accomplish by their own initiative and industry and give it to the community, so also it is an injustice and at the same time a grave evil and disturbance of right order to assign to a greater and higher association what lesser and subordinate organizations can do. (*QA* 79)

Though it appeared first in Catholic social teaching, the term was soon adopted by sociology, political science, military science, and economics. It now appears in many national and federal constitutions around the world.

Pope Benedict XVI developed the idea more explicitly than any of his predecessors. In his encyclical *Caritas in Veritate* (57), he spoke of subsidiarity as a "manifestation of charity and a guiding criterion for fraternal cooperation between believers and nonbelievers." It is, he said, "an expression of inalienable human freedom."

Subsidiarity recognizes the "autonomy of intermediate bodies" and so places a healthy, natural limit on the state or the collective. Central authority comes into play only when individuals or small groups cannot accomplish something on their own. Thus, in Catholic teaching, government is at the service of the person and the family, rather than vice versa. Government assistance must always be "designed to achieve their emancipation." Pope Benedict XVI added: "By considering reciprocity as the heart of what it is to be a human being, subsidiarity is the most effective antidote against any form of all-encompassing welfare state."

Respect for subsidiarity is the surest and most peaceful way to oppose tyranny.

SOLIDARITY

The principle of subsidiarity is interdependent with, and practically inseparable from, yet another principle: *solidarity*. In *Caritas in Veritate* (58), Pope Benedict XVI stated that the "principle of subsidiarity must remain closely linked to the principle of solidarity and vice versa." Subsidiarity without solidarity, he explained, degenerates into "social privatism," which is little better than selfish individualism. Solidarity without subsidiarity, however, gives way to "paternalist social assistance that is demeaning to those in need."

Solidarity is the principle of unity in a society that extends beyond mere self-interest. In a nation, the bond may be ethnic, cultural, or racial. For Catholics, however, solidarity must be universal. The Catholic Church is not a national, tribal, or ethnic community. "Catholic" means universal, and Christ established his Church to encompass all humanity made in God's image.

Thus, Catholics must practice solidarity with the whole human race. This is a valuable witness today, as people everywhere suddenly find themselves living in a "global village," united by easy trade and communications. The world itself, long divided along national and ethnic lines, suddenly finds itself heading toward a "unification of humanity," which, Pope Benedict XVI said, should be connected with "the Christian ideal of a single family of peoples in solidarity and fraternity."[8] The *Catechism* speaks of solidarity in terms of "friendship" and "social charity" (CCC 1939).

St. John Paul II spoke often of the importance of solidarity in society. He emphasized that it was not enough to claim a vague, philosophical bond with others. Solidarity must manifest itself in deeds and in a way of life. It manifests itself in *participation* in society.

St. John Paul II received Lech Walesa, leader of the anti-communist Solidarity movement in Poland, at the Vatican in January 1981. John Paul's support of the Solidarity movement was a considerable force behind the collapse of Soviet domination in Poland.

The exercise of solidarity within each society is valid when its members recognize one another as persons. Those who are more influential, because they have a greater share of goods and common services, should feel responsible for the weaker and be ready to share with them all they possess. Those who are weaker, for their part, in the same spirit of solidarity, should not adopt a purely passive attitude or one that is destructive of the social fabric, but, while claiming their legitimate rights, should do what they can for the good of all. The intermediate groups, in their turn, should not selfishly insist on their particular interests, but respect the interests of others. (*SRS* 39)

The *Catechism* puts it briefly:

Solidarity is manifested in the first place by the distribution of goods and remuneration for work. It also presupposes the effort for a more just social order where tensions are better able to be reduced and conflicts more readily settled by negotiation. (CCC 1940)

Both St. John Paul II and the *Catechism* noted that solidarity provides a way of overcoming socio-economic problems.[9] When the poor work with one another, they are stronger. When the poor work together with the rich—rather than perceiving them as enemies in some Marxist class struggle—they can accomplish still more. Christian charity offers a way of overcoming social circumstances that are usually divisive.

St. John Paul II's teachings on solidarity profoundly influenced the rise of labor unions in the so-called Eastern Bloc countries dominated by Soviet communism. It was the Polish trade union named *Solidarnosc* ("Solidarity") that precipitated the country's first movements toward democracy. Its founders traced their inspiration to Catholic social teaching and specifically to St. John Paul II.

LECH WALESA AND THE POWER OF SOLIDARITY

Lech Walesa (b. 1943) was trained as an electrician in vocational school. He never went to college. He worked as an auto mechanic and served in the Polish military when he was young. In 1967 he got a steady job at the Lenin Shipyard in Gdansk, Poland. With good employment in place, he married in 1969 and started a family. Lech and his wife Danuta would eventually have eight children.

Early in life, he recognized a certain hypocrisy in the rhetoric of Poland's communist leaders. They talked about the state as a "worker's democracy," but they cared little about the actual conditions of laborers, whose complaints about workplace hazards, low wages, and ill treatment were routinely ignored.

He began to organize trade unions, which were against the law, and he led his co-workers in strikes and work shutdowns. The secret police began following and threatening him. He was often arrested. His home was placed under electronic surveillance. He lost his job and then bounced from one position to another, as the government pressured his employers to fire him. His family suffered from his irregular income and frequent absences. Once he was jailed for almost an entire year. But they bore their hardships patiently, knowing that Lech was doing the right thing.

In 1978, for the first time in history, a Pole was elected Pope: Karol Wojtyla, the Archbishop of Krakow, who took the name John Paul II. The following year, the Polish Pope visited his homeland and gave international visibility and tremendous moral support to the union and its leaders.

Soon afterward, Walesa cofounded a trade union and gave it a name taken straight from Catholic social doctrine: Solidarity. "Solidarity" also became a byword of papal teaching during St. John Paul II's pontificate. For Walesa, the term represented the power people gain when they overcome fear and work together. Walesa has always credited the Catholic Faith as his strength and inspiration.

Walesa's movement made the most of the international notice. Their strikes, especially the 1980 Gdansk Shipyard strike, pressured the government to address workers' real concerns, and the government soon found itself in the difficult position of having to negotiate with organizations that were technically illegal. The Polish people saw the sacrifices Walesa and other union leaders were willing to make for the common good. Solidarity soon enjoyed far greater respect than did the government.

In 1981, the Polish government cracked down on the movement, declaring martial law and jailing Walesa. In 1983, while the turmoil still raged, Walesa was awarded the Nobel Peace Prize.

By the end of that decade, thanks to Walesa's persistent, courageous witness and work, Poland had its first free parliamentary elections in a half-century. By 1989, Solidarity was more than a trade union; it had become a nationwide, pro-democracy political movement—and it was elected to take the reins of government. In 1990, Walesa was elected first president of the newly free Poland.

A Catholic of profound faith, Walesa was able to distinguish the good from the bad of the modern world as he led his country into democracy and free enterprise after years of communist despotism. He said he would resign rather than ever sign a bill legalizing abortion in Poland.

Since leaving office in 1995, he has lectured widely, received many honors, and founded an institute for the promotion of democracy in the world.

SECONDARY PRINCIPLES

From those four basic principles—human dignity, the common good, subsidiarity, and solidarity—the Church derives other important principles. Such "secondary" principles are important for our understanding of the major themes discussed in the next chapter.

Catholic tradition speaks of *the universal destination of goods*: namely, that God entrusted the care of the earth to the human race as a whole and he created the goods of the earth to be shared in common by all people. The goods of the earth are meant to be enjoyed not just by a few people, but by all. Creation is God's gift to mankind, meant to be shared in common.

Yet, human beings do have a right to possess *private property*, as long as they acquire and keep it in ways that are legal and moral. The right to private property does not contradict—and should not impede—the universal destination of goods. It is God who appoints men and women as stewards over creation. They possess and manage goods for the sake of others, beginning with family and extending to the community and then beyond. The Bible, in both the Old and New Testaments, condemns the practice of hoarding wealth while one's neighbors live without the necessities of a decent life (see, for example, Luke 16:19-31; 12:16-21). It is the criminal Cain who dares to ask the Lord God: "Am I my brother's keeper?" (Gn 4:9). The *Catechism* clearly teaches:

> "In his use of things man should regard the external goods he legitimately owns not merely as exclusive to himself but common to others also, in the sense that they can benefit others as well as himself."[10] The ownership of any property makes its holder a steward of Providence, with the task of making it fruitful and communicating its benefits to others, first of all his family. (CCC 2404)

Child Begging in India.
The goods of the earth are meant to be enjoyed not just by a few people, but by all.

The right of private property is not absolute or inalienable. It is not like the right to life. The state has the right, and even the duty, to regulate the rights of ownership. For the sake of the common good, the state may impose just taxes for the responsible redistribution of wealth and goods.

Such redistribution, however, must be carried out prudently and moderately, so that people do not fall into habits of passivity, which would also be detrimental to society. The principle of subsidiarity works only if people take active responsibility for their roles in society. This principle is called *participation*. The Church encourages forms of government that maximize the contributions of all members of society. People participate in social life by voting, working, expressing their opinions respectfully, volunteering, and in many other ways—in short, by sharing the responsibilities for day-to-day life. This dynamic is implicit in the principles of subsidiarity and solidarity.

All these principles of healthy social life, both primary and secondary, depend upon strong values and moral attitudes. They presuppose a respect for others as human beings, a desire to live with integrity, a respect for the truth and a desire to help others to know the truth. They assume that free will is supremely important; for Christians believe that God's gift of free will is the clearest sign that human beings are made in God's image and likeness. They presuppose also a desire for justice.

The Church teaches that laws, by themselves, can never bring about a just society. That can only come from the love known as charity. It is expressed in the closest relationships, and so is safeguarded by the principle of subsidiarity. But it extends beyond those, through a more universal solidarity with people of all conditions.

SHAHBAZ BHATTI:
Solidarity Among Persecuted Minorities

Shahbaz Bhatti was one of six children born to a family that was proud to be Pakistani. His father served his country in the military. The Bhattis were also Roman Catholic in a predominantly Muslim country, however, and for this they suffered misunderstanding and even persecution.

While he was still a teenager, Shahbaz determined he would do everything he could to overcome religious oppression. He worked with other marginalized people to found, first, the Christian Liberation Front and, later, the All Pakistan Minorities Alliance. His special concern was for religious minorities—in Pakistan, that meant Christians, Hindus, Sikhs, and Parsis. He was a tireless promoter of interreligious dialogue and understanding.

In 2008, he was appointed by President Asif Ali Zardari as the country's minister for the defense of minorities, a newly elevated cabinet position.

Bhatti pledged his life to "struggle for human equality, social justice, religious freedom, and to uplift and empower the religious minorities' communities."

"Jesus is the nucleus of my life," he said, "and I want to be his true follower through my actions by sharing the love of God with poor, oppressed, victimized, needy and suffering people of Pakistan." He devoted himself fully to his vocation, never marrying and owning few possessions.

He began several initiatives designed to overcome ignorance of other religions and the resulting prejudice. He spearheaded the development of a school curriculum that would help members of all religions to understand one another. He also arranged for changes in law that allowed minorities greater representation in government. He brought together many religious leaders to issue a joint condemnation of terrorism, an issue that was sorely dividing his country.

He regularly received death threats. "I believe in Jesus Christ," he said, "who has given his own life for us, and I am ready to die for a cause. I'm living for my community…and I will die to defend their rights."

He was assassinated in 2011 by Muslim extremists who considered him a "blasphemer" because of his practice of Christianity.

When his family showed up to empty his apartment, there was little to carry away. On the stand by his bed were his Bible, his Rosary, and an image of the Blessed Virgin Mary.

The Catholic bishops of Pakistan have petitioned the Pope to include Bhatti's name in the martyrology of the universal Church.

Shahbaz Bhatti (1968-2011)
"I'm living for my community…and I will die to defend their rights."

This way of love requires people to be patient with one another, and not merely just but also understanding and merciful. St. Paul gave such love its classic expression.

> If I speak in the tongues of men and of angels, but have not love, I am a noisy gong or a clanging cymbal. And if I have prophetic powers, and understand all mysteries and all knowledge, and if I have all faith, so as to remove mountains, but have not love, I am nothing. If I give away all I have, and if I deliver my body to be burned, but have not love, I gain nothing.
>
> Love is patient and kind; love is not jealous or boastful; it is not arrogant or rude. Love does not insist on its own way; it is not irritable or resentful; it does not rejoice at wrong, but rejoices in the right.
>
> Love bears all things, believes all things, hopes all things, endures all things. Love never ends. (1 Cor 13:1-8)

CONCLUSION

Catholic social doctrine is a reasoned and systematic reflection that lends itself to practical application. It has been elaborated to a remarkable degree, casting light on questions of government, economics, warfare, and industry. It has, moreover, exercised a significant influence on international relations and the development of treaties and constitutions.

The Church provides a moral clarity that is inaccessible apart from Divine Revelation. Because the Church recognizes the origins of human weakness, its doctrine is also eminently practical. Apart from the Christian doctrine of divine love, the practices of mercy and forgiveness (for example) are not self-evident virtues; indeed, they were condemned in some pre-Christian societies as signs of weakness and vice. Yet they remain the only way to lasting peace.

St. John Paul II and Bl. Teresa of Calcutta give comfort to a patient at the Nirmal Hriday (Home of the Pure Heart) run by the Missionaries of Charity in Calcutta, India. People brought to the home receive medical attention and are given a loving sanctuary where they can die with dignity. "In Nirmal Hriday, the mystery of human suffering meets the mystery of faith and love."
—*St. John Paul II, February 3, 1986*

Christ left us an example of his divine love and mercy by forgiving those who persecuted him. Instead of seeking revenge, or trying to get even, he calls us to forgive and to love, and we can be assured that he will give us the grace to follow him no matter how difficult it may seem. The numerous martyrs who gave their lives for Christ show us the strength and power of faith and God's grace.

Because Catholic social doctrine is systematic, it has been able to articulate basic philosophical concepts and define them in a way that is appealing and convincing even to nonbelievers. Its most basic principles are *human dignity*, the *common good*, *subsidiarity*, and *solidarity*. From these principles the Church derives important secondary principles, which will be elaborated in the themes we will study in the next chapter. Implicit in these principles are values common to all people of good will.

The most distinctive element in Christian social doctrine, however, is self-giving love—true charity. All the principles and values, all the teachings of the Popes and councils, find their origin and perfection in love. The *Catechism* says:

> Respect for the human person proceeds by way of respect for the principle that "everyone should look upon his neighbor (without any exception) as 'another self,' above all bearing in mind his life and the means necessary for living it with dignity."[11] No legislation could by itself do away with the fears, prejudices, and attitudes of pride and selfishness which obstruct the establishment of truly fraternal societies. Such behavior will cease only through the charity that finds in every man a "neighbor," a brother. (CCC 1931)

The Saints
PILLARS OF THE CHURCH

BL. JUANA MARIA CONDESA LLUCH

Bl. Juana Maria Condesa Lluch was born in 1862 into a wealthy family in Valencia, Spain. As an adolescent, she already had a deep prayer life.

She was especially sensitive to the plight of the exploited factory workers in her city. With the rapid growth of industrialization in the nineteenth century, men and women were forced to leave the countryside to seek work in the cities. Their only option was to work on the assembly line. They were often treated as mere "tools" and stripped of their human dignity. Juana wanted to help them materially, morally, and spiritually. When she was eighteen, she felt called to found a religious order that would assist exploited workers and their families.

Her archbishop thought she was too young to begin a congregation, but in 1884 she received permission to open a shelter where workers could go for spiritual formation and other basic needs. A few months later, Juana opened a school for the workers' children. Soon she was joined by other young women who felt called to "live and give their all for the good of the workers."

In 1892, the Congregation of the Handmaids of the Immaculate Conception, Protectress of Workers, received Church approval. The number of its members rapidly increased, and the Handmaids spread into other cities affected by the Industrial Revolution.

Mother Juana died in 1916. Her congregation continues its work today.

SUPPLEMENTARY READING

Dorothy Day: Social Security and Subsidiarity

The Servant of God Dorothy Day wrote an incisive critique of government assistance, based on papal teaching and appealing to the principles of dignity, the common good, subsidiarity, and solidarity. The following is excerpted from the article "More About Holy Poverty," *which appeared in* The Catholic Worker *newspaper, February 1945, pages 1-2.*

We believe that social security legislation, now hailed as a great victory for the poor and for the worker, is a great defeat for Christianity. It is an acceptance of the idea of force and compulsion. It is an acceptance of Cain's statement, on the part of the employer: "Am I my brother's keeper?" Since the employer can never be trusted to give a family wage, nor take care of the worker as he takes care of his machine when it is idle, the state must enter in and compel help on his part. Of course, economists say that business cannot afford to act on Christian principles. It is impractical, uneconomic. But it is generally coming to be accepted that such a degree of centralization as ours is impractical, and that there must be decentralization. In other words, business has made a mess of things, and the state has had to enter in to rescue the worker from starvation.

Of course, Pope Pius XI said that, when such a crisis came about, in unemployment, fire, flood, earthquake, etc., the state had to enter in and help.

But we in our generation have more and more come to consider the state as bountiful Uncle Sam. "Uncle Sam will take care of it all. The race question, the labor question, the unemployment question." We will all be registered and tabulated and employed or put on a dole, and shunted from clinic to birth control clinic. "What right have people who have no work to have a baby?" How many poor Catholic mothers heard that during those grim years before the war!

Of course, it is the very circumstances of our lives that lead us to write as we do. We see these ideas worked out all around us. We see the result of this way of thinking on all sides. We live with the poor; we are of the poor. We know their virtues and their vices. We know their generosities and their extravagances. Their very generosity makes them extravagant and improvident.

Please do not think we are blaming the poor when we talk so frankly about their failings, which they, too, will acknowledge. They do not want people to be sentimental about them. They do not want people to idealize them. I think they realize pretty well that they are but dust, and one of our jobs, too, is to make them realize that they are also a little less than the angels.

We are not being uncharitable to them when we talk about a binge of department store buying. Did I say that? What I meant was installment-plan buying. Who do we blame for such installment-plan buying, for the movies, cigarettes, radio, magazines, or all the trash, the worthless trash with which they try to comfort their poor hard lives? We do not blame them, God knows. We blame the advertising men, the household loan companies, the cheap stores, the radio, the movies.

The people are seduced, robbed, stupefied, drugged and demoralized daily. They are robbed just as surely as though those flat pocketbooks of those shabby mothers were pilfered of the pennies, dimes and nickels by sneak thieves…

But who is to take care of them if the government does not? That is a question in a day when all are turning to the state, and when people are asking, "Am I my brother's keeper?" Certainly we all should know that it is not the province of the government to practice the works of mercy, or go in for insurance. Smaller bodies, decentralized groups, should be caring for all such needs.

The first unit of society is the family. The family should look after its own and, in addition, as the early fathers said, "Every home should have a Christ room in it, so that hospitality may be practiced." "The coat that hangs in your closet belongs to the poor." "If your brother is hungry, it is your responsibility."

"When did we see Thee hungry, when did we see Thee naked?" People either plead ignorance or they say, "It is none of my responsibility." But we are all members one of another, so we are obliged in conscience to help each other.

SUPPLEMENTARY READING Continued

The parish is the next unit, and there are local councils of the St. Vincent de Paul Society. Then there is the city, and the larger body of charitable groups. And there are the unions, where mutual aid and fraternal charity is also practiced. For those who are not Catholics there are lodges, fraternal organizations, where there is a long tradition of charity. But now there is a dependence on the state. Hospitals once Catholic are subsidized by the state. Orphanages once supported by Catholic charity receive their aid from community chests. And when it is not the state it is bingo parties!...

Pope Pius XII: On the Unity of Human Society

Just days before the outbreak of World War II, Pope Pius XII issued his encyclical letter Summi Pontificatus, *on the unity of human society. The following is from sections 42-43.*

In the light of this unity of all mankind, which exists in law and in fact, individuals do not feel themselves isolated units, like grains of sand, but united by the very force of their nature and by their internal destiny, into an organic, harmonious mutual relationship which varies with the changing of times.

And the nations, despite a difference of development due to diverse conditions of life and of culture, are not destined to break the unity of the human race, but rather to enrich and embellish it by the sharing of their own peculiar gifts and by that reciprocal interchange of goods which can be possible and efficacious only when a mutual love and a lively sense of charity unite all the sons of the same Father and all those redeemed by the same Divine Blood.

Compendium of the Social Doctrine of the Church:
Subsidiarity and Participation

185. *Subsidiarity is among the most constant and characteristic directives of the Church's social doctrine* and has been present since the first great social encyclical.[12] It is impossible to promote the dignity of the person without showing concern for the family, groups, associations, local territorial realities; in short, for that aggregate of economic, social, cultural, sports-oriented, recreational, professional and political expressions to which people spontaneously give life and which make it possible for them to achieve effective social growth.[13] This is the realm of *civil society*, understood as the sum of the relationships between individuals and intermediate social groupings, which are the first relationships to arise and which come about thanks to "the creative subjectivity of the citizen."[14] This network of relationships strengthens the social fabric and constitutes the basis of a true community of persons, making possible the recognition of higher forms of social activity.[15]

187. *The principle of subsidiarity protects people from abuses by higher-level social authority and calls on these same authorities to help individuals and intermediate groups to fulfill their duties. This principle is imperative because every person, family and intermediate group has something original to offer to the community.* Experience shows that the denial of subsidiarity, or its limitation in the name of an alleged democratization or equality of all members of society, limits and sometimes even destroys the spirit of freedom and initiative.

The principle of subsidiarity is opposed to certain forms of centralization, bureaucratization, and welfare assistance and to the unjustified and excessive presence of the State in public mechanisms. "By intervening directly and depriving society of its responsibility, the Social Assistance State leads to a loss of human energies and an inordinate increase of public agencies, which are dominated more by bureaucratic ways of thinking than by concern for serving their clients, and which are accompanied by an enormous increase in spending."[16] An absent or insufficient recognition of private initiative—in economic matters also—and the failure to recognize its public function, contribute to the undermining of the principle of subsidiarity, as monopolies do as well.

In order for the principle of subsidiarity to be put into practice there is a *corresponding need* for: respect and effective promotion of the human person and the family; ever greater appreciation of associations and intermediate organizations in their fundamental choices and in those that cannot be delegated to or exercised by others; the encouragement of private initiative so that every social entity remains at the service of the common good, each with its own distinctive characteristics; the presence of pluralism in society and due representation of its vital components; safeguarding human rights and the rights of minorities; bringing about bureaucratic and administrative decentralization; striking a balance between the public and private spheres, with the resulting recognition of the *social* function of the private sphere; appropriate methods for making citizens more responsible in actively "being a part" of the political and social reality of their country.

Pope Benedict XVI: Subsidiarity and Solidarity

From his 2009 encyclical *Caritas in Veritate*, 57-58.

Fruitful dialogue between faith and reason cannot but render the work of charity more effective within society, and it constitutes the most appropriate framework for promoting *fraternal collaboration between believers and non-believers* in their shared commitment to working for justice and the peace of the human family. In the Pastoral Constitution *Gaudium et Spes*, the Council fathers asserted that "believers and unbelievers agree almost unanimously that all things on earth should be ordered towards man as to their center and summit."[17] For believers, the world derives neither from blind chance nor from strict necessity, but from God's plan. This is what gives rise to the duty of believers to unite their efforts with those of all men and women of good will, with the followers of other religions and with non-believers, so that this world of ours may effectively correspond to the divine plan: living as a family under the Creator's watchful eye. A particular manifestation of charity and a guiding criterion for fraternal cooperation between believers and non-believers is undoubtedly the *principle of subsidiarity*,[18] an expression of inalienable human freedom. Subsidiarity is first and foremost a form of assistance to the human person via the autonomy of intermediate bodies. Such assistance is offered when individuals or groups are unable to accomplish something on their own, and it is always designed to achieve their emancipation, because it fosters freedom and participation through assumption of responsibility. Subsidiarity respects personal dignity by recognizing in the person a subject who is always capable of giving something to others. By considering reciprocity as the heart of what it is to be a human being, subsidiarity is the most effective antidote against any form of all-encompassing welfare state. It is able to take account both of the manifold articulation of plans—and therefore of the plurality of subjects—as well as the coordination of those plans. Hence the principle of subsidiarity is particularly well-suited to managing globalization and directing it towards authentic human development. In order not to produce a dangerous universal power of a tyrannical nature, *the governance of globalization must be marked by subsidiarity*, articulated into several layers and involving different levels that can work together. Globalization certainly requires authority, insofar as it poses the problem of a global common good that needs to be pursued. This authority, however, must be organized in a subsidiary and stratified way,[19] if it is not to infringe upon freedom and if it is to yield effective results in practice.

The principle of subsidiarity must remain closely linked to the principle of solidarity and vice versa, since the former without the latter gives way to social privatism, while the latter without the former gives way to paternalist social assistance that is demeaning to those in need. This general rule must also be taken broadly into consideration when addressing issues concerning *international development aid*. Such aid, whatever the donors' intentions, can sometimes lock people into a state of dependence and even foster situations of localized oppression and exploitation in the receiving country. Economic aid, in order to be true to its purpose, must not pursue secondary objectives. It must be distributed with the involvement not only of the governments of receiving countries, but also local economic agents and the bearers of culture within civil society, including local

SUPPLEMENTARY READING Continued

Churches. Aid programs must increasingly acquire the characteristics of participation and completion from the grass roots. Indeed, the most valuable resources in countries receiving development aid are human resources: herein lies the real capital that needs to accumulate in order to guarantee a truly autonomous future for the poorest countries. It should also be remembered that, in the economic sphere, the principal form of assistance needed by developing countries is that of allowing and encouraging the gradual penetration of their products into international markets, thus making it possible for these countries to participate fully in international economic life. Too often in the past, aid has served to create only fringe markets for the products of these donor countries. This was often due to a lack of genuine demand for the products in question: it is therefore necessary to help such countries improve their products and adapt them more effectively to existing demand. Furthermore, there are those who fear the effects of competition through the importation of products—normally agricultural products—from economically poor countries. Nevertheless, it should be remembered that for such countries, the possibility of marketing their products is very often what guarantees their survival in both the short and long term. Just and equitable international trade in agricultural goods can be beneficial to everyone, both to suppliers and to customers. For this reason, not only is commercial orientation needed for production of this kind, but also the establishment of international trade regulations to support it and stronger financing for development in order to increase the productivity of these economies.

VOCABULARY

COMMON GOOD
The total of social conditions that will allow both individuals and groups to reach their human and spiritual fulfillment more easily.

DEVELOPMENT OF DOCTRINE
The process by which Christian teaching becomes gradually more explicit and detailed, though later statements of doctrine remain consistent with earlier statements.

PARTICIPATION
The principle by which people take active responsibility for their roles in society—by means of labor, voting, community life, and so on.

PRIVATE PROPERTY, RIGHT TO
The right of a person or community of persons to own, govern, and otherwise dispose of some part of creation.

SOLIDARITY
The quality of communities or individuals being united in interests, sympathies, and aspirations. Also, the principle of "friendship" or "social charity" manifested first in the distribution of goods and the remuneration of work.

SUBSIDIARITY
An organizing principle in society, subsidiarity proposes that matters should be handled by the smallest and most local competent authority, rather than being handled default by a central authority.

TECHNOCRATIC
Describes a form of government in which experts in industry, science, and technology are in control of all decision-making.

UNIVERSAL DESTINATION OF GOODS
Catholic doctrine that God created the goods of the earth to be shared in common by all people.

STUDY QUESTIONS

1. What are the four permanent principles of Catholic social doctrine, and what makes them so important?

2. What is the common good, and how is it often confused or misunderstood?

3. What is subsidiarity?

4. In what ways do modern forms of government tend to limit or cripple subsidiarity?

5. What is solidarity?

6. What is participation, and how is it related to solidarity?

7. What is private property, and how does it relate to the universal destination of goods?

8. Is private property an absolute right? If not, why not?

9. Does the state have the right to levy taxes? What principle of Catholic social doctrine allows for this?

10. Why is truth important to the healthy functioning of society?

11. How can love help a society to function more efficiently and effectively?

12. What are the limits of solidarity for a Catholic?

PRACTICAL EXERCISES

1. What gives human beings their inherent dignity? Is human dignity possible apart from this factor? If so, explain how. If not, explain why.

2. Find a national constitution or international treaty that uses the term "subsidiarity" or "solidarity." Explain how the term is used and whether its usage is in harmony with Catholic doctrine. Explain how Catholic social doctrine could have influenced the development of the text under consideration.

3. Take one of the four primary or "permanent" principles of Catholic social doctrine and trace it, by way of the Church documents, back to its origins in Scripture. Then trace its development forward in one of the secondary principles. Use this pattern to explain how Christian doctrine develops, but does not change.

4. Research the ways in which different political philosophers have understood the right to private property. Compare and contrast these views with Catholic doctrine.

THE SOCIAL DOCTRINE OF THE CATHOLIC CHURCH

FROM THE CATECHISM

1907 First, the common good presupposes *respect for the person* as such. In the name of the common good, public authorities are bound to respect the fundamental and inalienable rights of the human person. Society should permit each of its members to fulfill his vocation. In particular, the common good resides in the conditions for the exercise of the natural freedoms indispensable for the development of the human vocation, such as "the right to act according to a sound norm of conscience and to safeguard…privacy, and rightful freedom also in matters of religion."[20]

1908 Second, the common good requires the *social well-being* and *development* of the group itself. Development is the epitome of all social duties. Certainly, it is the proper function of authority to arbitrate, in the name of the common good, between various particular interests; but it should make accessible to each what is needed to lead a truly human life: food, clothing, health, work, education and culture, suitable information, the right to establish a family, and so on.[21]

1909 Finally, the common good requires *peace*, that is, the stability and security of a just order. It presupposes that authority should ensure by morally acceptable means the *security* of society and its members. It is the basis of the right to legitimate personal and collective defense.

2405 Goods of production—material or immaterial—such as land, factories, practical or artistic skills, oblige their possessors to employ them in ways that will benefit the greatest number. Those who hold goods for use and consumption should use them with moderation, reserving the better part for guests, for the sick and the poor.

2406 *Political authority* has the right and duty to regulate the legitimate exercise of the right to ownership for the sake of the common good.[22]

The more blessed we are with wealth and prosperity, the greater the obligation to share those blessings with the poor and suffering.

ENDNOTES – CHAPTER FOUR

1. Cf. Congregation for Catholic Education, *Guidelines for the Study and Teaching of the Church's Social Doctrine in the Formation of Priests*, 29-42, Vatican Polyglot Press, Rome 1988, pp. 35-43.
2. Cf. John XXIII, Encyclical Letter *Mater et Magistra*: AAS 53 (1961), 453.
3. Congregation for the Doctrine of the Faith, Instruction *Libertatis Conscientia*, 72: AAS 79 (1987), 585.
4. *GS* 29 § 3.
5. *Letter of Barnabas* 4.10.
6. *GS* 26 § 1; cf. *GS* 74 § 1.
7. Cf. *GS* 26 § 2.
8. *CV* 13.
9. See CCC 1941; *LE* 8.
10. *GS* 69 § 1.
11. *GS* 27 § 1.
12. Cf. *RN*.
13. Cf. CCC 1882.
14. *SRS* 15; cf. *QA, MM, GS* 65; Congregation for the Doctrine of the Faith, Instruction *Libertatis Conscientia*, 73, 85-86; *CA* 48; CCC 1883-1885.
15. Cf. John Paul II, Encyclical Letter *Centesimus Annus*, 49: AAS 83 (1991), 854-856; John Paul II, Encyclical Letter *Sollicitudo Rei Socialis*, 15: AAS 80 (1988), 528-530.
16. *CA* 48.
17. *GS* 12.
18. Cf. *QA*; *CA* 48: CCC 1883.
19. Cf. *PT*, loc. cit., 274.
20. *GS* 26 § 2.
21. Cf. *GS* 26 § 2.
22. Cf. *GS* 71 § 4; *SRS* 42; *CA* 40; 48.

Social Doctrine of the Catholic Church
CHAPTER 5

Major Themes in Catholic Social Doctrine

The entire body of Catholic social doctrine is founded upon the principle of the inherent dignity of the human person.

Social Doctrine of the Catholic Church

CHAPTER FIVE

Major Themes in Catholic Social Doctrine

CLEAR MESSAGES DELIVERED WITH URGENCY AND FREQUENCY

Men and women of today, humanity come of age yet often still so frail in mind and will, let the Child of Bethlehem take you by the hand! Do not fear; put your trust in him! The life-giving power of his light is an incentive for building a new world order based on just ethical and economic relationships. May his love guide every people on earth and strengthen their common consciousness of being a "family" called to foster relationships of trust and mutual support. A united humanity will be able to confront the many troubling problems of the present time: from the menace of terrorism to the humiliating poverty in which millions of human beings live, from the proliferation of weapons to the pandemics and the environmental destruction which threatens the future of our planet.

—Pope Benedict XVI, *Urbi et Orbi Message*, Christmas 2005

IN THIS CHAPTER, WE WILL ADDRESS SEVERAL QUESTIONS:

- What themes recur in recent Catholic social doctrine?
- What gives human life its special dignity—and warrants its special protection?
- What is a family, and what is the family's place in society?
- What are our basic human rights and duties?
- Why do Christians show preference for the poor?
- What is the value of human work?
- How can solidarity help society?
- What are our responsibilities toward the environment?

The principles discussed in the last chapter play out in themes that recur in the Church's teaching and preaching. The themes are as old as the Gospel, but they have come to the fore in the last century and a half, as the world underwent (and continues to undergo) its age of revolutions.

Creation of Adam by Michelangelo.
Most philosophers, governments, and ordinary people agree that human beings possess some special dignity among the inhabitants of the earth.

THE DIGNITY OF HUMAN LIFE

The most fundamental theme in Catholic social doctrine is that of the dignity of human life. We have discussed the subject of human dignity at length in the last chapter, as well as in the book's introduction. Here we will build upon those discussions to show the distinctiveness of the Catholic approach.

Most philosophers, governments, and ordinary people agree that human beings possess some special dignity among the inhabitants of the earth. Though some people deny the equality of all human beings, most will affirm that men, women, and children have something that sets them apart from other animal species. They acknowledge rights for humans that they would deny to dogs, cats, monkeys, lions, squirrels, or snails.

Non-Christian thinkers differ, however, about what exactly is the quality that gives human beings their special dignity and thus their unique rights. Some say it is the capacity for free will. All other animals are bound to obey their innate instincts. Only human beings can deny such instincts for the sake of a greater, abstract good. Still, not all philosophers agree that human beings *have* free will. Behaviorists say that a man is bound just as much by his conditioning as an animal is by instinct. There are even thinkers in other religions who believe that God pre-determines every human action.

Apart from Divine Revelation, it is difficult to gather a consensus on the *reasons* for human dignity. Even those who recognize the *fact* of humanity's special dignity do not agree about the *origin or limits* of that dignity. The founders of the United States believed that human equality is "self-evident," and that universal human rights follow upon the fact (which, again, seemed obvious to them) of human equality.

Yet, these principles do not enjoy universal acceptance. Many non-Christian philosophers have taught, on the contrary, that *inequality* is a self-evident fact: people possess different gifts, to different degrees, and this produces a sort of natural aristocracy. From there, some argue that people with gifts that are more useful to society should enjoy a wider range of rights and freedoms.

Chapter Five

The Catholic Faith rejects such ideas as false. Human beings have no right to assign relative values to other human beings based on usefulness, attractiveness, or other criteria. This is the ancient teaching of the Church. In the fourth century, St. Basil the Great affirmed in clear terms the universal equality of all human beings:

> To every man belongs by nature equality of like honor with all men…Superiorities in us are not according to family, nor according to excess of wealth, nor according to the body's constitution, but according to the superiority of our fear of God. (Letter 262.1)

Nor, St. Basil added, can one race or nation claim superiority to another:

> The saints do not all belong to one country. Each is venerated in a different place. So what does that imply? Should we call them city-less, or citizens of the whole world? Just as at a common meal those things laid before the group by each are regarded as available to all who meet together, so among the saints, the homeland of each is common to all, and they give to each other everywhere whatever they have to hand. (Homily 338.2)

Catholic teaching on human dignity is based on the doctrine of Creation, which is implicit in the first pages of the Bible:

> Then God said, "Let us make man in our image, after our likeness; and let them have dominion over the fish of the sea, and over the birds of the air, and over the cattle, and over all the earth, and over every creeping thing that creeps upon the earth." So God created man in his own image, in the image of God he created him; male and female he created them. And God blessed them, and God said to them, "Be fruitful and multiply, and fill the earth and subdue it; and have dominion over the fish of the sea and over the birds of the air and over every living thing that moves upon the earth." And God said, "Behold, I have given you every plant yielding seed which is upon the face of all the earth, and every tree with seed in its fruit; you shall have them for food. And to every beast of the earth, and to every bird of the air, and to everything that creeps on the earth, everything that has the breath of life, I have given every green plant for food." And it was so. And God saw everything that he had made, and behold, it was very good. (Gn 1:26-31)

From the account of Creation in the Book of Genesis, we learn that human beings possess special dignity because they alone, of all the creatures on the earth, are created in God's image.

Catholic doctrine applies this status universally and equally, to every human being, from conception to natural death, because the Creation story makes no distinctions based on usefulness, race, or other characteristics. The creation of Adam and Eve is presented as the common origin of the entire human race. All their offspring share in their special dignity, dominion, rights, and goods, as well as the consequences of their fall from grace. This Fall, which we call the "Original Sin," has wounded human nature—weakened the will and darkened the intellect—but has not destroyed its essential dignity.

Human dignity is confirmed, in fact, by God's constant love for human beings in spite of their sustained disobedience. Throughout the Old Testament, God manifests his love and concern by sending prophets, mediators, and kings to help his people correct their moral course. At the culmination of history, God sent his divine, coeternal Son to assume human nature and

Allegory of Freewill and Sin, Illustration, *City of God* by St. Augustine.
Human dignity is confirmed, in fact, by God's constant love for human beings in spite of their sustained disobedience.

offer himself as an expiating sacrifice for the love of all people. Through the Incarnation—by the act of taking on flesh (cf. Jn 1:14)—God identified himself with each and every human being, even those who would be counted "least" by all earthly measures. Christ said: "Truly, I say to you, as you did it to one of the least of these my brethren, you did it to me" (Mt 25:40; see also Acts 9:4).

Christ on the Cross by El Greco.
It was for *all* human beings, and for *each* human being, that Christ shed his blood.

It was for *all* human beings, and for *each* human being, that Christ shed his blood (2 Cor 5:14-15; 1 Tm 2:6). Each human being, then, is worth the inestimable price of redemption, of God's redeeming action, of Christ's suffering and Death.

Apart from God's revelation that man is the pinnacle of his creation, made in the Creator's own image and likeness, it is difficult to defend a special dignity and equality applicable to all human beings. When states or individuals deny the transcendent basis of human dignity, they must look for other criteria for personhood—for example, mental capacity, physical ability, or the very elusive "quality of life." The inevitable result is that some human beings are denied status as human *persons*, and so they are denied possession of human rights and membership in the human community. This happens most often to those who are most defenseless: children in the womb and newborn babies, persons with developmental disabilities, the very old and infirm, or people who are in a coma (even those who might some day regain consciousness). These people do not have the capacity to assert their status as human beings, and so they are denied their rights, sometimes even their right to life.

Throughout world history, different rulers have argued that human rights should be assigned based on class, caste, race, or physical or mental ability. In ancient Sparta, all babies deemed "imperfect" were drowned or simply left to die. More recently, the eugenic programs of the Nazis denied the right to bear children to people who were deemed "unfit" because of perceived imperfections. Such people were deemed "life unworthy of life," and were rendered infertile by surgical sterilization—or killed outright.

Even today, as prenatal genetic testing becomes more common, some people—and even some governments—are denying the right to life to children in the womb. By government decision or parental choice, some children, deemed unworthy of life, are killed before they can be born.

The right to life is fundamental and should be protected and defended at every stage. It is the prerequisite of all other rights: Denied this most fundamental right, it follows that a person can exercise no other rights. And if this fundamental right can be denied, then no rights are secure.

There can be no sliding scale of humanity. Human rights are universal, based on some transcendent quality, or they are a sham. Rights are either conferred by God or they are subject to human whims and are utterly fungible. State-conferred "rights" today are almost certainly temporary, and may be proscribed at a time when they are no longer convenient.

Any social order that is based on a principle other than the respect for transcendent human dignity is not truly ordered, but, to varying degrees, disordered. As the *Catechism* observes:

> Social justice can be obtained only in respecting the transcendent dignity of man. The person represents the ultimate end of society, which is ordered to him:
>> What is at stake is the dignity of the human person, whose defense and promotion have been entrusted to us by the Creator, and to whom the men and women at every moment of history are strictly and responsibly in debt.[1] (CCC 1929)

> Respect for the human person entails respect for the rights that flow from his dignity as a creature. These rights are prior to society and must be recognized by it. They are the basis of the moral legitimacy of every authority: by flouting them, or refusing to recognize them in its positive legislation, a society undermines its own moral legitimacy.² If it does not respect them, authority can rely only on force or violence to obtain obedience from its subjects. It is the Church's role to remind men of good will of these rights and to distinguish them from unwarranted or false claims. (CCC 1930)

Because of the clarity of its teaching on human dignity and human rights, the Church has much to contribute to the development of thought on these matters. Human dignity is a theme that appears in almost all the documents related to the Church's social doctrine. It is a special focus in Pope Pius XI's *Mit Brennender Sorge*, Pope Pius XII's *Humani Generis*, the Second Vatican Council's *Dignitatis Humanæ*, Pope Paul VI's *Humanae Vitæ*, and St. John Paul II's *Evangelium Vitæ*.

THE CALL TO FAMILY, COMMUNITY, AND PARTICIPATION

Community begins with the family; and the family begins, in the created order, with marriage.

God launched human society with the creation of our first parents, Adam and Eve, who raised children. The family's priority in time reflects a primacy in importance in society. In the words of the Second Vatican Council: "Since the Creator of all things has established the conjugal partnership as the beginning and basis of human society," the family is "the first and vital cell of society."³

The family is where social life begins for most human beings. Pope Benedict XVI told a conference on the family:

> It is within a family that one experiences for the first time how the human person was created to live, not closed up in himself, but in relationship with others. (Address at World Meeting on Families, Milan, Italy, June 1, 2012)

Holy Family by Coello.
The family is where social life begins for most human beings.

In Scripture and throughout history, the word *family* has had a commonly accepted meaning. It is built upon marriage, which also means something very specific. We find its classic expression in the Gospel according to Matthew (19:4-9), where Christ explained the Creation account of the Book of Genesis (1:27-28 and 2:21-25):

> Have you not read that he who made them from the beginning made them male and female, and said, "for this reason a man shall leave his father and mother and be joined to his wife, and the two shall become one flesh"? So they are no longer two but one flesh. What therefore God has joined together, let not man put asunder.

Though the ancient peoples often counted the "family" as a large, tribal arrangement, each tribe was built from households that began with a couple—a husband and wife—and grew through their children.

The family's form is evident in nature; but, as Christ pointed out, it is vulnerable to misunderstanding—sometimes willful misunderstanding and perversion. God established marriage as a lifelong and exclusive bond, but couples rejected the divine plan and practiced divorce, abandonment, adultery, and polygamy. Even in the Old Testament, we can already see the sad societal effects of these abuses.

Christ clarified the matter. His teaching is echoed by St. Paul, who described marriage as a Sacrament, a profound mystery (cf. Eph 5:32), a living sign of God's abiding and fruitful love for his people and a sign of the union of Christ and his Church.

It was important, then, for Christ to communicate very precisely the nature of marriage and family. The *Catechism* reflects further on the Scripture passages to produce definitions.

> A man and a woman united in marriage, together with their children, form a family. This institution is prior to any recognition by public authority, which has an obligation to recognize it. It should be considered the normal reference point by which the different forms of family relationship are to be evaluated. (CCC 2202)

> In creating man and woman, God instituted the human family and endowed it with its fundamental constitution. Its members are persons equal in dignity. For the common good of its members and of society, the family necessarily has manifold responsibilities, rights, and duties. (CCC 2203)

The family is the fundamental unit of society. If the family suffers disorder, society cannot know peace; for peace, according to St. Augustine, is "tranquility in order." When the family breaks down, society suffers the way a body suffers when its very cells are attacked by disease. For it is in the family that human beings normally have their first experience of society and their first instruction in the social virtues. St. John Paul II put the matter succinctly:

> The family has vital and organic links with society, since it is its foundation and nourishes it continually through its role of service to life: it is from the family that citizens come to birth and it is within the family that they find the first school of the social virtues that are the animating principle of the existence and development of society itself.[4]

Families do not live in isolation, but, rather, alongside other families. They interact with other families and individuals in the neighborhood. By their behavior and their outreach, they improve their local environment, they influence other families, and they exercise stewardship over the portion of society that is under their control. Perhaps they cannot change national laws, but they can establish the conditions for an orderly and happy household, and in doing so they are contributing to the improvement of society.

As the Popes have consistently pointed out, this does not mean that a household will be closed in on itself. Strong families must help weaker families to grow in strength. Strong families also witness to life's best possibilities. Writing in the fourth century, St. Jerome said:

The family is the fundamental unit of society. If the family suffers disorder, society cannot know peace.

> The eyes of all are turned upon you. Your house is set upon a watchtower. Your life establishes for others the limits of their self-control.[5]

Yet there is great confusion today about the meaning and constitution of the family. This has had catastrophic effects on society, and especially on the lives of children.

Society is based upon family, and family is based upon marriage. Marriage is a lifelong, indissoluble union between one man and one woman. God has revealed this. Nature and history confirm it. Recent trends away from this norm have, by their ill effects, demonstrated the truth of God's word. A same-sex partnership cannot be a marriage. A true marriage can never be dissolved, by individuals or by the state. Violations of the marriage bond—divorce, adultery, sterilization—bring unhappiness not only

Society should protect the dignity and the flourishing of the traditional family. No other institution has stood as steadfastly for the traditional family and the rights of children and spouses as the Church.

to individuals and households but to society, for the family is where participation in society begins. When families are healthy, society benefits from a better economy, a more motivated workforce, gains in education, and reductions in street crime.

For all of these reasons, society should protect the dignity and the flourishing of the traditional family. In fact, St. John Paul II called for governments to respect the freedom of families and provide support as needed:

> The family and society have complementary functions in defending and fostering the good of each and every human being. But society—more specifically the State—must recognize that "the family is a society in its own original right" (Second Vatican Council, *Dignitatis Humanæ*, 5), and so society is under a grave obligation in its relations with the family to adhere to the principle of subsidiarity.
>
> By virtue of this principle, the State cannot and must not take away from families the functions that they can just as well perform on their own or in free associations; instead it must positively favor and encourage as far as possible responsible initiative by families. In the conviction that the good of the family is an indispensable and essential value of the civil community, the public authorities must do everything possible to ensure that families have all those aids—economic, social, educational, political and cultural assistance—that they need in order to face all their responsibilities in a human way.[6]

Community begins with the family and cannot thrive apart from healthy families. When societies began to reject the traditional family—beginning with the communist experiments early in the twentieth century—the Church frequently and decisively addressed the issue. No other institution has stood so steadfastly for the rights of children and spouses. Key documents for understanding Church doctrine are Pope Paul VI's *Humanæ Vitæ* and St. John Paul II's *Familiaris Consortio* and *Letter to Families*. Also illuminating are the Vatican's interventions on the subject of the family at the United Nations' conferences on population, on women, and on development.

RESPONSIBILITIES AND RIGHTS

Human rights are a necessary corollary to human dignity. Rights, as we saw in Chapter 2, are the goods that are owed to a person simply for the fact that he or she is human. We possess the right to life because we are human. We also possess rights that enable us to fulfill our human nature, as created by God, as well as our divine vocation.

Human rights are discernible through the natural law, the light of intellect infused in human beings by God. By the natural law, we know—to varying degrees, based upon on the peculiarities of culture and other circumstances that either strengthen or weaken the intellect and moral imagination—what must be done and what must be avoided. People have always intuited the inalienable right to life, and so murder has been forbidden in every society, even among the most primitive peoples. People also instinctively recognize the right to private property, and so every society prohibits theft. And people have an innate sense of justice—of that which is their due—and hence the ubiquitous role of judge throughout history, transcending time and place.

The natural law expresses the dignity of the person and lays the foundations of the person's fundamental rights and duties. Even though people are divided by language and culture, the natural law can serve to unite them around some basic common moral standards. Natural-law reasoning was helpful and influential for many international bodies in the twentieth century as they sought consensus among member states that were widely diverse—communist, capitalist, Islamist, Jewish, Christian, socialist, monarchist, democratic, and republican.

The natural law is not always discerned accurately or recognized. In fact, some people reject the very idea of a natural law. Nevertheless, even they must appeal to natural-law principles in order to promote or defend their own natural rights.

The social upheavals and revolutions of recent centuries have often arisen from a concern for human rights. This was the constant theme in the negotiations and propaganda before and during the revolutions in North America, France, Russia, China, and elsewhere. The movement to identify and proclaim human rights is a distinguishing mark of the modern era, and it has been affirmed and supported by the Church.

The Church teaches that the ultimate source of human rights is not found in the will of human beings, in the decisions of the State, or in the consensus of a group, but rather are innate in every human being and endowed by God the Creator. Human rights are universal, inviolable, and inalienable. No one can legitimately deprive another person—any person—of these rights, since this would do violence to their very nature.

Rights must be respected, then, because they correspond to the demands of human dignity. They represent the goods that fulfill the basic needs, spiritual and material, of human nature.

Jesus Before Pilate, Second Interview (detail) by Tissot. "Jesus answered him, 'You would have no power over me unless it had been given you from above; therefore he who delivered me to you has the greater sin.'" (Jn 19:11)

The Church and the Popes have spoken often to promote or defend human rights. In his encyclical *Centesimus Annus* (47), St. John Paul II drew up a list of fundamental human rights:

> The right to life, an integral part of which is the right of the child to develop in the mother's womb from the moment of conception; the right to live in a united family and in a moral environment conducive to the growth of the child's personality; the right to develop one's intelligence and freedom in seeking and knowing the truth; the right to share in the work which makes wise use of the earth's material resources, and to derive from that work the means to support oneself and

THE SOCIAL DOCTRINE OF THE CATHOLIC CHURCH

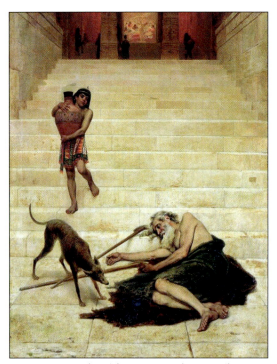

Lazarus at the Rich Man's Gate by Bronnikov. All people are coresponsible, responsible together, for the common good.

one's dependents; and the right freely to establish a family, to have and to rear children through the responsible exercise of one's sexuality. In a certain sense, the source and synthesis of these rights is religious freedom, understood as the right to live in the truth of one's faith and in conformity with one's transcendent dignity as a person.

For Christians, respect for human rights derives from a commandment of the Lord: "You shall love your neighbor as yourself" (Mt 22:39). The *Catechism* adds:

> Respect for the human person considers the other "another self." It presupposes respect for the fundamental rights that flow from the dignity intrinsic of the person. (CCC 1944)

Rights "belong to human nature and are inherent in the person by virtue of the creative act from which the person took his origin"[7] (CCC 2273). But with rights come duties: "Every one to whom much is given, of him will much be required" (Lk 12:48). Thus, rights and duties are complementary and inextricably linked to one another. If we are given rights, we have the obligation to recognize, respect, and defend those same rights on behalf of others. As St. John XXIII wrote in his encyclical *Pacem in Terris* (30):

> Those, therefore, who claim their own rights, yet altogether forget or neglect to carry out their respective duties, are people who build with one hand and destroy with the other.

The rich who possess much must recognize and address the needs of the destitute who lack life's necessities. The right to own property comes with the obligation to manage it well for God, who is sovereign over all creation. All people are coresponsible, responsible together, for the common good. Cain's defense, "Am I my brother's keeper" (Gn 4:9), is consistently deplored in any biblically based ethics, Jewish or Christian.

Though the Church has praised the historical movement to recognize human rights, St. John Paul II observed that there is sometimes a great gap between the "letter" and the "spirit" of the laws that affirm human rights (see his encyclical *Redemptor Hominis*, 17). If they are not enforced—if they are, in fact, ignored or routinely suspended, or abrogated by the state—then the laws are empty promises.

PREFERENTIAL OPTION FOR THE POOR

There can be no doubt that Christ showed a special love for people who were poor, oppressed, and outcast. He touched those who were considered ritually "unclean" and marginalized by society—lepers, for example, and tax collectors. He counseled his disciples to favor the disadvantaged over the well-off:

> But when you give a feast, invite the poor, the maimed, the lame, the blind. (Lk 14:13)

In fact, he defined his earthly life as a mission to the poor:

> The Spirit of the Lord is upon me, because he has anointed me to preach good news to the poor. He has sent me to proclaim release to the captives and recovering of sight to the blind, to set at liberty those who are oppressed. (Lk 4:18)

Christ addressed the poor directly and called them "blessed":

> Blessed are you poor, for yours is the kingdom of God. Blessed are you that hunger now, for you shall be satisfied. (Lk 6:20-21)

Parable of Lazarus and Dives (Latin for "Rich Man") (detail), *Codex* Illumination.
Top panel: Lazarus' soul is carried to Paradise by two angels, and Lazarus sits in Abraham's bosom.
Bottom panel: Dives' soul is carried off by two devils to Hell, and Dives cries out to Abraham for help.

The other side of this blessing, moreover, is a curse, a "woe" pronounced upon the rich and those whose bellies are full (Lk 6:24-25). Christ told one wealthy man:

> If you would be perfect, go, sell what you possess and give to the poor, and you will have treasure in heaven; and come, follow me. (Mt 19:21)

His parable of the rich man and the beggar Lazarus stands as a warning to the rich:

> The poor man died and was carried by the angels to Abraham's bosom. The rich man also died and was buried. (Lk 16:22)

The contrast in destinies is striking: The man marginalized on earth is welcomed by angels; the man who had ease on earth was buried in the ground, and that is the best thing that could be said about the matter.

The Lord did not condemn wealth in itself, but rather the hoarding of wealth and neglect of the poor. He had many wealthy and generous friends, and he showed them great love: Nicodemus, for example, who was a ruler and a man of means (cf. Jn 3:1, 19:39); Zacchaeus, the tax collector who gave half of his possessions to the poor (cf. Lk 19:8); and Joanna, the wife of Herod's steward, who helped to fund Christ's ministry (cf. Lk 8:3).

This predilection for the poor has always been a distinguishing mark of Christians and of the Church. Throughout this book we have studied many examples of individuals and programs that exemplified such charity. In 1968, the superior general of the Jesuits, Fr. Pedro Arrupe, coined a phrase to describe this Christian tendency. He called it the "option for the poor." The bishops of Latin America further developed the idea as a "*preferential* option for the poor." The *Catechism* explains:

> "In its various forms—material deprivation, unjust oppression, physical and psychological illness and death—*human misery* is the obvious sign of the inherited condition of frailty and need for salvation in which man finds himself as a consequence of original sin. This misery elicited the compassion of Christ the Savior, who willingly took it upon himself and identified himself with the least of his brethren. Hence, those who are oppressed by poverty are the object of a preferential love on the part of the Church which, since her origin and in spite of the failings of many of her members, has not ceased to work for their relief, defense, and liberation through numerous works of charity which remain indispensable always and everywhere."[8] (CCC 2448)

The phrase "preferential option for the poor" (or some variation of it) appears often in the works of Popes John Paul II and Benedict XVI. In *Sollicitudo Rei Socialis*, St. John Paul II defined this option as "a special form of primacy in the exercise of Christian charity.…It affects the life of each Christian inasmuch as he or she seeks to imitate the life of Christ."[9] It applies, he said, to one's entire manner of living, one's ownership and use of goods. And the range of a Christian's concern should be not merely local, but global, reaching out to "the immense multitudes of the hungry, the needy, the homeless, those without medical care and, above all, those without hope of a better future. It is impossible not to take account of the existence of these realities. To ignore them would mean becoming like the 'rich man' who pretended not to know the beggar Lazarus lying at his gate."[10]

Who are the poor? Who are the rich? Many people continue to live in squalor, despite improvements in technology and international commitments to human rights.

Who are the poor? Who are the rich? It is useful to consider that many, if not most, citizens living in the "developed" nations of the West enjoy a better quality of life than the wealthiest citizens of Christ's land and times. The ancients did not have centralized heat in winter or air conditioning in summer. They could not take aspirin or other medicines to relieve pain with any degree of effectiveness. Travel was hard and dangerous. Life expectancy was around thirty-five years old. Many people alive today would qualify as "rich" by Christ's standards.

Yet, many other people continue to live in squalor, despite improvements in technology and international commitments to human rights. Those who enjoy the benefits of a global economy must also share the duty of relieving global poverty.

Nevertheless, most individual actions will normally be directed to the local community. In St. John Paul II's encyclical *Centesimus Annus*, he asks that Christians' "love for the poor" be directed toward "different forms of poverty" suffered "by groups which live on the margins of society, by the elderly and the sick, by the victims of consumerism, and even more immediately by so many refugees and migrants."[11]

Private Property and the Universal Destination of Goods

Because every person has an inherent right to life, nourishment, and shelter, among other things, the created goods of the earth are destined to benefit everyone, not just a small segment of the population. This concept is generally referred to as the "universal destination of goods." Ownership of created goods goes hand-in-hand with the moral obligation to help those in need. These ideas are summarized in the *Catechism*:

> In the beginning God entrusted the earth and its resources to the common stewardship of mankind to take care of them, master them by labor, and enjoy their fruits.[12] The goods of creation are destined for the whole human race. (CCC 2402)

In emphasizing that the goods of this world are intended for the benefit of all, the Church also indicates that each person also has the right to his own possessions—a right founded on human nature itself:

PILLARS OF THE CHURCH

ST. GREGORY OF NAZIANZUS: We Are All Poor and Needy

A Father of the early Church, St. Gregory of Nazianzus, made the case for solidarity with the poor.

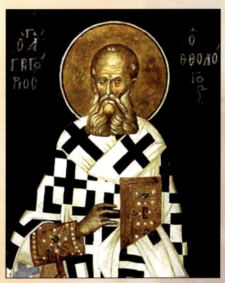

St. Gregory of Nazianzus
(ca. 329-390)

My brothers and fellow paupers—for we are all poor and needy where divine grace is concerned, even though, measured by our paltry standards one man may seem to have more than another…We must open our hearts, then, to all the poor, to those suffering evil for any reason at all, according to the Scripture that commands us to "rejoice with those who rejoice and weep with those who weep." Because we are human beings, we must offer the favor of our kindness first of all to other human beings, whether they need it because they are widows or orphans, or because they are exiles from their own country, or because of the cruelty of their masters, or the harshness of their rulers, or the inhumanity of their tax-collectors, or because of the bloody violence of robbers or the insatiable greed of thieves, or because of the legal confiscation of their property, or shipwreck—all are wretched alike, and so all look toward our hands, as we look towards God's, for the things we need.

—*On the Love of the Poor*, 1, 6.

Shanty town in the Philippines. The goods of the earth are created by God to benefit every person.

> However, the earth is divided up among men to assure the security of their lives, endangered by poverty, and threatened by violence. The appropriation of property is legitimate for guaranteeing the freedom and dignity of persons and for helping each of them to meet his basic needs and the needs of those in his charge. It should allow for a natural solidarity to develop between men. (CCC 2402)

How, then, does the Catholic Magisterium reconcile these two fundamental human rights—the right to own property, and the right to a fair distribution of goods so that the dignity of every human person is respected by having his or her basic material needs of food, water, and shelter met?

The Catholic Faith affirms a natural right to private property but emphasizes that this right is subordinate to the universal destination of goods. If there is a dispute between private property and its destination, the social principle prevails over the private because God created goods for the use of all people. When only a few people possess most of the goods, it becomes impossible for the majority of people to live in accordance with basic human dignity. In such instances, the Father's plan is not fulfilled.

> The *universal destination of goods* remains primordial, even if the promotion of the common good requires respect for the right to private property and its exercise. (CCC 2403)

The goods of the earth are created by God to benefit every person. If some people have more of these goods, they should look upon the goods as given in trust by God. They are stewards of wealth owned by God, and he expects them to share what he has given them. The Parable of the Talents makes it clear: God demands more from those who have received more (cf. Mt 25:29). In case anyone missed the point of the Parable of the Talents, Christ followed immediately with the Parable of the Sheep and the Goats, which teaches that God will judge each of us based on our treatment of the poor. This includes those who are "spiritually poor."

Thus, the ownership of private property does not conflict with the common good when it is placed at the service of the common good and goods are distributed according to a proper understanding of every human being as a steward of God's Creation.

> The goods of creation are destined for the entire human race. The right to private property does not abolish the universal destination of goods. (CCC 2452)

If a person lacks basic needs such as shelter, clothing, nourishment, and tools for work, he or she cannot function properly as a free being. The Church recognizes the right (and duty) of the state to intervene when necessary to ensure that private property does not oppose the common good, but rather makes a positive contribution for the good of society. To this end, the state can claim certain goods for use by the public. The state has the right to impose taxes upon citizens in order to fund programs that benefit others who are less fortunate. The state can also use the right of *eminent domain* to claim private property—with just payment to the owner—because of a legitimate and overriding public concern, such as when a farmer's land is needed to build a highway that will benefit the common good.

St. John Paul II always addressed the "preferential option for the poor" in terms of love: "love for others, and in the first place love for the poor."[13]

He went on to explain:

> Justice will never be fully attained unless people see in the poor person, who is asking for help in order to survive, not an annoyance or a burden, but an opportunity for showing kindness and a chance for greater enrichment. Only such an awareness can give the courage needed to face the

> risk and the change involved in every authentic attempt to come to the aid of another. It is not merely a matter of "giving from one's surplus," but of helping entire peoples which are presently excluded or marginalized to enter into the sphere of economic and human development. For this to happen, it is not enough to draw on the surplus goods which in fact our world abundantly produces; it requires above all a change of life-styles, of models of production and consumption, and of the established structures of power which today govern societies. Nor is it a matter of eliminating instruments of social organization which have proved useful, but rather of orienting them according to an adequate notion of the common good in relation to the whole human family.[14]

The preferential option for the poor is an antidote to *laissez-faire* capitalism's neglect of the poor; but it is also a peaceful alternative to Marxism's murderous doctrine of class struggle. It is a way of solidarity, acknowledging that differences and inequalities exist for the sake of mutual support and solidarity. In Christian life, all benefactors are beneficiaries, because they will be rewarded for their charity, at least in eternal life; and all beneficiaries are benefactors, because they make possible such great spiritual rewards.

THE DIGNITY OF WORK

"Human work," said St. John Paul II, "is a key, probably the essential key, to the whole social question."[15]

Work, like society, is part of human nature. We are made for it. It is difficult for us to be fulfilled apart from it. We find this truth in the beginning of the Book of Genesis. When God created man, he gave him "dominion" over the earth, with all its plants and animals; God instructed Adam to "fill the earth and subdue it" (Gn 1:28). Earth itself was made for this purpose, and it is not fulfilled until there is "man to till the ground" (Gn 2:5).

The Lord God took the man and put him in the Garden of Eden to till it and keep it. (Gn 2:15)

Adam and Eve's Life of Toil by Master Bertram. Work, like society, is part of human nature.

This is the condition of human beings as they were created by God—before Original Sin. Work, then, is an integral part of being human. After the Fall, work becomes more arduous (cf. Gn 3:17-19), but it remains part of human nature, and so it is "very good" (Gn 1:31). Because it is integrally human, it shares in human dignity.

Throughout the Old Testament, people were often identified by the work they did: herdsmen, farmers, potters, merchants, priests, soldiers, blacksmiths, cooks, scholars, sailors, architects and builders, kings and cabinet ministers. The Book of Proverbs is famous for its praise of the work of women, in the home, in the fields, and in the marketplace (cf. Prv 31:10-31). The Old Testament Scriptures praise industry and condemn idleness (cf. Prv 6:6-11).

When God became man, he became a worker, a craftsman. Tradition tells us Christ was a carpenter, and he grew up working in St. Joseph's workshop. In his parables he drew lessons from the work of shepherds, farmers, judges, sowers, householders, servants and stewards, and homemakers. He drew disciples from a wide range of fields of endeavor: fishermen, a tax collector, legal scholars, rulers. The God-man divinized work by doing it, and he spoke of work as something godlike: "My Father is working still, and I am working" (Jn 5:17). He addressed his Gospel to people who worked hard: "Come to me, all who labor and are heavy laden, and I will give you rest" (Mt 11:28).

Jesus Grew Strong in Spirit and Wisdom by Unknown Master.
In work, people can fulfill their human nature, imitate Jesus Christ, and participate in God's creation.

Christ's disciples respected work, and they themselves worked with diligence. St. Paul, who supported himself in his apostleship as a tent-maker, could say to his followers in Thessalonika: "For you remember our labor and toil, brethren; we worked night and day, that we might not burden any of you, while we preached to you the gospel of God" (1 Thes 2:9). He urged them to follow his example: "aspire to live quietly, to mind your own affairs, and to work with your hands" (1 Thes 4:11); and he warned them not to associate with people who refused to work (cf. 2 Thes 3:7-12). St. Paul gloried in the fact that he was a manual laborer (cf. 1 Cor 4:12).

For Christ and for St. Paul, all honest work had dignity precisely because it was done by human beings. As St. John Paul II observed: "The basis for determining the value of human work is not primarily the kind of work being done but the fact that the one who is doing it is a person."[16]

The early Church attracted workers of every sort. A second-century opponent of Christianity, Celsus, disdained the Church because it included "wool-workers, cobblers, [and] laundry-workers," and because it paid homage to the Holy Family, "a poor woman of the country, who gained her subsistence by spinning, and [whose husband was] a carpenter by trade."

Work is as old as humanity itself; but, for many people, its conditions have changed radically since the Industrial Revolution. Certain trades were completely automated, taken over by machines. Whereas many people formerly found work on farms, now they found opportunities in factories, in cities. St. John Paul II said that this new situation "calls for the discovery of the new meanings of human work. It likewise calls for the formulation of the new tasks that in this sector face each individual, the family, each country, the whole human race, and, finally, the Church herself."[17]

In work, people can fulfill their human nature, imitate Jesus Christ, and participate in God's creation. Work can be arduous; but even this situation, with all its suffering, can redound to the benefit of the worker. The Christian knows how to unite his difficulties with the Passion of Christ, so that they become redemptive. As St. Paul said: "Now I rejoice in my sufferings for your sake, and in my flesh I complete what is lacking in Christ's afflictions for the sake of his body, that is, the Church" (Col 1:24).

THE ROOTS OF THE EUROPEAN UNION

The European Union (EU) is a confederation of many member states located across the continent of Europe. In the first half of the twentieth century, most of these states fought one another in devastating wars. In the aftermath of World War II, many statesmen sought a way to unify the peoples of Europe, economically and (to a limited degree) politically, to ensure mutual support, peace, and prosperity—in short, to maximize the common good. Most of the leaders of this movement were devout Catholics who based their political approach on the social encyclicals of the Popes and on the philosophical works of Jacques Maritain and Emmanuel Mounier. Of the seven men usually called "Founders of the European Union," five were Catholic.

It was Robert Schuman,[18] a Catholic Frenchman, who first called for a "European Coal and Steel Community," basing his proposal on the work of another Catholic Frenchman, Jean Monnet. The success of this endeavor led, in the years that followed, to increased cooperation and more formal bonds among the nations of Europe. Monnet became the first president of the European "High Authority." Schuman later served as president of the European Parliament. A scholar of Scripture and the philosophy of St. Thomas Aquinas, Schuman lived a celibate life so that he could dedicate himself completely to the work he saw as his vocation from God. He died in 1963, and his cause for sainthood has been introduced in Rome.

Also counted among the EU's Founders is Konrad Adenauer,[19] who served as chancellor of West Germany from 1949 to 1963. He was largely responsible for the country's re-emergence as a world power in the postwar peace. Even before the war, he had enjoyed a long career in government, promoting good morals and social order. The mayor of Cologne at the time of Hitler's electoral victory, he was soon removed from office and was imprisoned twice during the Fuhrer's reign. After Hitler's downfall, West Germany turned to Adenauer as a leader of unimpeachable integrity and hard-won wisdom. He assumed the office of chancellor at age seventy-two.

A third man prominent among the Founders was Alcide De Gasperi,[20] Italy's prime minister in the years immediately after World War II. During a 2008 visit to his tomb, Pope Benedict XVI described him as "a wise and balanced guide for Italy during the difficult years of the postwar reconstruction and, at the same time, a distinguished statesman capable of looking to Europe with a broad Christian vision."

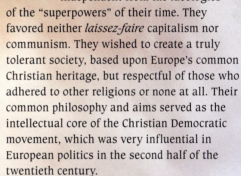

All of these men cited *Rerum Novarum* as the great influence on the formative years of their lives. They sought, through their work in government, to put Catholic social doctrine into practice. They wanted to establish a European identity and unity that was distinct and independent from the ideologies of the "superpowers" of their time. They favored neither *laissez-faire* capitalism nor communism. They wished to create a truly tolerant society, based upon Europe's common Christian heritage, but respectful of those who adhered to other religions or none at all. Their common philosophy and aims served as the intellectual core of the Christian Democratic movement, which was very influential in European politics in the second half of the twentieth century.

The influence of these men also shows in the governing document of the European Union, the 1993 Treaty of Maastricht, which often employs the language of Catholic social thought, expressing the desire "to deepen the solidarity between peoples" and pledging to order international relations "in accordance with the principle of subsidiarity."[21]

St. John Paul II could study human work and conclude:

> Work is a good thing for man—a good thing for his humanity—because through work man *not only transforms nature*, adapting it to his own needs, but he also *achieves fulfillment* as a human being and indeed, in a sense, becomes "more a human being."²²

The Second Vatican Council spoke of human work as an exercise of priesthood, because all Christians share in the priesthood of Christ (cf. 1 Pt 2:5, 9). When we work, our desk, our field, our stove, our cash register become like altars where we offer sacrifice.

> For all their works, prayers and apostolic endeavors, their ordinary married and family life, their daily occupations, their physical and mental relaxation, if carried out in the Spirit, and even the hardships of life, if patiently borne—all these become "spiritual sacrifices acceptable to God through Jesus Christ" (1 Pt 2:5). Together with the offering of the Lord's Body, they are most fittingly offered in the celebration of the Eucharist. Thus, as those everywhere who adore in holy activity, the laity consecrate the world itself to God. (*LG* 34)

Those who labor are "God's fellow workers" (1 Cor 3:9), and they are honored as such in the Church, which observes an annual feast in honor of St. Joseph the Worker.

The challenge for Catholic social teaching is to advocate for working conditions that respect human dignity. If work is part of human nature, then all people have a natural right to work. They have a right to learn a trade so that they can support a family or otherwise fulfill their vocation. They have a right to access to employment, education, training, and tools. These are matters of fundamental social justice.

UNIVERSAL SOLIDARITY

Society is not a mere gathering of individuals. All human beings are united by a common nature, by mutual need, by complementary skills, and by their strivings toward common goals. God created people with differences so that they would come together in their need for one another. The interests and concerns of each member cannot be alien to the rest.

Dorothy Day's last arrest at the age of seventy-five for picketing in support of farmworkers. The principles of social justice call for action, and Dorothy opened the first of what would become "houses of hospitality" for the homeless and hungry.

Solidarity, a term we introduced in Chapter 4, is the name we give to the social unity formed by common interests, goals, or standards. Solidarity is the integration of people with their neighbors. It represents the "ties that bind" people to one another in society.

For a Christian this bond comes *not* from tribalism, nationalism, or provincialism, but from our common humanity before God. Among Christians, said St. Paul, "There is neither Jew nor Greek, there is neither slave nor free, there is neither male nor female; for you are all one in Christ Jesus" (Gal 3:28). Thus, a Christian recognizes a bond of solidarity uniting the whole human race.

Political leaders will sometimes try to unite citizens against a common enemy—even a subgroup within their society. Marxists foment "class struggle" and "class warfare." Revolutionaries try to exploit a "generation gap" between young and old. Racial supremacists have imposed regimes of "ethnic cleansing" and genocide. Rather than divide society by class or caste, the Catholic notion of solidarity aims to unite all people in their common humanity.

Solidarity benefits society in many ways. Cooperation makes it easier for people to achieve common goals.

Universal solidarity makes sense not only in religious terms, but also in the context of a global economy, with shared interests, shared resources, and shared consequences.

St. John Paul II used the term so often he was often called "the Pope of solidarity." He invited people to recognize their interdependence and then to commit themselves to mutual self-giving, so that they could achieve together what they could never accomplish separately. Solidarity marks a sensible way to approach world peace. It is a sensible approach even for those who do not share the Christian Faith. For believers, however, it imposes a special obligation. Christian love—charity—impels Christians to pledge solidarity with all others.

John Paul II saw solidarity as a "system" of interdependence that determines economic, cultural, political, and religious elements in the modern world.[23] When solidarity is understood in this way, the moral response becomes a virtue. It is a sense of solidarity that drives a Christian to feed, clothe, and shelter those who are in need. It is solidarity that drives a Christian to share the Gospel with others and bring them to the Sacraments. As the *Catechism* puts it:

> Solidarity is an eminently Christian virtue. It practices the sharing of spiritual goods even more than material ones. (CCC 1948)

All people are duty-bound to work together for the common good. Their sense of solidarity enables them to coordinate efforts, overcoming partisan positions that divide and cause confrontations.

> Such solidarity, open, dynamic, and universal by nature, will never be negative. It will not be a "solidarity against" but a positive and constructive one, a "solidarity for," for work, for justice, for peace, for well-being and for truth in social life.[24]

Another great benefit of solidarity is the acknowledgment of mutual rights and duties. This leads people to look out for one another, identifying needs and defending and protecting one another through a network of mutual relations.

Solidarity does not end at national borders. Nations and peoples, too, are called to live in solidarity with one another. Though each culture is distinctive and different from all others, all peoples are equal before God. We must make this equality effective, however, and not merely theoretical. To this end, wealthier nations have a grave obligation to provide for the needs of the less developed nations, which also means helping them to help themselves: e.g., by introducing to them better agricultural systems and models of government. It is an offense against justice and a grievous neglect of basic human rights to ignore groups of people suffering misery and destitution while other nations have a surplus of riches at their disposal. As the *Catechism* says:

Homeless Children in Bangladesh. Wealthier nations have a grave obligation to provide for the needs of less developed nations.

> Rich nations have a grave moral responsibility toward those which are unable to ensure the means of their development by themselves or have been prevented from doing so by tragic historical events. It is a duty in solidarity and charity; it is also an obligation in justice if the prosperity of the rich nations has come from resources that have not been paid for fairly. (CCC 2439)

A globalized economy has the potential to help poorer nations, but it also leaves them vulnerable to exploitation by multinational corporations that make use of their resources and labor forces without care for stewardship and human rights.

> Various causes of a religious, political, economic, and financial nature today give "the social question a worldwide dimension."[25] There must be solidarity among nations which are already

> politically interdependent. It is even more essential when it is a question of dismantling the "perverse mechanisms" that impede the development of the less advanced countries.[26] In place of abusive if not usurious financial systems, iniquitous commercial relations among nations, and the arms race, there must be substituted a common effort to mobilize resources toward objectives of moral, cultural, and economic development, "redefining the priorities and hierarchies of values."[27] (CCC 2438)
>
> *Direct aid* is an appropriate response to immediate, extraordinary needs caused by natural catastrophes, epidemics, and the like. But it does not suffice to repair the grave damage resulting from destitution or to provide a lasting solution to a country's needs. It is also necessary to *reform* international economic and financial *institutions* so that they will better promote equitable relationships with less advanced countries.[28] (CCC 2440)

Solidarity affects the way a Christian will approach many issues—immigration, for example. The *Catechism* recognizes the complexity of the issue, affirming a nation's right to limit immigration, but also requiring compassion and generosity for those fleeing their homelands in order to ensure their basic human dignity.

The more prosperous nations are obliged, to the extent they are able, to welcome "strangers" in search of the security and the means of livelihood that they cannot find in their country of origin. Public authorities should see to it that the natural right is respected that places a guest under the protection of those who receive him.

> Political authorities, for the sake of the common good for which they are responsible, may make the exercise of the right to immigrate subject to various juridical conditions, especially with regard to the immigrants' duties toward their country of adoption. Immigrants are obliged to respect with gratitude the material and spiritual heritage of the country that receives them, to obey its laws and to assist in carrying civic burdens. (CCC 2241)

The Miracle of the Loaves and Fishes by Lombard.
"As he went ashore he saw a great throng; and he had compassion on them, and healed their sick. When it was evening, the disciples came to him and said, 'This is a lonely place, and the day is now over; send the crowds away to go into the villages and buy food for themselves.' Jesus said, 'They need not go away; you give them something to eat.'" (Mt 14:14-16)

ST. LUIGI GUANELLA: Helping People with Disabilities Enjoy Life Abundantly

Luigi Guanella was born in Italy in 1842 to a family that raised sheep and cattle. Called to the priesthood, he was ordained a priest in 1866. He served faithfully as a parish priest, but always felt God wanted more from him. He discerned a special call to serve the poor and disadvantaged. His first efforts, however, were frustrated. He founded a school for poor children, but local authorities shut it down. He wondered what God's will for his life was.

Clarity came with a new assignment in 1881. At his new parish he found an active group of young women already dedicated to helping the needy. Father Guanella's group soon expanded its outreach beyond the local town and into the nearby city of Como. This group would, before long, develop into a religious order founded by Father Guanella: the Daughters of St. Mary of Providence. In time, he also founded an order of priests, the Servants of Charity, to work alongside the sisters. The need was great, and so both orders spread out to the cities of Italy and beyond to Switzerland.

Father Guanella showed special concern for people with developmental disabilities. They had few opportunities to live with dignity—to exercise their right to work, for example, or receive an education. Father Guanella treated them with respect. Once, while he was playing cards with a group of these boys, the bishop of Como arrived to see him. The boys were enjoying the game, so Father Guanella played to the end while the bishop waited. The bishop, who was accustomed to being treated as a dignitary, was deeply moved by the priest's fatherly love.

The Guanellians, as they are commonly called, established schools and residences for people with developmental disabilities. These institutions are today counted among the most respected facilities of their kind.

St. Luigi Guanella.
Father Guanella was beatified in 1964 by Pope Paul VI and canonized a saint on October 23, 2011, by Pope Benedict XVI.

Hearing about the poverty of many Italian immigrants living in the United States, Father Guanella went by ship to North America in 1912, at age 70. Even when he was very old, he worked tirelessly on behalf of the poor. He died in 1915 and was canonized a saint in 2011.

In the New Testament we read: "If a brother or sister is ill-clad and in lack of daily food, and one of you says to them, 'Go in peace, be warmed and filled,' without giving them the things needed for the body, what does it profit? So faith by itself, if it has no works, is dead" (Jas 2:15-17).

It was not enough for St. Luigi Guanella merely to recognize a need and feel sympathy. It was not enough for him merely to acknowledge that children with developmental disabilities possessed human dignity and human rights. He worked to give those children access to the means of fulfillment of their rights—so that they could enjoy life abundantly.

STEWARDSHIP OF GOD'S CREATION

When God gave Adam dominion over the earth, he delegated responsibility not simply for the *use* of creation, but for its *care* and *custody* as well. Adam was to exercise stewardship over all earthly goods: animals, plants, soil, and water. God made these to serve and delight not only Adam, but all future generations. The universal destination applied to all the goods of nature from the first moment of their creation.

Thus, to abuse the earth's resources—to overuse them, mishandle them, or unduly deplete them—is really to steal them from others to whom they are due.

> The seventh commandment enjoins respect for the integrity of creation. Animals, like plants and inanimate beings, are by nature destined for the common good of past, present, and future humanity.[29] Use of the mineral, vegetable, and animal resources of the universe cannot be divorced from respect for moral imperatives. Man's dominion over inanimate and other living beings granted by the Creator is not absolute; it is limited by concern for the quality of life of his neighbor, including generations to come; it requires a religious respect for the integrity of creation.[30] (CCC 2415)

Since the environment is the world common to all people, it should be respected.

Recent Popes have expressed grave concern for a situation they have, since 1990, called an "ecological crisis." St. John Paul II spoke of an "urgent moral need for a new solidarity"[31]—a bond of concern for future generations and also for those who share our ecosystem. For water and air do not observe national boundaries. What one nation does to these common resources affects many other nations' ability to use them.

Pope Benedict XVI sustained his predecessor's sense of alarm. He spoke to it urgently for the World Day of Peace in 2010, in a statement titled "If You Want to Cultivate Peace, Protect Creation."

To abuse the earth's resources—to overuse them, mishandle them, or unduly deplete them—is really to steal them from others to whom they are due.

> Sad to say, it is all too evident that large numbers of people in different countries and areas of our planet are experiencing increased hardship because of the negligence or refusal of many others to exercise responsible stewardship over the environment. The Second Vatican Ecumenical Council reminded us that "God has destined the earth and everything it contains for all peoples and nations."[32] The goods of creation belong to humanity as a whole. Yet the current pace of environmental exploitation is seriously endangering the supply of certain natural resources not only for the present generation, but above all for generations yet to come.[33] It is not hard to see that environmental degradation is often due to the lack of far-sighted official policies or to the pursuit of myopic economic interests, which then, tragically, become a serious threat to creation. To combat this phenomenon, economic activity needs to consider the fact that "every economic decision has a moral consequence"[34] and thus show increased respect for the environment. When making use of natural resources, we should be concerned for their protection and consider the cost entailed—environmentally and socially—as an essential part of the overall expenses incurred. The international community and national governments are responsible for sending the right signals in order to combat effectively the misuse of the environment. To protect the environment, and to safeguard natural resources and the climate, there is a need to act in

Human beings are the only animals that can will to care for other creatures and find a way to exercise such care with maximal effectiveness.

> accordance with clearly-defined rules, also from the juridical and economic standpoint, while at the same time taking into due account the solidarity we owe to those living in the poorer areas of our world and to future generations.

The Holy Father presented stewardship over creation not merely as obedience to a divine command, but as a requirement of human solidarity. While claiming no special expertise in the technical questions of environmental management, he nonetheless spoke for the Church, which is an "expert in humanity," and he called upon individuals, states, and the international community to take up responsibility for conservation of the earth's resources. "Natural resources should be used in such a way that immediate benefits do not have a negative impact on living creatures, human and not, present and future," he said, adding that the protection of private property should not conflict with the universal destination of goods. "The ecological crisis shows the urgency of a solidarity which embraces time and space."

The Church consistently bases this teaching upon God's charge to Adam in the opening chapters of Genesis. Adam receives dominion, the sort of authority that parents have in a home. Adam must tend, maintain, observe, conserve, reserve, allot, and plan for the wise use of all the resources he has been given.

Disorder came to earth when Adam refused to obey God. Pope Benedict XVI explained:

> "Human beings let themselves be mastered by selfishness; they misunderstood the meaning of God's command and exploited creation out of a desire to exercise absolute domination over it. But the true meaning of God's original command, as the Book of Genesis clearly shows, was not a simple conferral of authority, but rather a summons to responsibility…Man thus has a duty to exercise responsible stewardship over creation, to care for it and to cultivate it."

It is important, however, to recognize that God created all the goods of the earth for the service of humanity. Some ecological proposals fail to acknowledge this fundamental fact, asserting instead that

Legend of St. Francis, 2: St. Francis Giving His Mantle to a Poor Man by Giotto.
It is this utmost respect for human life and our status as creatures made in the image and likeness of God that animates all Catholic reflection on how people must relate to one another and to the physical world.

humanity occupies no special place in the natural order, and that the life of a human being is equivalent to that of other animals or even plants. This is contrary to Christian doctrine as well as common sense. Human beings are unique in all of the material world, in that they have spiritual souls and are created in God's image. This confers a unique dignity upon them. With that dignity comes responsibility for the care of other creatures. Human beings are the only animals that can will to care for other creatures and find a way to exercise such care with maximal effectiveness.

CONCLUSION

The entire body of Catholic social doctrine is founded upon the principle of the inherent dignity of the human person. It is this utmost respect for human life and our status as creatures made in the image and likeness of God that animates all Catholic reflection on how people must relate to one another and to the physical world. Out of this consideration of human dignity flows Catholic teaching on such matters as concern for the common good, the centrality of family life, the role of the faithful in society, the principles of solidarity and subsidiarity, the proper role and scope of civil government, the preferential option for the poor, the dignity of human work, and our responsibility for stewardship of the earth.

Sometimes those who are critical of Catholic social teaching like to attack certain aspects they find problematic. Some tend to elevate certain elements of this teaching, such as the defense of private ownership of property, without balancing them with other considerations, such as the universal destination of goods and the preferential option for the poor. When viewed and practiced as a whole, however, Catholic social doctrine represents a comprehensive and eminently reasonable system that fosters justice and celebrates the God-given dignity for all human persons.

The Saints
PILLARS OF THE CHURCH

ST. JOHN CHRYSOSTOM:
A Warning to the Wealthy

St. John Chrysostom, an early Church Father and Archbishop of Constantinople, was shocked to find rich families spending large sums of money for luxurious toilets while the poor were cold and hungry.

St. John Chrysostom
(ca. 347-407)

What can be more senseless than wealthy people…who make chamber pots of silver? You should be ashamed, who make these things. When Christ is famishing, do you revel in luxury?…

For it is not proper for a soul devoted to wisdom to have silver dishes, which themselves would be a luxury. But making silver vessels for filth, is this luxury? No, I will not call it luxury, but senselessness. Nor even senselessness, but madness; or, rather, worse than madness…

Another person, made after the image of God, is dying in the cold; and you furnish yourself with such things as these? O the senseless pride! What more would a madman have done? Do you pay such honor to your excrement, as to deposit it in silver? I know that you are shocked at hearing this; but those who make such things ought to be shocked.…For this is wantonness, and savageness, and inhumanity, and brutishness.

—*Homilies on Colossians* 7.5

SUPPLEMENTARY READING

Payback for Unjust Payment

Come now, you rich, weep and howl for the miseries that are coming upon you. Your riches have rotted and your garments are moth-eaten. Your gold and silver have rusted, and their rust will be evidence against you and will eat your flesh like fire. You have laid up treasure for the last days. Behold, the wages of the laborers who mowed your fields, which you kept back by fraud, cry out; and the cries of the harvesters have reached the ears of the Lord of hosts. You have lived on the earth in luxury and in pleasure; you have fattened your hearts in a day of slaughter. You have condemned, you have killed the righteous man; he does not resist you.

— James 5:1-6

Compendium of the Social Doctrine of the Church

I. The Family, The First Natural Society

209. *The importance and centrality of the family with regard to the person and society is repeatedly underlined by Sacred Scripture.* "It is not good that the man should be alone" (Gen 2:18). From the texts that narrate the creation of man (cf. Gen 1:26-28, 2:7-24) there emerges how—in God's plan—the couple constitutes "the first form of communion between persons."[35] Eve is created like Adam as the one who, in her otherness, completes him (cf. Gen 2:18) in order to form with him "one flesh" (Gen 2:24; cf. Mt 19:5-6).[36] At the same time, both are involved in the work of procreation, which makes them co-workers with the Creator: "Be fruitful and multiply, and fill the earth" (Gen 1:28). The family is presented, in the Creator's plan, as "the *primary place of 'humanization'* for the person and society" and the "cradle of life and love."[37]

210. *It is in the family that one learns the love and faithfulness of the Lord, and the need to respond to these* (cf. Ex 12:25-27, 13:8, 14-15; Deut 6:20-25, 13:7-11; 1 Sam 3:13). It is in the family that children learn their first and most important lessons of practical wisdom, to which the virtues are connected (cf. Prov 1:8-9, 4:1-4, 6:20-21; Sir 3:1-16, 7:27-28). Because of all this, the Lord himself is the guarantor of the love and fidelity of married life (cf. Mal 2:14-15).

Jesus was born and lived in a concrete family, accepting all its characteristic features[38] *and he conferred the highest dignity on the institution of marriage*, making it a sacrament of the new covenant (cf. Mt 19:3-9). It is in this new perspective that the couple finds the fullness of its dignity and the family its solid foundation.

211. *Enlightened by the radiance of the biblical message, the Church considers the family as the first natural society, with underived rights that are proper to it, and places it at the center of social life*. Relegating the family "to a subordinate or secondary role, excluding it from its rightful position in society, would be to inflict grave harm on the authentic growth of society as a whole."[39] The family, in fact, is born of the intimate communion of life and love founded on the marriage between one man and one woman.[40] It possesses its own specific and original social dimension, in that it is the principal place of interpersonal relationships, *the first and vital cell of society*.[41] The family is a divine institution that stands at the foundation of life of the human person as the prototype of every social order.

Importance of the Family for Society

213. *The family, the natural community in which human social nature is experienced, makes a unique and irreplaceable contribution to the good of society*. The family unit, in fact, is born from the communion of persons. "'Communion' has to do with the personal relationship between the 'I' and the 'thou.' 'Community' on the other hand transcends this framework and moves towards a 'society,' a 'we.' The family, as a community of persons, is thus the first human 'society.'"[42]

A society built on a family scale is the best guarantee against drifting off course into individualism or collectivism, because within the family the person is always at the center of attention as an end and never as a means. It is patently clear that the good of persons and the proper functioning of society are closely connected "with the healthy state of conjugal and family life."[43] Without families that are

SUPPLEMENTARY READING (Continued)

strong in their communion and stable in their commitment, peoples grow weak. In the family, moral values are taught starting from the very first years of life; the spiritual heritage of the religious community and the cultural legacy of the nation are transmitted. In the family one learns social responsibility and solidarity.[44]

214. *The priority of the family over society and over the State must be affirmed*. The family in fact, at least in its procreative function, is the condition itself for their existence. With regard to other functions that benefit each of its members, it proceeds in importance and value the functions that society and the State are called to perform.[45] The family possesses inviolable rights and finds its legitimization in human nature and not in being recognized by the State. *The family, then, does not exist for society or the State, but society and the State exist for the family.*

Every social model that intends to serve the good of man must not overlook the centrality and social responsibility of the family. In their relationship to the family, society and the State are seriously obligated to observe the principle of subsidiarity. In virtue of this principle, public authorities may not take away from the family tasks which it can accomplish well by itself or in free association with other families; on the other hand, these same authorities have the duty to sustain the family, ensuring that it has all the assistance that it needs to fulfil properly its responsibilities.[46]

St. John Paul II: Apostolic Exhortation *Familiaris Consortio*

The Family as the First and Vital Cell of Society

42. "Since the Creator of all things has established the conjugal partnership as the beginning and basis of human society," the family is "the first and vital cell of society."[47]

The family has vital and organic links with society, since it is its foundation and nourishes it continually through its role of service to life: it is from the family that citizens come to birth and it is within the family that they find the first school of the social virtues that are the animating principle of the existence and development of society itself.

Thus, far from being closed in on itself, the family is by nature and vocation open to other families and to society, and undertakes its social role.

Family Life as an Experience of Communion and Sharing

43. The very experience of communion and sharing that should characterize the family's daily life represents its first and fundamental contribution to society.

The relationships between the members of the family community are inspired and guided by the law of "free giving." By respecting and fostering personal dignity in each and every one as the only basis for value, this free giving takes the form of heartfelt acceptance, encounter and dialogue, disinterested availability, generous service and deep solidarity.

Thus the fostering of authentic and mature communion between persons within the family is the first and irreplaceable school of social life, and example and stimulus for the broader community relationships marked by respect, justice, dialogue and love.

The family is thus, as the Synod Fathers recalled, the place of origin and the most effective means for humanizing and personalizing society: it makes an original contribution in depth to building up the world, by making possible a life that is properly speaking human, in particular by guarding and transmitting virtues and "values." As the Second Vatican Council states, in the family "the various generations come together and help one another to grow wiser and to harmonize personal rights with the other requirements of social living."[48]

Consequently, faced with a society that is running the risk of becoming more and more depersonalized and standardized and therefore inhuman and dehumanizing, with the negative results of many forms of escapism—such as alcoholism, drugs, and even terrorism—the family possesses and continues still to release formidable energies capable of taking man out of his anonymity, keeping him conscious

SUPPLEMENTARY READING Continued

of his personal dignity, enriching him with deep humanity and actively placing him, in his uniqueness and unrepeatability, within the fabric of society.

The Social and Political Role

44. The social role of the family certainly cannot stop short at procreation and education, even if this constitutes its primary and irreplaceable form of expression.

Families therefore, either singly or in association, can and should devote themselves to manifold social service activities, especially in favor of the poor, or at any rate for the benefit of all people and situations that cannot be reached by the public authorities' welfare organization.

The social contribution of the family has an original character of its own, one that should be given greater recognition and more decisive encouragement, especially as the children grow up, and actually involving all its members as much as possible.[49]

In particular, note must be taken of the ever greater importance in our society of hospitality in all its forms, from opening the door of one's home and still more of one's heart to the pleas of one's brothers and sisters, to concrete efforts to ensure that every family has its own home, as the natural environment that preserves it and makes it grow. In a special way the Christian family is called upon to listen to the Apostle's recommendation: "Practice hospitality,"[50] and therefore, imitating Christ's example and sharing in His love, to welcome the brother or sister in need: "Whoever gives to one of these little ones even a cup of cold water because he is a disciple, truly, I say to you, he shall not lose his reward."[51]

The social role of families is called upon to find expression also in the form of political intervention: families should be the first to take steps to see that the laws and institutions of the State not only do not offend but support and positively defend the rights and duties of the family. Along these lines, families should grow in awareness of being "protagonists" of what is known as "family politics" and assume responsibility for transforming society; otherwise families will be the first victims of the evils that they have done no more than note with indifference. The Second Vatican Council's appeal to go beyond an individualistic ethic therefore also holds good for the family as such."[52]

Society at the Service of the Family

45. Just as the intimate connection between the family and society demands that the family be open to and participate in society and its development, so also it requires that society should never fail in its fundamental task of respecting and fostering the family.

The family and society have complementary functions in defending and fostering the good of each and every human being. But society—more specifically, the State—must recognize that "the family is a society in its own original right,"[53] and so society is under a grave obligation in its relations with the family to adhere to the principle of subsidiarity.

By virtue of this principle, the State cannot and must not take away from families the functions that they can just as well perform on their own or in free associations; instead it must positively favor and encourage as far as possible responsible initiative by families. In the conviction that the good of the family is an indispensable and essential value of the civil community, the public authorities must do everything possible to ensure that families have all those aids—economic, social, educational, political, and cultural assistance—that they need in order to face all their responsibilities in a human way.

The Charter of Family Rights

46. The ideal of mutual support and development between the family and society is often very seriously in conflict with the reality of their separation and even opposition.

In fact, as was repeatedly denounced by the Synod, the situation experienced by many families in various countries is highly problematical, if not entirely negative: institutions and laws unjustly ignore the inviolable rights of the family and of the human person; and society, far from putting itself at the service of the family, attacks it violently in its values and fundamental requirements. Thus the

SUPPLEMENTARY READING Continued

family, which in God's plan is the basic cell of society and a subject of rights and duties before the State or any other community, finds itself the victim of society, of the delays and slowness with which it acts, and even of its blatant injustice.

For this reason, the Church openly and strongly defends the rights of the family against the intolerable usurpations of society and the State. In particular, the Synod Fathers mentioned the following rights of the family:

— the right to exist and progress as a family, that is to say, the right of every human being, even if he or she is poor, to found a family and to have adequate means to support it;

— the right to exercise its responsibility regarding the transmission of life and to educate children;

— the right to the intimacy of conjugal and family life;

— the right to the stability of the bond and of the institution of marriage;

— the right to believe in and profess one's faith and to propagate it;

— the right to bring up children in accordance with the family's own traditions and religious and cultural values, with the necessary instruments, means and institutions;

— the right, especially of the poor and the sick, to obtain physical, social, political, and economic security;

— the right to housing suitable for living family life in a proper way;

— the right to expression and to representation, either directly or through associations, before the economic, social, and cultural public authorities and lower authorities;

— the right to form associations with other families and institutions, in order to fulfill the family's role suitably and expeditiously;

— the right to protect minors by adequate institutions and legislation from harmful drugs, pornography, alcoholism, etc.;

— the right to wholesome recreation of a kind that also fosters family values;

— the right of the elderly to a worthy life and a worthy death;

— the right to emigrate as a family in search of a better life.[54]

"The family, which in God's plan is the basic cell of society and a subject of rights and duties before the State or any other community, finds itself the victim of society, of the delays and slowness with which it acts, and even of its blatant injustice." (*FC* 46)

VOCABULARY

DIGNITY
The quality of being worthy or honorable; worthiness, nobility, excellence. Every human person, by reason of his or her creation in the image and likeness of God, has an intrinsic dignity. Certain characteristics that are distinctive in human beings—such as work and freedom—are endowed by God with a special dignity.

ECOLOGY
From the Greek *oikos* meaning a house or dwelling, this science deals with the relations of living organisms (especially humans) to their surroundings or habitats. This field also studies environmental issues.

EMINENT DOMAIN
This legal principle of civil law states that a government can claim private property, with compensation to the owner, because of a legitimate and overriding public concern. It is consonant with Catholic social doctrine when exercised in a just way, i.e., for the common good and with just compensation to the owner.

FAMILY
The fundamental unit of society and of the Church. The family is based upon the marriage of a man and a woman and includes their children. A Catholic family is a "domestic Church."

MARRIAGE (MATRIMONY)
A covenant or partnership for life between one man and one woman. Marriage is ordered to the good of the spouses and the procreation and upbringing of children. When validly contracted between two baptized persons, marriage is a Sacrament.

PERSON
An individual substance of a rational nature. Complete in itself, uncommunicable, and possessing responsibilities and rights as well as the essential elements of distinctiveness, uniqueness, intelligence, and will. A human person is an "individual, made in the image of God; he or she is not some thing but some one, a unity of spirit and matter, soul and body, capable of knowledge, self-possession, and freedom, who can enter into communion with other persons-- and with God (357, 362; cf. 1700)" (CCC Glossary).

POVERTY
The condition of want experienced by those who are poor, whom Christ called blessed, and for whom he had a special love. Poverty of spirit signifies humility and detachment from worldly things.

PROCREATION
The formation of new life through a married couple's cooperation with God and in response to their vocation.

PRO-LIFE
Term commonly used to identify individuals and organizations that oppose abortion and other affronts to human dignity.

RACISM
The theory that distinctive human characteristics and abilities are determined by race. This can be manifested in the different treatment of people based solely on race; in this way, it is a violation of human dignity and a sin against justice.

STEWARDSHIP
The responsible and just use of the world's resources.

STUDY QUESTIONS

1. What are the major themes of Catholic social doctrine discussed in this chapter?

2. What is the special dignity of human persons?

3. What is a family?

4. What is marriage?

5. Of what is marriage a sign?

6. Why is stable, lifelong marriage good for society?

7. What is the relationship between rights and responsibilities?

8. Why must Christians have a preferential love for the poor? What does this mean for individuals and societies?

9. Why do Christians consider work to be especially honorable?

10. What is a human being's relationship to natural resources? What rights and duties are implicit in this relationship?

PRACTICAL EXERCISES

1. Choose one: either (a) China's policy of one child per family or (b) the United States' abortion license (on-demand, unrestricted access to abortion). Research and analyze the social circumstance of this phenomenon and explain how it violates the principles of human dignity, the common good, subsidiarity, and solidarity. Consider each principle individually.

2. Choose one: either (a) homosexual unions, or (b) "no-fault" divorce. Research and analyze the social circumstance and explain how it works against the principles of human dignity, the common good, subsidiarity, and solidarity. Consider each principle individually.

3. How might the "preferential option for the poor" affect everyday consumer decisions in a global economy? How might poverty in "developing nations" influence a family's purchases in the "developed nations"? Give examples.

4. How might your "stewardship of God's creation" affect your everyday consumer decisions and household practices? How might consumption in "developed" nations affect the quality of everyday life in "developing" nations? Give examples.

Presentation in the Temple (detail) by Champaigne.
Every human person, by reason of his or her creation in the image and likeness of God, has an intrinsic dignity.

FROM THE CATECHISM

1882 Certain societies, such as the family and the state, correspond more directly to the nature of man; they are necessary to him. To promote the participation of the greatest number in the life of a society, the creation of voluntary associations and institutions must be encouraged "on both national and international levels, which relate to economic and social goals, to cultural and recreational activities, to sport, to various professions, and to political affairs."[55] This *"socialization"* also expresses the natural tendency for human beings to associate with one another for the sake of attaining objectives that exceed individual capacities. It develops the qualities of the person, especially the sense of initiative and responsibility, and helps guarantee his rights.[56]

1883 Socialization also presents dangers. Excessive intervention by the state can threaten personal freedom and initiative. The teaching of the Church has elaborated the principle of *subsidiarity*, according to which "a community of a higher order should not interfere in the internal life of a community of a lower order, depriving the latter of its functions, but rather should support it in case of need and help to coordinate its activity with the activities of the rest of society, always with a view to the common good."[57]

1978 The natural law is a participation in God's wisdom and goodness by man formed in the image of his Creator. It expresses the dignity of the human person and forms the basis of his fundamental rights and duties.

2237 *Political authorities* are obliged to respect the fundamental rights of the human person. They will dispense justice humanely by respecting the rights of everyone, especially of families and the disadvantaged.

The political rights attached to citizenship can and should be granted according to the requirements of the common good. They cannot be suspended by public authorities without legitimate and proportionate reasons. Political rights are meant to be exercised for the common good of the nation and the human community.

ENDNOTES – CHAPTER FIVE

1. St. John Paul II, *SRS* 47.
2. Cf. St. John XXIII, *PT* 65.
3. Second Vatican Council, *Apostolicam Actuositatem*, 11.
4. *FC* 42.
5. *Letter* 60.14.
6. *FC* 45.
7. CDF, *Donum Vitæ* III.
8. CDF, instruction, *Libertatis Conscientia*, 68.
9. *SRS* 42.
10. Ibid.
11. *CA* 57.
12. Cf. Gn 1:26-29.
13. *CA* 58.
14. Ibid.
15. *LE* 3
16. *LE* 6.
17. *LE* 2.
18. Cf. Fimister, Alan Paul, *Robert Schuman: Neo-Scholastic Humanism and the Reunification of Europe* (Brussels, Belgium: P.I.E. Peter Lang S.A., Editions scientifiques internationals, 2008), p. 33.
19. Cf. Entz, Geza, "Architects of the New Democracies, Jozsef Antall and Konrad Adenauer," *Hungarian Review*, Volume III., No. 3, May 14, 2012; cf. Williams, Charles, *Adenauer: The Father of a New Germany* (New York, New York: John Wiley & Sons, 2000), p. 221.
20. Cf. "The Christian Democracy for Freedom and Justice: The Address of Alcide De Gasperi on the Anniversary of *Rerum Novarum*," Rome, May 15, 1949.
21. "Preface of the 1993 Treaty of Maastricht," Official Journal of the European Communities (OJEC). July 29, 1992, No C 191. [s.l.], pp. 4, 5.
22. *LE* 9.
23. *SRS* 38.
24. St. John Paul II, "Address to Workers and Businessmen in Barcelona," November 7, 1982.
25. *SRS* 9.
26. Cf. *SRS* 17; 45.
27. *CA* 28; cf. 35.
28. Cf. *SRS* 16.
29. Cf. Gn 1:28-31.
30. Cf. *CA* 37-38.
31. *Message for the 1990 World Day of Peace*, 10.
32. *GS* 69.
33. Cf. *SRS* 34.
34. *CV* 37.
35. *GS* 12.
36. Cf. CCC 1605.
37. *CL* 40.
38. The Holy Family is an example of family life: "May Nazareth remind us what the family is, what the communion of love is, its stark and simple beauty, its sacred and inviolable character; may it help us to see how sweet and irreplaceable education in the family is; may it teach us its natural function in the social order. May we finally learn the lesson of work": Pope Paul VI, Address at Nazareth (January 5, 1964).
39. St. John Paul II, Letter to Families *Gratissimam Sane*, 17.
40. Cf. *GS* 48.
41. Cf. Second Vatican Ecumenical Council, Decree *Apostolicam Actuositatem*, 11.
42. St. John Paul II, Letter to Families *Gratissimam Sane*, 7; cf. CCC 2206.
43. *GS* 47; cf. CCC 2210.
44. Cf. CCC 2224.
45. Cf. Holy See, *Charter of the Rights of the Family*, Preamble, D-E (Rome: Vatican Polyglot Press, 1983), 6.
46. Cf. St. John Paul II, Apostolic Exhortation *Familiaris Consortio* 45; CCC 2209.
47. *AA* 11.
48. *GS* 52.
49. Cf. *DH* 5.
50. Rom. 12:13.
51. Mt. 10:42.
52. Cf. *GS* 30.
53. *DH* 5.
54. Cf. *Propositio* 42.
55. St. John XXIII, *MM* 60.
56. Cf. *GS* 25 § 2; *CA* 12.
57. *CA* 48 § 4; cf. Pius XI, *Quadragesimo Anno* I, 184-186.

Social Doctrine of the Catholic Church
CHAPTER 6

Law, Love, Sin, and Virtue

The Beatitudes are complementary to the Ten Commandments, and they fulfill and complete them, often in a more positive way.

Social Doctrine of the Catholic Church

CHAPTER SIX

Law, Love, Sin, and Virtue

THE COMMANDMENTS AND THE BEATITUDES: CLASSIC BIBLICAL EXPRESSIONS OF SOCIAL DOCTRINE

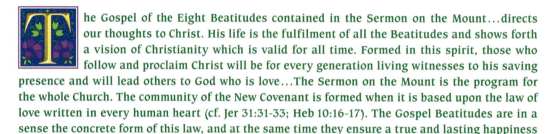he Gospel of the Eight Beatitudes contained in the Sermon on the Mount…directs our thoughts to Christ. His life is the fulfilment of all the Beatitudes and shows forth a vision of Christianity which is valid for all time. Formed in this spirit, those who follow and proclaim Christ will be for every generation living witnesses to his saving presence and will lead others to God who is love…The Sermon on the Mount is the program for the whole Church. The community of the New Covenant is formed when it is based upon the law of love written in every human heart (cf. Jer 31:31-33; Heb 10:16-17). The Gospel Beatitudes are in a sense the concrete form of this law, and at the same time they ensure a true and lasting happiness which springs from purity and peace of heart, the fruits of reconciliation with God and men.

— St. John Paul II
  Meeting with Polish Bishops' Conference, June 11, 1999

IN THIS CHAPTER, WE WILL ADDRESS SEVERAL QUESTIONS:

- What is "social sin"?
- What are "structures of sin"?
- What are the Ten Commandments?
- What is the social dimension of each Commandment?
- What are the Beatitudes?
- What is the social dimension of each Beatitude?

Movement in the physical world follows certain laws of physics. An object at rest tends to remain at rest unless acted upon by some external force. Every action brings about an equal and opposite reaction.

In the moral world, too, people tend to move according to certain laws. Ultimately, it is an *individual person* who makes a decision to act in a particular way. The individual is responsible for the action. In making the decision to act, however, the individual is influenced by many factors. These factors may include the advice and encouragement of other people, the promise of reward, the threat of punishment, the memory of past experience, and the limitations of environment. These factors can increase or

LAW, LOVE, SIN, AND VIRTUE

Christ Walking on the Waters by Klever.
"The Gospel Beatitudes…ensure a true and lasting happiness which springs from purity and peace of heart, the fruits of reconciliation with God and men." —St. John Paul II

mitigate personal guilt if the individual makes a bad decision. Good or bad, the decision will, in turn, influence *other* decisions made by *other* individuals.

No one is an island. When we act, our acts (or failures to act) have consequences. Our decisions affect others, and we bear some responsibility for their effects. With our everyday choices, we inevitably influence, impress, inspire, disgust, mislead, or corrupt those around us.

We are moral by nature because we have free will, the freedom to choose how to act.

We are social by nature because we live with others and depend upon them, and likewise they depend upon us.

There is, moreover, an inescapable social dimension to our moral life, as there is a necessary moral dimension to our social life.

PERSONAL SIN AND SOCIAL SIN

Though moral responsibility is always personal, it is often shared. Since we are social, we act with others in various ways, some passive and some active. Sometimes we cooperate with others by our action, and sometimes by our inaction. This is how the *Catechism* expresses the matter:

> Sin is a personal act. Moreover, we have a responsibility for the sins committed by others when we *cooperate in them*:
>
> —by participating directly and voluntarily in them;
>
> —by ordering, advising, praising, or approving them;
>
> —by not disclosing or not hindering them when we have an obligation to do so;
>
> —by protecting evil-doers. (CCC 1868)
>
> Thus sin makes men accomplices of one another and causes concupiscence, violence, and injustice to reign among them. Sins give rise to social situations and institutions that are contrary to the divine goodness. "Structures of sin" are the expression and effect of personal sins. They lead their victims to do evil in their turn. In an analogous sense, they constitute a "social sin."[1] (CCC 1869)

St. John Paul II, in his apostolic exhortation on reconciliation and penance, emphasized that sin is always "personal and untransferable" and can be called "social" only by analogy. People may be conditioned or influenced by external factors, but each person remains free. We should never try to transfer the blame for any sin to anyone or anything beyond ourselves.

Nevertheless, the Pope recognized that, because of human solidarity, we must acknowledge that each individual's sin in some way affects others. In this sense, he said, "every sin can undoubtedly be considered as social sin."[2]

Some sins, however, are social also because they are committed by one person against another person or persons. Such sins always have victims or accomplices—or both. For this reason, murder, adultery, and theft are always "social sins," because they invariably involve victims. The only aspect of these sins that is purely private is the decision to commit the evil deed.

By analogy, "social sin" can also be applied to institutions and structures. People speak colloquially of "evil corporations" when a company's executives choose to violate pollution standards, illegally fix prices, or deceive customers. A corporation cannot really commit a sin, because all sin is personal, an act of the human will. Sinners, however, can certainly conspire together; and they can construct organizations, processes, procedures, laws, and even societies that make it easy to commit sin and difficult to resist it. St. John Paul II described such situations as "sinful structures" or "structures of sin."

Dred Scott (1799-1858) was a slave who unsuccessfully sued the U.S. government for his freedom. The U.S. Supreme Court found that he, nor any person of African ancestry, could claim citizenship and therefore could not bring suit in a federal court.

Take an example from United States history. For years, many states had laws that denied basic rights to some citizens based on their race. Nonwhites could not vote, marry freely, or hold elected office. Those who enforced such laws were actively cooperating in evil, even though they were doing what the law required. The law itself compelled people to sin, as did the structures of society that supported the law. The evil of racism affected everything from voter registration to marriage licenses. The law "taught" a pervasive racist attitude that was reinforced through generations.

When laws are unjust, people are duty-bound to resist the laws and even disobey them. St. Augustine said that an unjust law has no compulsory power and, thus, does not have to be obeyed: "An unjust law is no law at all."[3]

This is a grave matter. The decision to resist or disobey a law should always be undertaken with serious spiritual reflection. Nevertheless, a Christian may not comply or cooperate with a law that requires actions that are objectively sinful.

This is why it is important for citizens to take as active an interest—and as active a part—in the legislative process as they can. The law is a teacher, said Aristotle; and saints such as St. Thomas More have invoked that same principle. Laws require people to do some things and forbid them to do other things. Every law implies that some course of action is right and another is wrong. Therefore, every law is implicitly "moral" in the sense that it makes a moral judgment. Laws teach citizens which behaviors will be accepted or tolerated by the community, and which will not—which actions are "good," and which actions are "evil," by the state's standards. Eventually, the state will tend to raise society, or drag it down, to the level of its legal standards. Over time, the law will change attitudes and practices—and society itself.

LAW, LOVE, SIN, AND VIRTUE

Pilate Washing His Hands (detail) by Duccio.
We must answer for our actions—and, in the end, we are answerable not to our employer, our government, or even our parents, but to God.

Take another example from the recent past. Through most of U.S. history, there was a general societal consensus against abortion. It was widely considered an immoral action, and the law reflected this consensus. Most states had laws severely restricting abortion. This was overturned abruptly by the United States Supreme Court in 1973. The court's decision in *Roe v. Wade* that year effectively nullified all national, state, and local laws restricting abortion.

If the law permits abortion or even requires government funding of the procedure, then it is teaching its citizens that a murderous action is not merely tolerable, but necessary, praiseworthy, and worthy of taxpayer support. It is a lesson learned too well. The number of abortions increased dramatically under the new, post-*Roe* legal climate. The law is a teacher, as Aristotle noted, and *Roe* taught many pregnant women, their boyfriends and husbands, many physicians, and many others—wrongly—that killing an unborn child is an acceptable solution to a wide range of problems.

Racial laws and abortion laws are just two examples of "sinful structures" that must be rejected by Christian conscience. As unjust laws, they are no laws at all, and, thus, they demand resistance. Christians must be prepared to suffer the consequences of unjust laws, and never give the appearance of approving or complying with them.

At the root of all such "social sins" are the personal sins of many people, who are complicit in making the system run. Also guilty are those who stand idly by and never raise their voices in protest, thus allowing injustice to happen. In the *Confiteor* that begins every Mass, we confess our sins "in what I have done, and what I have failed to do." We sin by the evil we do (sins of commission) as well as by the good that we fail to do (sins of omission).

It is a personal choice to submit to coercion. It is a personal choice to resist it, in spite of the consequences. But one person's courageous choice can inspire many others. That is the life story of many of the leaders profiled throughout this book—people like Cesar Chavez, John Howard Griffin, and King Baudouin of Belgium.

Catholics who would participate in society should be adept at identifying "structures of sin"—situations that could lead us to do what is wrong or deny what is right. We should judge all social structures by the measures of natural law and divine justice. We must answer for our actions—and, in the end, we are answerable not to our employer, our government, or even our parents, but to God.

Chapter Six

Tables of the Law with the Golden Calf (detail) by Rosselli.
In the Decalogue, God revealed the most fundamental moral law even though it had always been accessible by reason alone.

THE TEN COMMANDMENTS

The true standard for social conduct is to be found in God's will, which we find codified in various ways in Scripture. The most basic, binding, universal expression of the divine will is the Decalogue, or Ten Commandments. These simple laws describe the requirements for true worship and morality; they express the natural law engraved by God on the human heart (cf. Rom 2:14-15). The *Catechism* explains:

> The word "Decalogue" means literally "ten words."[4] God revealed these "ten words" to his people on the holy mountain. They were written "with the finger of God,"[5] unlike the other commandments written by Moses.[6] They are pre-eminently the words of God. They are handed on to us in the books of *Exodus*[7] and *Deuteronomy*.[8] Beginning with the Old Testament, the sacred books refer to the "ten words,"[9] but it is in the New Covenant in Jesus Christ that their full meaning will be revealed. (CCC 2056)

> The "ten words" sum up and proclaim God's law: "These words the LORD spoke to all your assembly at the mountain out of the midst of the fire, the cloud, and the thick darkness, with a loud voice; and he added no more. And he wrote them upon two tables of stone, and gave them to me."[10] For this reason these two tables are called "the Testimony." In fact, they contain the terms of the covenant concluded between God and his people. These "tables of the Testimony" were to be deposited in "the ark."[11] (CCC 2058)

The stone tablets of the Law were kept with the most sacred relics of Israel's exodus from Egypt, the nation's liberation from slavery. They were reserved for veneration first in Israel's Tabernacle, a portable tent that served as a center of worship during their journey through the wilderness en route to the Promised Land, and then in the innermost sanctuary of the Temple in Jerusalem. It was a reminder of God's manifestation to Moses and the Chosen People.

In the Decalogue, God revealed the most fundamental moral law even though it had always been accessible by reason alone. The Commandments are simply a summary of the demands of the natural law. The human person has an innate sense of certain moral truths of right and wrong. For example, even apart from special revelation, people know within their hearts that murder, adultery, and theft are wrongful acts. Even apart from special revelation, people can come to know that there is divinity to which we owe worship.

Humanity, however, was in such a state of sin that they could not discern true worship and true morality. Sin darkens the intellect and weakens the will. Sin smothers the voice of conscience. So a summary explanation of morality was necessary (see CCC 2071).

This is how the Ten Commandments appear in the Book of Deuteronomy (5:6-21):

> I am the LORD your God, who brought you out of the land of Egypt, out of the house of bondage. You shall have no other gods before me.
>
> You shall not take the name of the LORD your God in vain:...
>
> Observe the Sabbath day, to keep it holy,...
>
> Honor your father and your mother,...
>
> You shall not murder.
>
> Neither shall you commit adultery.
>
> Neither shall you steal.
>
> Neither shall you bear false witness against your neighbor.
>
> Neither shall you covet your neighbor's wife; and you shall not desire your neighbor's house, his field, or his manservant, or his maidservant, his ox, or his ass, or anything that is your neighbor's.

In the fullness of time, with the coming of Christ, the Law would be once again clearly inscribed "not on tablets of stone but on tablets of human hearts" (2 Cor 3:1).

All of the Commandments have a social dimension. It is explicit in the Commandments pertaining to moral behavior, but it is also present, though implicit, in the first three Commandments related to worship.

THE FIRST THREE COMMANDMENTS

The Commandments are often divided into two groups: the first contains the laws related to divine worship (the First, Second, and Third Commandments); the second contains the laws for human behavior, or the moral law (the Fourth through the Tenth Commandments).

The first three Commandments are concerned primarily with each human being's relationship to God. The First Commandment prescribes worship and reserves it to God alone, forbidding the worship of idols. The Second Commandment requires the respectful use of God's name and forbids the swearing of vain oaths. The Third Commandment enjoins Israel to observe the Sabbath as a day of rest and divine worship.

Though they impose a duty on individuals, they presume participation by a *people*—a community of faith.

> The duty to offer God authentic worship concerns man both as an individual and as a social being. (CCC 2136)

Moses and the Burning Bush by Brugger. The Second Commandment requires the respectful use of God's name.

The Adoration of the Golden Calf by Poussin.
The First Commandment prescribes worship and reserves it to God alone, forbidding the worship of idols.

Israel's worship was communal, sacrificial, and liturgical. When God commanded worship, he intended it to be according to the prescribed forms, in the prescribed assembly.

The content of this Commandment did not change with the New Testament, though the ritual forms were fulfilled in the Paschal Mystery of Jesus Christ. Christ established the Sacraments as the new order of worship, still communal, sacrificial, and liturgical. Now they take place not in a nation, or among one ethnic group, but are universal—that is, *catholic*—and take place in the Church. With his own command, "Do this in memory of me," Christ instituted the Mass as the Church's authentic worship, to be celebrated on the Lord's Day. The Apostles urged all Christians not to neglect "to meet together" (Heb 10:25). Thus the Church requires attendance at Mass on Sundays and Holy Days of Obligation.

Worship is communal, so the First and Third Commandments entail a certain social obligation. The *Catechism* speaks of another social obligation implicit in the First Commandment—to bring all people to know, love, and worship the one true God.

> The social duty of Christians is to respect and awaken in each man the love of the true and the good. It requires them to make known the worship of the one true religion which subsists in the Catholic and apostolic Church.[12] Christians are called to be the light of the world. Thus, the Church shows forth the kingship of Christ over all creation and in particular over human societies.[13] (CCC 2105)

The Second Commandment also assumes a social context. Oaths are sworn in courts of law or to seal agreements or treaties between two parties. They are public acts, public witnesses, that invoke God's name. Believers must use God's name respectfully and honor the commitments they make when they call God as their witness. Many martyrs suffered death rather than swear a false oath or simulate false worship. For example, St. Thomas More was condemned for treason because he would not swear an oath that claimed the King of England was the supreme head of the Church in that country.

It is important that society's authorities ensure the free exercise of religion. Christians should be vigilant in defending this right for themselves and protecting it for others. All people should be free to worship and conduct their lives according to the dictates of rightly formed consciences.

Thus, there is a social dimension even to the Commandments that deal with divine matters. God created men and women to be social by nature. He accommodates human nature even as he requires worship.

THE FAMILY: WHERE SOCIAL ORDER BEGINS

In response to the question about the first of the commandments, Jesus says: "The first is, 'Hear, O Israel: The Lord our God, the Lord is one; and you shall love the Lord your God with all your heart, and with all your soul, and with all your mind, and with all your strength.' The second is this, 'You shall love your neighbor as yourself.' There is no other commandment greater than these."[14]

The apostle St. Paul reminds us of this: "He who loves his neighbor has fulfilled the law. The commandments, *You shall not commit adultery, You shall not kill, You shall not steal, You shall not covet,* and any other commandment, are summed up in this sentence, 'You shall love your neighbor as yourself.' Love does no wrong to a neighbor; therefore love is the fulfilling of the law."[15] (CCC 2196)

The second group of Commandments—the last seven Commandments—focus on relationships between and among human beings. Here the moral teaching of the Catholic Faith is brought into people's everyday interactions. Each Commandment may be considered in terms of its positive and negative requirements: Each Commandment requires certain behaviors (at least by implication) and prohibits others.

The first of these, the Fourth Commandment, is very important in Catholic social thought. It marks the necessary foundation of order in society, since the family is society's fundamental unit. The Commandment states: "Honor your father and your mother, that your days may be long in the land which the Lord your God gives you" (Ex 20:12), and St. Paul noted that it is "the first commandment with a promise" (Eph 6:1). The implication for St. Paul was very clear: "Children, obey your parents in the Lord, for this is right" (Eph 6:1).

Christ himself serves as a model for such respect. Regarding his relationship with his parents, the Gospel reports that he "was obedient to them" (Lk 2:51). As he was dying on the Cross, Christ made arrangements for the care of his mother (cf. Jn 19:26-27). If anyone could be exempt from obligations of obedience and subservience, it would be Christ, who is God incarnate. But he willingly took up these duties as he assumed human nature. To honor one's parents is to live in a truly human way; and in his obedience and care Christ showed himself to be truly human as well as truly divine.

The Child Jesus Going down with His Parents to Nazareth by Dobson.
To honor one's parents is to live in a truly human way.

Salvation came by way of the family. Jesus Christ was born of a human Mother, the Blessed Virgin Mary, and reared by her and St. Joseph. Their household, revered as "The Holy Family" is a model for all families. "The Christian family is a communion of persons, a sign and image of the communion of the Father and the Son in the Holy Spirit" (CCC 2205). St. John Paul II explained:

> In the light of the New Testament it is possible to discern how the primordial model of the family is to be sought in God himself, in the Trinitarian mystery of his life. The divine "We" is the eternal pattern of the human "we," especially of that "we" formed by the man and the woman created in the divine image and likeness.[16]

The family fails to correspond to the divine model when there is discord or disobedience in the home. Christ was always obedient to his Father in Heaven (cf. Phil 2:8), and he was likewise obedient to his parents on earth, Mary and Joseph (cf. Lk 2:51).

THE SOCIAL DOCTRINE OF THE CATHOLIC CHURCH

In his public ministry, Christ made some provocative statements about the relationship between children and parents. "Call no man your father on earth," he said, "for you have one Father, who is in heaven" (Mt 23:9). He also told the multitudes: "If any one comes to me and does not hate his own father and mother…he cannot be my disciple" (Lk 14:25).

Here, as in all verses of Scripture, we need to read these statements in light of the rest of the New Testament (and, indeed, the whole Bible). Christ loved his parents and paid them due honor. He kept all the Commandments, including the Fourth. By no means did he annul or undermine parental authority. In fact, his statements made the contrary point: As important as parental authority is, God's authority is still greater. Sons and daughters owe far less, in terms of love and obedience, to their parents than they owe to God, who created and redeemed them. God is more a Father to Christians than their human fathers ever can be.

Christian teaching has always understood the Fourth Commandment as enjoining obedience beyond the family as well as to all legitimate authorities. St. Paul told the Romans (13:1-2):

> Let every person be subject to the governing authorities. For there is no authority except from God, and those that exist have been instituted by God. Therefore he who resists the authorities resists what God has appointed, and those who resist will incur judgment.

And the *Catechism* explains:

> The fourth commandment is addressed expressly to children in their relationship to their father and mother, because this relationship is the most universal. It likewise concerns the ties of kinship between members of the extended family. It requires honor, affection, and gratitude toward elders and ancestors. Finally, it extends to the duties of pupils to teachers, employees to employers, subordinates to leaders, citizens to their country, and to those who administer or govern it.

> This commandment includes and presupposes the duties of parents, instructors, teachers, leaders, magistrates, those who govern, all who exercise authority over others or over a community of persons. (CCC 2199)

Civil authority, then, is analogous to parental authority, and it is intended to be a participation in God's governance over creation. The common good is the reason why we have human authority and laws. Human laws participate in the divine law when they apply natural precepts to specific circumstances. Thus, the effect of civil law exceeds its own reach—and becomes a moral obligation—only when it fulfills the moral function that legitimizes it. On the other hand, when a civil law claims absolute value and is severed from the natural moral order, it must be rejected in conscience.

Based on the Fourth Commandment, the Church stands opposed to tyranny, anarchy, corruption in government, and any other sinful circumstance that undermines legitimate authority.

Peace is tranquility in order. No society can enjoy peace if its families are in disarray or dissolution. A healthy society is invariably composed of healthy families. This is the most basic application of the principle of subsidiarity. The home is also the place where solidarity begins, in the bonds of filial and parental love.

The family, society's most basic unit, is where social order begins.

The Rest on the Return from Egypt by Barocci. The home is the place where solidarity begins, in the bonds of filial and parental love.

CHOOSE LIFE

I call heaven and earth to witness against you this day, that I have set before you life and death, blessing and curse; therefore choose life, that you and your descendants may live. (Dt 30:19)

A profound respect for life set Christianity apart from the traditional cultures of the ancient world. Pagan religion offered little in the way of moral reflection. The leading lights of classical philosophy offered no significant qualms about the routine taking of human life. Abortion, infanticide, and euthanasia were widespread. Suicide was counted a virtuous act. Capital punishment was meted out for many crimes. Executions were arranged as public entertainment—spotlight moments in the circus or in a dramatic portrayal of mythic stories. Condemned criminals would be forced to play starring roles in cosmic tragedies that ended with their own fiery or bloody demise. Warfare was uninhibited; and torture, humiliation, and slaughter were visited upon civilian populations. Human life was cheap, and killing was seen as an acceptable way of coping with personal or social problems.

Rest on Flight to Egypt (detail) by Caravaggio. There can be no true peace in a society that permits the killing of its vulnerable members.

In such a world, Christianity set itself apart as a way of life, and the only saving alternative to a pervasive culture of death. Christianity defended those who were chronically ill, disabled, or otherwise vulnerable. These poor souls would have been routinely left for dead in the Greco-Roman world, but instead they found care—following the legalization of Christianity—in the new, rising institutions established by Christians: orphanages, hospices, shelters, and hospitals.

Christian morality—consistently and from the start—has been characterized by what we might call a preferential option for life. The right to life is sacred. It is fundamental—the precondition of all other rights—and it is inalienable. The Fifth Commandment forbids the taking of human life by murder, abortion, infanticide, euthanasia, or suicide. The sacredness of human life, which begins at the moment of conception and extends through natural death, also forbids such practices as human cloning and genetic manipulation. If a society tolerates or promotes any of these sins, then no rights will be secure because no life will be safe. There can be no true peace in a society that permits the killing of its vulnerable members or violations of the sanctity of life.

The gravity of such sins is evident from the earliest pages of Scripture.

> In the account of Abel's murder by his brother Cain,[17] Scripture reveals the presence of anger and envy in man, consequences of original sin, from the beginning of human history. Man has become the enemy of his fellow man. God declares the wickedness of this fratricide: "What have you done? The voice of your brother's blood is crying to me from the ground. And now you are cursed from the ground, which has opened its mouth to receive your brother's blood from your hand."[18] (CCC 2259)

> The covenant between God and mankind is interwoven with reminders of God's gift of human life and man's murderous violence:
>
>> For your lifeblood I will surely require a reckoning....Whoever sheds the blood of man, by man shall his blood be shed; for God made man in his own image.[19]
>
>> The Old Testament always considered blood a sacred sign of life.[20] This teaching remains necessary for all time. (CCC 2260)

Scripture elaborates on the Commandment, specifying: "Do not slay the innocent and the righteous" (Ex 23:7; cf. CCC 2261). Christ quoted the Commandment and went farther still, proscribing even anger, hatred, and the desire for revenge, which are often preconditions of murder (see Mt 5:22-39, 44; CCC 2262).

BAUDOUIN: A King and His Conscience

Baudouin was the eldest son and heir apparent of King Leopold III of Belgium. Born in 1930, he was just twenty years old when he assumed the throne as king. It was 1951, and his country was still in disarray in the aftermath of World War II. The young king was a unifying figure for Belgium, beloved by his people. He reigned during a difficult time, managing Belgium's transition from a colonial power to a modern European state. Baudouin even attended the festivities when the African nation of Congo, a former Belgian colony, was declared independent.

Queen Fabiola and King Baudouin of Belgium.

In 1960, he married a Spanish noblewoman, Doña Fabiola de Mora y Aragón. The couple were known for their deep Catholic faith. They made regular pilgrimages to a favorite shrine in France, and they were active in the Catholic Charismatic Renewal.

In modern constitutional monarchies, the king serves a mostly ceremonial role, but ceremony counts for something. In Belgium, the king's signature is required on every law passed by the legislature.

In 1990, when Belgium's Parliament passed a law permitting abortion, Baudouin refused to give royal assent. This threatened to create a constitutional crisis. The king's approval was necessary for a law to be enacted, but it had always been considered a mere formality.

Baudouin stood firmly in opposition to the measure, though he saw that the standoff had the potential to bring down the monarchy. Yet, he could not compromise. He noted that the bill approved of abortion if the child to be born suffers "a particularly grave anomaly recognized as incurable at the moment of diagnosis." Baudouin asked: "Have we considered how such a message will be perceived by the handicapped and their families?…I fear that this law will contribute to a palpable diminution of respect for the lives of the weakest among us." In a letter to Parliament, he asked: "Does freedom of conscience apply to everyone except the king?"

Baudouin brought in world-renowned experts, such as the geneticist Dr. Jerome Lejeune, to help him make his case. It was to no avail. He could not sway Parliament's majority.

The government declared him temporarily unable to reign. On that day, the members of government signed the infamous bill; the next day, parliamentarians restored Baudouin to the throne.

King Baudouin was criticized by some for going along with the evasion. But he saw no better alternative. As long as he was king, he could at least exercise some moral influence on a country that was taking a turn for the worse. He managed to remain in office, publicly arguing the pro-life cause, while the world media listened, at least out of curiosity. He strove to take no action that would offend God.

King Baudouin died suddenly of heart failure in 1993. At his funeral, the Archbishop of Brussels said: "For him, conscience was absolute. It was the voice of the deepest part of the human person and the voice of God. He always followed it, even at the risk of his personal interests, even at the risk of putting the monarchy into question. He knew that human life was worth such a price."

As Abel's murder cried out to God, so does the taking of innocent life to this day. The Church has focused her teaching particularly on anti-life practices that have become increasingly pervasive and tolerated in recent years.

Abortion

The most grievous direct offense against human life today is arguably that of *abortion*, the deliberate termination of a pregnancy by the killing of the unborn child. Human life begins at the moment of conception and must be protected absolutely from that moment forward. This is implicit in both the Old and New Testaments, and it has been the consistent teaching of the Church since the first century. Anyone who procures an abortion is automatically excommunicated (see CCC 2272), as are those who participate or cooperate in the action—performing the procedure, assisting at it, paying for it, providing transportation, and so on. The Church attaches the most severe penalties to this practice because of its great gravity and the irreparable harm it causes.

Euthanasia, Suicide, and Assisted Suicide

A sin against the Fifth Commandment at the other end of the life cycle is the practice of *euthanasia*, an action or omission that causes the death of a handicapped, sick, or dying person. (Refusing to prolong a dying person's life by extraordinary or unnatural means—i.e., beyond providing basic sustenance—is not contrary to Church teaching, however.) It is sometimes justified as "mercy killing," because it aims to end suffering. Euthanasia arises from a devaluing of human life—a belief that certain lives are not worth living because they involve conditions that are difficult, painful, or simply embarrassing. Suffering has profound meaning in Christian life. The Cross of Jesus Christ, with all its pain and humiliation, is the symbol of human redemption, and everyone is called to "take up his cross" (Mt 16:24), in order to share the life of the Son of God. St. Paul explained:

Christ Carrying the Cross by Titian. The Cross of Jesus Christ, with all its pain and humiliation, is the symbol of human redemption, and everyone is called to "take up his cross."

> We are children of God, and if children, then heirs, heirs of God and fellow heirs with Christ, provided we suffer with him in order that we may also be glorified with him. (Rom 8:16-17)

The Fifth Commandment extends even to the respect for our own lives and bodies. *Suicide*, the willful taking of one's own life, offends this commandment. God alone is the master of life, therefore, we are forbidden to take human life, even our own. Suicide is a denial of God's sovereignty, his plan, and his ability to bring good out of suffering. It also brings lasting harm to those left behind.

The Church does recognize, however, that there may be many attenuating circumstances that could diminish the subjective gravity of this kind of tragic action. For example, severe psychological problems many diminish responsibility for suicide. For this reason, "the Church prays for persons who have taken their own lives" (CCC 2283).

It is a grave offense to help another person commit suicide. Thus, *assisted suicide*, which sometimes is practiced even under the auspices of health-care professionals who provide the means for taking one's own life, is also forbidden by the Commandment.

Self-Defense and Capital Punishment

The giving and taking of life is at God's discretion and his alone. The Church, however, recognizes limited exceptions. One of these involves the *right of self-defense*, which may sometimes involve lethal force. St. Thomas Aquinas explained that such actions have "double effect": the preservation of one's own life, or the life of another innocent person, and the killing of the aggressor. One is intended, while the other is not (cf. CCC 2263).

Self-defense can be not only a right but a grave duty for someone who bears responsibility for the lives of others—parents, for example, who must guard their children, or police, who must protect entire communities.

Christ Taken Prisoner by Cesari.
The act of self-defense is compatible with the Fifth Commandment as long as its purpose is to respect and protect innocent life.

Capital punishment is the execution by the state of individuals who have committed particularly heinous crimes. The Church has always recognized the authority of the state "to inflict punishment proportionate to the gravity of the offense" (CCC 2266; cf. Rom 13:4). The state has the authority even to inflict the ultimate penalty, the death penalty, if there is no other way to defend innocent lives from harm and murder. In recent years, however, the Popes and bishops have advocated consistently for mercy in such cases. The *Catechism* spells out the Church's pastoral position:

> Assuming that the guilty party's identity and responsibility have been fully determined, the traditional teaching of the Church does not exclude recourse to the death penalty, if this is the only possible way of effectively defending human lives against the unjust aggressor.
>
> If, however, non-lethal means are sufficient to defend and protect people's safety from the aggressor, authority will limit itself to such means, as these are more in keeping with the concrete conditions of the common good and more in conformity to the dignity of the human person.
>
> Today, in fact, as a consequence of the possibilities which the state has for effectively preventing crime, by rendering one who has committed an offense incapable of doing harm—without definitely taking away from him the possibility of redeeming himself—the cases in which the execution of the offender is an absolute necessity "are very rare, if not practically nonexistent."[21] (CCC 2267)

The Church clearly prefers and urges that the state *not* impose the death penalty if the criminal can be securely incarcerated and kept from harming others. There is a presumption in favor of preserving the life even of capital offenders, in part out of hope for their eventual reform and conversion. One could argue convincingly that capital punishment is not an "absolute necessity" in politically stable developed nations that have effective prison systems. We will always hear the Pope and other Church leaders advocating for sparing the life of those sentenced to death.

Scandal

The Church also considers *scandal*—an attitude or behavior that tempts or leads other people to sin—among the offenses against the Fifth Commandment. Why is this considered alongside the stealing of life? Because if we set a bad example—if, for instance, by our words and actions, we lead someone else to try drugs, engage in sinful sexual practices, or take up criminal activity, we are diminishing their capacity for life. We are taking their good life away from them and leading them into destructive behaviors that may indeed shorten their lifespan and could certainly estrange them from God (see CCC 2284-2287).

JUST WAR

Just as individuals have a right to self-defense, so do nations. Christians are obligated to work for peace and do everything possible to avoid going to war. But the Church recognizes that governments cannot be denied the right to defend themselves by military means. Nevertheless, their reasons must be sound, and their cause must be just. To guide people in discerning such circumstances, the Church has developed its just-war doctrine.

Philosophers in the ancient world had grappled with the question of when war was justified, but their speculations produced little effect in the real world. Armies going to war did not need to justify their actions. All was considered fair on the battlefield, and ordinary moral restraints could be suspended. Civilians were targeted as much as warriors. Mercy, in the pagan world, was considered a sign of weakness.

Moreover, conquest and plunder were the bread and butter of imperial powers. Stronger peoples made a business of invading weaker peoples to steal their treasure, take over their lands, and enslave their populations.

The Church opposed such warfare. Early Church Fathers such as St. Augustine argued that terrible evils always accompany war, and in order for it to be justified, the effects of *not* going to war must be even worse. War must always be for the sake of peace; and all the moral laws that apply in peace must also be observed on the battlefield.

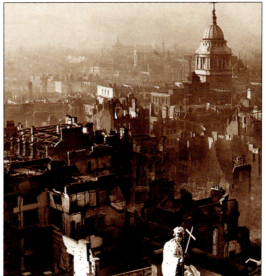

Ruins of St. Paul's Cathedral after the London Blitz. Starting on September 7, 1940, London was bombed by Germany for fifty-seven consecutive nights. More than one million London houses were destroyed or damaged, and more than 40,000 civilians were killed, almost half of them in London.

In the thirteenth century, St. Thomas Aquinas developed the principles of just-war theory, and they have been refined over the centuries to be very restrictive. In Catholic doctrine, there are four criteria that must *all* be met before it is legitimate to consider going to war (see CCC 2309):

✤ the damage inflicted by the aggressor on the nation or community of nations must be lasting, grave, and certain;

✤ all other means of putting an end to it must have been shown to be impractical or ineffective;

✤ there must be serious prospects of success;

✤ the use of arms must not produce evils and disorders graver than the evil to be eliminated. The power of modern means of destruction weighs very heavily in evaluating this condition.

The decision to go to war is always a prudential judgment resting with a country's legitimate authorities, and Catholics may differ about whether a particular conflict should be called "just." But there is a standard now, as there was not in the pre-Christian world. Even the most aggressive dictators know that some show of justice is essential for their standing among the nations, and that some show of proportionality in fighting the war is the only thing that will keep them from being shunned by the world community.

Even in the prosecution of a just war, however, authorities should accommodate those who declare themselves to be conscientious objectors (cf. CCC 2311). The state, however, may require them to serve their country in some alternative way.

HOLY PURITY

As we turn to the second half of the Ten Commandments, we find two that are closely related to one another, the Sixth and Ninth Commandments. The Sixth promotes chaste love and forbids the misuse of sexuality. The Ninth forbids attitudes and dispositions that would incline a person toward sexual sin.

Why does human sexuality merit two Commandments? Because it is supremely important. God made man and woman with complementary bodies and souls, so that they would seek a measure of fulfillment in their love for one another. Joining together in this way, they would also share in God's power to bring new life into being. Their act would not be mere "mating," which all animals do, but *pro-creation*, which is participation in a divine activity: the creation of a new human being, with a spiritual soul.

When the marital act is used apart from its proper context, it is like a desecration of the sacred vessels used in the Mass.

God willed that the two should become "one flesh." He commanded Adam and Eve to fill the earth—to be fruitful and multiply. He pronounced their union to be "very good."

With great power, however, comes great responsibility. Thus, our sexual faculties are protected by *two* Commandments. Together, these precepts root out not only bad behaviors, but also the mental habits and attitudes that would predispose people to do bad things. Christ often gave his disciples this sort of practical spiritual direction. He confirmed the prohibition of murder, for example, but he also directed people not even to allow themselves to grow angry. Similarly, he confirmed the Sixth Commandment, but he also told his followers not even to *look* lustfully at another person:

> You have heard that it was said, "You shall not commit adultery." But I say to you that every one who looks at a woman lustfully has already committed adultery with her in his heart. (Mt 5:27-28)

Sex belongs to marriage. Outside marriage, sex tends to cause havoc—jealousy and betrayal, manipulation and insecurity, stunted communication. The Sixth and Ninth Commandments place a needed discipline on a drive that has been disordered by Original Sin.

St. Paul spoke of the one-flesh union of husband and wife as a great sign of the union of Christ and the Church. In Latin, the phrase is *magnum sacramentum*, which can also be translated as "great sacrament"; and so Christians have always honored marriage as a sacramental sign. Commentators from St. John Chrysostom to St. John Paul II have observed that the union of husband and wife, producing a child, provides an earthly image of the Blessed Trinity. And this is why sexual sins are all grave sins: because they involve a power so sublime, powerful, and beautiful. When the marital act is used apart from its proper context, it is like a desecration of the sacred vessels used in the Mass. The problem is not with sex itself, but with its misuse—its abuse. Like those sacred vessels, the marital act has a

BL. FRANZ JAGERSTATTER:
Conscientious Objector and Martyr

Franz Jagerstatter was born in 1907 in St. Radegund, Upper Austria, to his unmarried mother, Rosalia Huber, and to Franz Bachmeier, who was killed during World War I. After the death of his natural father, Rosalia married Heinrich Jagerstatter, who adopted Franz and gave the boy his surname in 1917.

*Bl. Franz Jagerstatter (1907-1943)
His conscience prevailed over the path of least resistance.*

Franz received a basic education in his village's one-room schoolhouse. His step-grandfather helped with his education and the boy became an avid reader.

While it seems Franz was unruly in his younger years—he was the first in his village to own a motorcycle—he is better known as an ordinary and humble Catholic who did not draw attention to himself.

After his marriage to Franziska in 1936 and their honeymoon in Rome, Franz grew in his faith but was not extreme in his piety.

Besides his farm work, in 1936 Franz became the local sexton—one who takes care of the parish church, from ringing the bell to digging graves—and began receiving the Eucharist daily. He was known to refuse the customary offering for his services at funerals, preferring the spiritual and corporal works of mercy over any remuneration. In 1940, Franz became a Third Order (Secular) Franciscan.

In the mid to late 1930s, while much of Austria was beginning to follow the tide of Nazism, Franz became ever more rooted in his Catholic faith and placed his complete trust in God.

While carrying out his duties as husband and bread-winner for his wife and three daughters, this ordinary man began thinking deeply about obedience to legitimate authority and obedience to God, about mortal life and eternal life and about Christ's suffering and Passion.

Franz was neither a revolutionary nor part of any resistance movement, but in 1938 he was the only local citizen to vote against the "Anschluss" (annexation of Austria by Germany), because his conscience prevailed over the path of least resistance.

Franz Jagerstatter was called up for military service and sworn in on June 17, 1940. Shortly thereafter, thanks to the intervention of his mayor, he was allowed to return to the farm. Later, he was in active service from October 1940 to April 1941, until the mayor's further intervention permitted his return home.

He became convinced that participation in the war was a serious sin and decided that any future call-up had to be met with his refusal to fight.

"It is very sad," he wrote, "to hear again and again from Catholics that this war waged by Germany is perhaps not so unjust because it will wipe out Bolshevism….But now a question: what are they fighting in this country—Bolshevism or the Russian People?

"When our Catholic missionaries went to a pagan country to make them Christians, did they advance with machine guns and bombs in order to convert and improve them?…

Continued

BL. FRANZ JAGERSTATTER:
Conscientious Objector and Martyr
Continued

If adversaries wage war on another nation, they have usually invaded the country not to improve people or even perhaps to give them something, but usually to get something for themselves....If we were merely fighting Bolshevism, these other things—minerals, oil wells or good farmland—would not be a factor."

Jagerstatter was at peace with himself despite the alarm he could have experienced witnessing the masses' capitulation to Hitler. Mesmerized by the National Socialist propaganda machine, many people knelt when Hitler made his entrance into Vienna. Catholic Churches were forced to fly the swastika flag and subjected to other abusive laws.

In February 1943 Franz was called up again for military service. He presented himself at the induction center and announced his refusal to fight, offering to carry out nonviolent services. His offer was denied.

Held in custody at Linz and eventually tried in Berlin on July 6, 1943, he was condemned to death for sedition. The prison chaplain was struck by the man's tranquil character. On being offered a copy of the New Testament, he replied, "I am completely bound in inner union with the Lord, and any reading would only interrupt my communication with my God."

On August 9, before being executed, Franz wrote: "If I must write…with my hands in chains, I find that much better than if my will were in chains. Neither prison nor chains nor sentence of death can rob a man of the Faith and his free will. God gives so much strength that it is possible to bear any suffering.... People worry about the obligations of conscience as they concern my wife and children. But I cannot believe that, just because one has a wife and children, a man is free to offend God."

Franz Jagerstatter, who would not bow his head to Hitler, bowed his head to God, and the guillotine took care of the rest. He was obviously called up to serve a higher order.

— *Adapted from the Vatican's biography for his beatification*

---

prominent place in God's design for our sacramental life. To use it in any other way is to violate his will—and prevent the "sign" of the Sacrament from signifying its true meaning.

If the marital act is intended to reflect the loving communion of the Trinity, its proper place is in the permanent, exclusive, faithful, loving relationship provided by the bond of marriage, and it must be open to the procreation of life.

Any sexual act that violates these qualities is unworthy of God's gift. Sexual sins are profoundly degrading. Among them are adultery, fornication, masturbation, homosexual acts, rape, prostitution, and the use of pornography (see CCC 2351-2356, 2514-2533).

All of these sins have serious social consequences, since they always involve more than one person. At the most basic level, sexuality affects every aspect of a person, including the ability to be in communion with and have relationships with other people. Integrating chastity allows a person to become truly human, which benefits relationships with others and thus society as a whole. The virtue of chastity bears fruit in the gift of self, leading to genuine friendship with others and to spiritual communion.

Some people claim that the use of pornography is "victimless," but that is not true. The industry exploits the desperation of many people who need money. They are the first victims, and those who use pornography are helping to victimize them. But users of pornography are also victimizing themselves and their families, since their habit will almost certainly affect their experience of marriage in a negative way. Also, those in thrall to the perverting effects of pornography have been motivated to commit heinous crimes.

Prostitution is contrary to the value of both parties involved, especially to the one who has been reduced to an instrument of sexual pleasure. Its proliferation and acceptance is accompanied often by more social sins of scandal and blackmail, which affect society. Rape, or the violation of another person's sexual intimacy by force, wounds the respect and freedom due to every person made in God's image. It can wound a victim for life, especially emotionally, which has great effects on his or her relationships with others, especially a (future) spouse.

Similarly, masturbation is not truly a solitary act. It is an injustice because it takes a faculty that properly belongs to one's (future) spouse and uses it for oneself. It is a result of and engenders lust, which is a disordered desire or enjoyment of sexual pleasure, sought for oneself and not placed at the service of communion.

Fornication, or sexual intercourse between an unmarried man and an unmarried woman, is contrary to the dignity of the person and marriage; it can also scandalize others in society as well as affect attitudes regarding the correct meaning of marriage and the marital act. Homosexual acts are contrary to marriage and the intended purposes of the marital act; their acceptance reduces attitudes in society about the purposes of human sexuality as if sexual pleasure were the highest good. Similarly, adultery, or marital infidelity, is contrary to human dignity, marriage, and the rights of the other spouse; it can sow discord between the spouses, with their children and families, and in their various societies.

We should strive to have very high standards in preserving purity. We should avoid viewing not only material that qualifies as pornography, but also any advertisements or television programs that show people immodestly dressed. In fact, even beyond that, we should not continue with any thought, word, or act that arouses sexual desire outside of the context of the married love of husband and wife.

It is sad but true that many of the dating practices that are considered "normal" in modern society routinely involve sins against the Sixth and Ninth Commandments. To live a good life—and a truly happy life—we must make a firm commitment to be counter-cultural, and not just blind followers. We do not need to abuse friendship and love by misusing our sexuality. Our friends deserve better treatment from us. Our dates deserve better treatment from us. God has placed these people in our lives, and he deserves the best we have.

A society will be healthy inasmuch as its families are healthy; and its families' health—your family's health—depends upon faithfulness to the Sixth and Ninth Commandments.

WHAT GOODS ARE GOOD FOR

With the Seventh Commandment, God seeks to restore humanity's just relationship to the material world. When God created the earth, he entrusted its resources to the human race. Adam was to exercise stewardship and mastery over the world and its goods.

> In the beginning God entrusted the earth and its resources to the common stewardship of mankind to take care of them, master them by labor, and enjoy their fruits.[22] The goods of creation are destined for the whole human race. However, the earth is divided up among men to assure the security of their lives, endangered by poverty and threatened by violence. The appropriation of property is legitimate for guaranteeing the freedom and dignity of persons and for helping each of them to meet his basic needs and the needs of those in his charge. It should allow for a natural solidarity to develop between men. (CCC 2402)

Original Sin, however, disturbed the relationship between humanity and the rest of creation. No longer in harmony with it, Adam found that the earth itself rebelled against his efforts, and work became arduous.

This lack of harmony with God's creation has important consequences. When someone's livelihood is based on his work, and his work seems insecure, he will be tempted to acquire more than he needs, hoarding goods against future scarcity. Through a curious reversal, man—who was created to exercise dominion over the earth—ends up dominated by it.

This is a disordered approach to the material world. It is so focused on acquiring property that it fails to see creation as a gift, a trust, and something to be shared. In its extreme form, this attitude becomes a worldview in which the material world completely eclipses the spiritual. It becomes *materialism*.

The Seventh and Tenth Commandments serve, together, as an antidote to that disordered worldview.

> The seventh commandment forbids unjustly taking or keeping the goods of one's neighbor and wronging him in any way with respect to his goods. It commands justice and charity in the care of earthly goods and the fruits of men's labor. For the sake of the common good, it requires respect for the universal destination of goods and respect for the right to private property. Christian life strives to order this world's goods to God and to fraternal charity. (CCC 2401)

Once again, we can see why there are two Commandments governing our custody of material things. As anger can lead to murder and lust can lead to adultery, so *coveting* can lead to *theft*. To nurture a disordered desire for material goods is itself a sin.

The Catholic Faith affirms the right to private property, and yet requires us to observe a certain detachment from material goods.

> The *right to private property*, acquired or received in a just way, does not do away with the original gift of the earth to the whole of mankind. The *universal destination of goods* remains primordial, even if the promotion of the common good requires respect for the right to private property and its exercise. (CCC 2403)

What we have, we must share with others.

> "In his use of things man should regard the external goods he legitimately owns not merely as exclusive to himself but common to others also, in the sense that they can benefit others as well as himself."²³ The ownership of any property makes its holder a steward of Providence, with the task of making it fruitful and communicating its benefits to others, first of all his family. (CCC 2404)

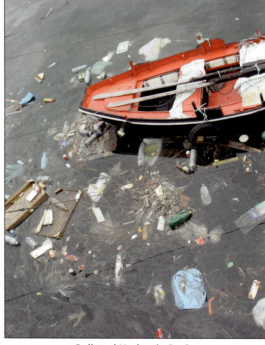

Polluted Harbor in Spain.
Everyone should strive to use environmental resources wisely, because we hold them in trust for future generations.

Those who find themselves materially rich must use their bounty for the benefit of many. Factory owners should manage their businesses so that their employees enjoy job security and receive just wages for their work. Everyone should strive to use environmental resources wisely, because we hold them in trust for future generations. If we waste or unnecessarily deplete resources today, we are stealing them from tomorrow—and thus violating the Seventh and Tenth Commandments.

The right to property is not absolute, however, and the *Catechism* affirms the state's right to regulate ownership for the sake of the common good (cf. CCC 2406).

Respect for private property means we should not take what belongs to someone else. The Seventh Commandment forbids the pilfering of supplies from one's employer.

It means, too, that we should be prudent in our spending, since the money we have should benefit others as well.

This does not mean we will always buy the lowest-priced item. Sometimes, such low prices are possible only because products are made by slave labor. If we cooperate in such a market, we perpetuate the poverty and oppression of people in faraway countries. Stewardship means we approach consumer decisions responsibly and critically. We should not make impulse purchases, even though "one-click ordering" seems so easy. We should not buy on whims. We should strive to live simply and not multiply "needs." When we own too much, our possessions own us. They weigh us down with concerns for maintenance, management, security, and upkeep. They leave us vulnerable to the envy of others—and to theft.

We should see goods for what they are: Good because God made them, they can make us happy only if they make us thankful to God.

Wealth, in itself, cannot confer happiness. Riches can only make us happy if we use them to enrich the lives of others and give greater glory to God.

TRUST AND TRUTH

Verbal communication is a distinctively human activity; and like all things human, it can be used well, or it can be abused. Words can be used for telling truth or lies. Words can be used to lovingly praise or viciously insult.

Pilate Questions Jesus by Ge.
"Jesus answered, '…Every one who is of the truth hears my voice.' Pilate said to him, 'What is truth?'"
(Jn 18:37-38)

When Christians communicate, they should always be "speaking the truth in love" (Eph 4:15)—exercising a civility that is based on charity. Even when we are speaking a hard truth—even when we are delivering a message that is critical—we should do so in a way that is sensitive to the dignity of the people involved, whether or not they are present to hear us.

Truth builds up trust, when truth is spoken in love, and trust makes solidarity possible. "You shall not bear false witness against your neighbor": The Eighth Commandment promotes truth-telling—in personal communication, in society, and in media—and it forbids practices that violate truth and charity in speech, such as lies, detraction, perjury, rash judgment, and the violation of professional secrets (cf. CCC 2464-2513).

Without trust, it is impossible to sustain a friendship, a happy marriage, or a lasting business partnership. We must never tell lies, as lies act like a cancer in human relationships. Truth-telling is a basic and essential element of Christian moral life and Catholic social doctrine. Without a generous measure of truth and trust, there can be no solidarity, no subsidiarity, and no common good. Lies are offenses against human dignity, insulting the person who receives them and degrading the person who tells them.

Truth-telling is important in every form of communication. However, it must be meticulously observed by those who work in the communications media. Their claims are distributed to many people, and so they serve to strengthen or sever the bonds of society. People who work conscientiously in this field observe a demanding code of professional ethics. Christians should judge themselves, furthermore, by the divine standard. Jesus Christ identified himself with "the truth" (Jn 14:6), and Christians have always worshiped a God who "is love" (1 Jn 4:16). Therefore, honesty and charity should be the hallmarks of all our conversations, all our communications.

In newsrooms it was once common to hang a sign where it could be seen by reporters and editors as they went about their daily work. The sign said: "Is it true? Is it kind?" Reporters know that their work will

GIORGIO LA PIRA: The Saintly Statist

Giorgio La Pira was born in 1904 to a devout, working-class Catholic family on the island of Sicily. He showed much promise in school, and his parents made great sacrifices to pay for Giorgio's education. He studied the classics as well as business, and he finished his degree in accounting. He went on to law school and eventually became a professor of law. Before he was thirty years old, he already held a prestigious chair at the University of Florence.

He was, however, an outspoken opponent of Italy's ruling party, the Fascists, led by dictator Benito Mussolini. Facing dire threats from the police, La Pira sought refuge within Vatican City. There, he wrote for the official newspaper, *L'Osservatore Romano*, and continued to criticize the Mussolini regime.

Giorgio La Pira, "an exemplary Christian."

By the end of World War II he had established a reputation for penetrating political analysis and personal courage. He emerged as one of the leaders of postwar reconstruction in Italy. He was influential in the drafting of the Italian constitution, arguing for the integrity of the family and against easy divorce. La Pira served in the government of Prime Minister Alcide De Gasperi as Undersecretary of Labor.

For decades after the war, Italian politics was defined by the struggle between the Christian Democrats and the Communists. Both sides included a loose coalition representing a wide range of opinion. La Pira was associated with the "left" wing of the Christian Democrats; and, though he favored local control in local matters, his policies leaned more toward statism than was typical of his party.

It was his unusual approach that made him attractive not only to the Christian Democrats' usual political base, but also to some voters who might be tempted to vote Communist. They saw La Pira as a man of principle, astute in fiscal matters, grounded in tradition, and proven in courage and charity.

In 1951, he was elected mayor of Florence, a city struggling to rebuild and suffering from wartime economic devastation. La Pira initiated public-works projects that employed many citizens for tasks that restored the city's infrastructure and its people's pride. He poured what money Florence had into bridges, public transportation, and (Florence's glory) the arts. He believed that all citizens had the right to enjoy not only basic material goods, but also—and more importantly—spiritual goods and cultural goods. He often said that everyone had a right to "a job, a house, and music."

In spite of Communist opposition, he won election to three terms as mayor. He enjoyed enormous popularity with ordinary people. He certainly had no airs about him: When he was very young, La Pira had become a Third Order (Lay) Dominican, and he took the life very seriously. A lifelong celibate, he lived in an unheated cell in the Dominican convent of San Marco. He sometimes arrived home barefoot because he had given his shoes to a beggar.

After finishing his final term as mayor in 1964, he spent a decade as a diplomat-at-large, promoting peace and economic cooperation among nations.

Continued

GIORGIO LA PIRA: The Saintly Statist
Continued

Alarmed by the increasing support for abortion in certain sectors of Italian government, La Pira returned to politics in 1976 and was elected to Italy's chamber of deputies. He returned to writing for *L'Osservatore Romano*, publishing that year a front-page manifesto titled "Confronting Abortion."

He fought for peace to the end of his life. He died in 1977, and his cause for canonization was launched by the Church of Florence.

Pope Benedict XVI recalled La Pira as an "exemplary Christian and an esteemed public administrator." In 2004, on the centenary of La Pira's birth, St. John Paul II wrote of him in fulsome detail:

> His spirituality was, as it were, "immanent" in his daily work. He went from Eucharistic communion to meditation, cultural commitment and social and political action without a break. He was intensely aware of the presence of the Most Holy Trinity who attracted him and gathered him, heart and soul, in contemplation and adoration. "The root of action," he wrote, "is always here: in this 'ecstasy' of the soul in love, shedding tears and saying to the Lord: "My God, my Lord! My God and my all!"
>
> Faithful to the Church's Magisterium, he had an authentic sense of the secularity and proper autonomy of the faithful in the area of the world's realities. He understood the public role as a service to the common good, free from the conditioning of power and the quest for prestige or personal interests.
>
> We like to think of him now, after his earthly life has ended, immersed forever in the contemplation of the Face of God as a citizen of that Heavenly Jerusalem that he so often pointed to as a model for the earthly city. Let us pray that his example may be an encouraging incentive to all who strive in contemporary society to witness with their lives to the Gospel and put themselves at the service of others, especially those "poor people" who always found in him a concerned and faithful friend.

La Pira fought for peace to the end of his life.

Judas' Betrayal (detail) by Giotto.
Lies are offenses against human dignity, insulting the person who receives them and degrading the person who tells them.

build up or destroy reputations, build up or destroy businesses, build up or destroy political careers. So they cannot be casual about what they publish.

Yet, this duty applies not only to professional communicators. Today, because of the proliferation of social media, everyone can be a publisher. Anyone's thoughts, posted on a blog or podcast or other online forum, have the potential to reach many people. Anyone's communications can have enormous potential to build up or tear down.

Christians should guard against forms of speech that dilute truth and diminish trust. Some are obvious: We should never tell a lie, uttering an intentional falsehood. We should never gossip, which spreads news that may be true, but which no one has a right to know.

These forms are obvious. Others are subtler. We should also avoid exaggeration, evasion, and the tendency to make a joke of every subject. A sense of humor is a valuable asset, and we can use it to make life more bearable for people. But we should not use it as a means of avoiding all serious conversation. Nor should we indulge excesses of sarcasm and irony. Christ spoke wisdom when he said: "Let what you say be simply 'Yes' or 'No'; anything more than this comes from evil" (Mt 5:37; see also Jas 5:12).

Nowhere is Christian respect for truth better exemplified than in the Sacrament of Penance, also known as Reconciliation or Confession. There we confess our sins plainly to the priest, who acts *in Persona Christi capitis* (in the Person of Christ the Head). The priest absolves us in God's name and keeps our sins secret forever. The seal of the confessional is absolute. Any priest who breaks the seal by repeating something he heard in the confessional brings automatic excommunication upon himself.

We should be deliberate about what we say—and choose not to say. Is it true? Is it kind? Does anyone really have a right or need to know it? "Speaking the truth in love" will make us not just better Christians, but better friends, better family members, and better professionals.

ABUNDANT LIFE: THE BEATITUDES

The Old Covenant was elevated and perfected by the New Covenant in Christ. The Beatitudes are an essential part of this New Law, which "fulfills the divine promises by elevating and orienting them toward the 'kingdom of heaven'" (CCC 1967).

The Beatitudes are the heart of Christ's Sermon on the Mount. They are a series of blessings pronounced upon people who keep certain attitudes and practice certain virtues. The name "Beatitudes" comes from the Latin word that begins every line: *Beati*…Blessed. They appear, with slight variations, in the Gospels of Matthew (5:3-12) and Luke (6:20-23).

> Blessed are the poor in spirit, for theirs is the kingdom of heaven.
>
> Blessed are those who mourn, for they shall be comforted.
>
> Blessed are the meek, for they shall inherit the earth.
>
> Blessed are those who hunger and thirst for righteousness, for they shall be satisfied.

> Blessed are the merciful, for they shall obtain mercy.
>
> Blessed are the pure in heart, for they shall see God.
>
> Blessed are the peacemakers, for they shall be called sons of God.
>
> Blessed are those who are persecuted for righteousness' sake, for theirs is the kingdom of heaven.
>
> Blessed are you when men revile you and persecute you and utter all kinds of evil against you falsely on my account.
>
> Rejoice and be glad, for your reward is great in heaven, for so men persecuted the prophets who were before you. (Mt 5:3-12)

Some commentators have wrongly portrayed the Beatitudes as somehow opposed to the Commandments. They speak as if blessings must somehow be the antitheses of laws. Pope Benedict XVI, in explaining the Beatitudes, rejects such a reading. "This approach," he says, "totally misconstrues these words of Jesus."[24]

Christ had no intention of abrogating or superseding the Ten Commandments. He reinforced them, fulfilled them, and added depth to them. In the Sermon on the Mount, Christ said: "Think not that I have come to abolish the law and the prophets; I have come not to abolish them but to fulfill them" (Mt 5:17).

Far from being "opposed" to the Law, the Beatitudes are, in fact, legal declarations. When Moses proclaimed the old Law, he said: "Behold, I set before you this day a blessing and a curse" (Dt 11:26). When people fulfill the Law, they receive "the blessing" and they are "blessed." When they disobey the Law and do not repent, they are "cursed." It is significant, in this regard, that St. Luke's version of the Beatitudes is followed by a series of curses, statements in which Christ pronounces "woe" upon those who fail to live rightly.

The Beatitudes, then, fulfill, refine, surpass, and lead the Old Law to perfection. Where the Commandments prohibit a certain vice, the Beatitudes affirm its opposing virtue.

Mount of Beatitudes hillside and Chapel of the Beatitudes on the northwestern shore of the Sea of Galilee, between Capernaum and Gennesaret in northern Israel. St. John Paul II celebrated a Mass at this site in March 2000. The Jesus Trail pilgrimage route connects the Mount to other sites from the life of Jesus.

Jesus Preaching on the Mount by Dore.
The Beatitudes give consolation to those who are persecuted for the sake of true worship.

If the Commandments (Seven and Ten) reject materialism as it is manifested in theft and covetousness, the Beatitudes affirm: "Blessed are the poor in spirit."

If the Commandments (Six and Nine) reject sensuality as it is manifested in adultery and lust, the Beatitudes affirm: "Blessed are the pure of heart."

While the Fifth Commandment forbids murder, the Beatitudes bless "the meek" and "the peacemakers."

While the Eighth Commandment condemns false witness, the Beatitudes bless those who hunger and thirst for righteousness and those who mourn because they recognize the hard truth.

As the Commandments (One through Three) require proper worship of the one true God, the Beatitudes give consolation to those who are persecuted for the sake of true worship.

The Beatitudes move us beyond the letter of the Law, to its spirit. They show us the way beyond minimalism, to an abundant life. As there is a social dimension to the Commandments, so there is also a social dimension to the Beatitudes.

Christ said, "Blessed are the poor in spirit," and so we should choose a lifestyle of simplicity. We should not indulge whims, but rather live in a way that benefits those who are most in need. Otherwise, we will tend to be materialistic, selfish, and treat others as mere means for our own gain and pleasure. Such a life makes love impossible.

Christ said, "Blessed are those who mourn," and so we will be blessed when we are compassionate to others in their pain. Compassion comes from the Latin words that mean "suffer together with." Even if we are not feeling the same sadness as others, we should accompany them in their grieving. In a world full of Christians, no one should ever feel alone and abandoned.

Christ said, "Blessed are the meek" and "Blessed are the peacemakers," and so he called us to be disciplined in the face of evil, responding with gentleness and unselfishness. This does *not* mean we should be pushovers. It does *not* mean we should tolerate injustice. It *does* mean we should never respond to evil with more evil. We should never respond to arrogance with arrogance, or return disrespect for disrespect. Christians bring people together and reconcile opponents. They should not be dividers, troublemakers, or warmongers.

Christ said, "Blessed are the merciful," and we too should be very forgiving and quick to ask forgiveness for our own faults. There is no place in Christian life for holding grudges, nursing bitterness, or imposing the "silent treatment." Only if we are merciful will we know mercy.

Christ said, "Blessed are those who hunger and thirst for righteousness," and that is the heart of Catholic social doctrine. We should desire justice, seek justice, pray for justice, work for justice, and not just sit around waiting for it to happen. Through prayer and study, we should develop a heart for others, a well-formed social conscience.

Christ said: "Blessed are the pure of heart." The Commandments condemned sins against sexual purity. The Beatitudes offer the reason behind the condemnations. Impurity renders one unfit for the vision of God—unable to find human fulfillment. We should live chaste lives and dress modestly so as not to scandalize others.

Christ said: "Blessed are those who are persecuted for righteousness' sake." We need to be constant in our witness to Christ and the Church. We must be prepared even to die for our faith as martyrs rather than offend God. The blessing is glory. The alternative is a shameful life, sick with cowardice, betrayal, and moral compromise.

THE CORPORAL WORKS OF MERCY	THE SPIRITUAL WORKS OF MERCY
✠ Feeding the hungry	✠ Counseling the doubtful
✠ Giving drink to the thirsty	✠ Instructing the ignorant
✠ Clothing the naked	✠ Admonishing sinners
✠ Sheltering the homeless	✠ Comforting the afflicted
✠ Visiting the sick	✠ Forgiving offenses
✠ Visiting the imprisoned	✠ Bearing wrongs patiently
✠ Burying the dead	✠ Praying for the living and the dead

CONCLUSION

A lawyer once asked Christ, "Teacher, which is the great commandment in the law?"

Christ responded:

> You shall love the Lord your God with all your heart, and with all your soul, and with all your mind. This is the great and first commandment. And a second is like it, You shall love your neighbor as yourself. On these two commandments depend all the law and the prophets. (Mt 22:36-40)

Christ's answer summed up the entire Law and the teachings of all the prophets. These two Great Commandments are the sum of the Ten Commandments and the Beatitudes.

The "Law of Love" is the essence of Catholic social doctrine, because it is the essence of the Gospel. It is a dual command to love God and love our neighbor. It contains, in the purest form, all the other commands of the Bible. As St. Augustine put it, "So that one commandment [love] contains two, those two contain ten, and those ten contain them all."[25]

The Saints
PILLARS OF THE CHURCH

ST. THOMAS AQUINAS
From his *Explanation of the Ten Commandments*

"You shall not covet your neighbor's goods." There is this difference between the divine and the human laws: human law judges only deeds and words, whereas the divine law judges also thoughts. The reason is because human laws are made by men who see things only exteriorly, but the divine law is from God, who sees both external things and the very interior of men. "God is the strength of my heart" (Ps 73:26). And again: "man looks on the outward appearance, but the Lord looks on the heart" (1 Sm 16:7).

Therefore, having considered those commandments that concern words and deeds, we now treat of the commandments about thoughts. For with God the intention is taken for the deed, and thus the words "You shall not covet" mean to include not only the taking by act, but also the intention to take. Therefore, it says: "You shall not even covet thy neighbor's goods." There are a number of reasons for this.

The first reason for the commandment is that man's desire has no limits, because desire itself is boundless. But he who is wise will aim at some particular end, for no one should have aimless desires: "He who loves money will not be satisfied with money" (Eccl 5:10). But the desires of man are never satisfied, because the heart of man is made for God. Thus, says St. Augustine: "You have made us for yourself, O Lord, and our hearts are restless until they rest in you." Nothing, therefore, less than God can satisfy the human heart: "who satisfies you with good" (Ps 103:5).

The second reason is that covetousness destroys peace of heart, which is indeed highly delightful. The covetous man is ever solicitous to acquire what he lacks, and to hold that which he has: "the surfeit of the rich will not let him sleep" (Sir 5:12). "For where your treasure is, there will your heart be also" (Mt 6:21). It was for this, says St. Gregory, that Christ compared riches to thorns (see Lk 8:14).

Thirdly, covetousness in a man of wealth renders his riches useless both to himself and to others, because he desires only to hold on to them: "Riches are not seemly for a stingy man; and of what use is property to an envious man?" (Sir 14:3). The fourth reason is that it destroys the equality of justice: "And you shall take no bribe, for a bribe blinds the officials, and subverts the cause of those who are in the right" (Ex 23:8). And again: "He who loves gold will not be justified" (Sir 31:5). The fifth reason is that it destroys the love of God and neighbor, for says St. Augustine: "The more one loves, the less one covets," and also the more one covets, the less one loves. Do not exchange your dear brother for the sake of gold (see Sir 7:20). And just as "no one can serve two masters," so neither can he serve "God and mammon" (Mt 6:24).

Finally, covetousness produces all kinds of wickedness. It is "the root of all evil," says St. Paul, and when this root is implanted in the heart it brings forth murder and theft and all kinds of evil. "Those who desire to be rich fall into temptation, into a snare, into many senseless and hurtful desires that plunge men into ruin and destruction. For the love of money is the root of all evils" (1 Tm 6:9-10). And note, furthermore, that covetousness is a mortal sin when one covets one's neighbor's goods without reason; and even if there be a reason, it is a venial sin.

SUPPLEMENTARY READING

St. John Paul II: Apostolic Exhortation *Reconciliatio et Paenitentia*

On Social Sin

16. Sin, in the proper sense, is always a personal act, since it is an act of freedom on the part of an individual person and not properly of a group or community. This individual may be conditioned, incited and influenced by numerous and powerful external factors. He may also be subjected to tendencies, defects and habits linked with his personal condition. In not a few cases such external and internal factors may attenuate, to a greater or lesser degree, the person's freedom and therefore his responsibility and guilt. But it is a truth of faith, also confirmed by our experience and reason, that the human person is free. This truth cannot be disregarded in order to place the blame for individuals' sins on external factors such as structures, systems or other people. Above all, this would be to deny the person's dignity and freedom, which are manifested—even though in a negative and disastrous way—also in this responsibility for sin committed. Hence there is nothing so personal and untransferable in each individual as merit for virtue or responsibility for sin.

As a personal act, sin has its first and most important consequences in the sinner himself: that is, in his relationship with God, who is the very foundation of human life; and also in his spirit, weakening his will and clouding his intellect.

At this point we must ask what was being referred to by those who during the preparation of the synod and in the course of its actual work frequently spoke of social sin.

The expression and the underlying concept in fact have various meanings.

To speak of social sin means in the first place to recognize that, by virtue of human solidarity which is as mysterious and intangible as it is real and concrete, each individual's sin in some way affects others. This is the other aspect of that solidarity which on the religious level is developed in the profound and magnificent mystery of the communion of saints, thanks to which it has been possible to say that "every soul that rises above itself, raises up the world."[26] To this law of ascent there unfortunately corresponds the law of descent. Consequently one can speak of a communion of sin, whereby a soul that lowers itself through sin drags down with itself the church and, in some way, the whole world. In other words, there is no sin, not even the most intimate and secret one, the most strictly individual one, that exclusively concerns the person committing it. With greater or lesser violence, with greater or lesser harm, every sin has repercussions on the entire ecclesial body and the whole human family. According to this first meaning of the term, every sin can undoubtedly be considered as social sin.

Some sins, however, by their very matter constitute a direct attack on one's neighbor and more exactly, in the language of the Gospel, against one's brother or sister. They are an offense against God because they are offenses against one's neighbor. These sins are usually called social sins, and this is the second meaning of the term. In this sense social sin is sin against love of neighbor, and in the law of Christ it is all the more serious in that it involves the Second Commandment, which is "like unto the first."[27] Likewise, the term social applies to every sin against justice in interpersonal

Jesus Washing Peter's Feet by Brown.
"Blessed are the meek, for they shall inherit the earth."

SUPPLEMENTARY READING Continued

relationships, committed either by the individual against the community or by the community against the individual. Also social is every sin against the rights of the human person, beginning with the right to and including the life of the unborn or against a person's physical integrity. Likewise social is every sin against others' freedom, especially against the supreme freedom to believe in God and adore him; social is every sin against the dignity and honor of one's neighbor. Also social is every sin against the common good and its exigencies in relation to the whole broad spectrum of the rights and duties of citizens. The term social can be applied to sins of commission or omission—on the part of political, economic or trade union leaders, who though in a position to do so, do not work diligently and wisely for the improvement and transformation of society according to the requirements and potential of the given historic moment; as also on the part of workers who through absenteeism or non-cooperation fail to ensure that their industries can continue to advance the well-being of the workers themselves, of their families and of the whole of society.

The third meaning of social sin refers to the relationships between the various human communities. These relationships are not always in accordance with the plan of God, who intends that there be justice in the world and freedom and peace between individuals, groups and peoples. Thus the class struggle, whoever the person who leads it or on occasion seeks to give it a theoretical justification, is a social evil. Likewise obstinate confrontation between blocs of nations, between one nation and another, between different groups within the same nation all this too is a social evil. In both cases one may ask whether moral responsibility for these evils, and therefore sin, can be attributed to any person in particular. Now it has to be admitted that realities and situations such as those described, when they become generalized and reach vast proportions as social phenomena, almost always become anonymous, just as their causes are complex and not always identifiable. Hence if one speaks of social sin here, the expression obviously has an analogical meaning.

However, to speak even analogically of social sins must not cause us to underestimate the responsibility of the individuals involved. It is meant to be an appeal to the consciences of all, so that each may shoulder his or her responsibility seriously and courageously in order to change those disastrous conditions and intolerable situations.

Having said this in the clearest and most unequivocal way, one must add at once that there is one meaning sometimes given to social sin that is not legitimate or acceptable even though it is very common in certain quarters today.[28] This usage contrasts social sin and personal sin, not without ambiguity, in a way that leads more or less unconsciously to the watering down and almost the abolition of personal sin, with the recognition only of social guilt and responsibilities. According to this usage, which can readily be seen to derive from non-Christian ideologies and systems—which have possibly been discarded today by the very people who formerly officially upheld them—practically every sin is a social sin, in the sense that blame for it is to be placed not so much on the moral conscience of an individual, but rather on some vague entity or anonymous collectivity such as the situation, the system, society, structures or institutions.

Whenever the church speaks of situations of sin or when she condemns as social sins certain situations or the collective behavior of certain social groups, big or small, or even of whole nations and blocs of nations, she knows and she proclaims that such cases of social sin are the result of the accumulation and concentration of many personal sins. It is a case of the very personal sins of those who cause or support evil or who exploit it; of those who are in a position to avoid, eliminate or at least limit certain social evils but who fail to do so out of laziness, fear or the conspiracy of silence, through secret complicity or indifference; of those who take refuge in the supposed impossibility of changing the world and also of those who sidestep the effort and sacrifice required, producing specious reasons of higher order. The real responsibility, then, lies with individuals.

SUPPLEMENTARY READING Continued

A situation—or likewise an institution, a structure, society itself—is not in itself the subject of moral acts. Hence a situation cannot in itself be good or bad.

At the heart of every situation of sin are always to be found sinful people. So true is this that even when such a situation can be changed in its structural and institutional aspects by the force of law or—as unfortunately more often happens by the law of force, the change in fact proves to be incomplete, of short duration and ultimately vain and ineffective—not to say counterproductive if the people directly or indirectly responsible for that situation are not converted.

The Book of Sirach 3:1-16
Honor Your Parents

Listen to me your father, O children;
> and act accordingly, that you may be kept in safety.

For the Lord honored the father above the children,
> and he confirmed the right of the mother over her sons.

Whoever honors his father atones for sins,
> and whoever glorifies his mother is like one who lays up treasure.

Whoever honors his father will be gladdened by his own children,
> and when he prays he will be heard.

Whoever glorifies his father will have long life,
> and whoever obeys the Lord will refresh his mother;
> he will serve his parents as his masters.

Honor your father by word and deed,
> that a blessing from him may come upon you.

For a father's blessing strengthens the houses of the children,
> but a mother's curse uproots their foundations.

Do not glorify yourself by dishonoring your father,
> for your father's dishonor is no glory to you.

For a man's glory comes from honoring his father,
> and it is a disgrace for children not to respect their mother.

O son, help your father in his old age,
> and do not grieve him as long as he lives;
> even if he is lacking in understanding, show forbearance;
> in all your strength do not despise him.

For kindness to a father will not be forgotten,
> and against your sins it will be credited to you;

in the day of your affliction it will be remembered in your favor;
> as frost in fair weather, your sins will melt away.

Whoever forsakes his father is like a blasphemer,
> and whoever angers his mother is cursed by the Lord.

Christ Discovered in the Temple by Martini.

SUPPLEMENTARY READING Continued

The Letter of St. Paul to the Romans (13:1-10)

The Authority of the State

Let every person be subject to the governing authorities. For there is no authority except from God, and those that exist have been instituted by God. Therefore he who resists the authorities resists what God has appointed, and those who resist will incur judgment. For rulers are not a terror to good conduct, but to bad. Would you have no fear of him who is in authority? Then do what is good, and you will receive his approval, for he is God's servant for your good. But if you do wrong, be afraid, for he does not bear the sword in vain; he is the servant of God to execute his wrath on the wrongdoer. Therefore one must be subject, not only to avoid God's wrath but also for the sake of conscience. For the same reason you also pay taxes, for the authorities are ministers of God, attending to this very thing. Pay all of them their dues, taxes to whom taxes are due, revenue to whom revenue is due, respect to whom respect is due, honor to whom honor is due.

Owe no one anything, except to love one another; for he who loves his neighbor has fulfilled the law. The commandments, "You shall not commit adultery, You shall not kill, You shall not steal, You shall not covet," and any other commandment, are summed up in this sentence, "You shall love your neighbor as yourself." Love does no wrong to a neighbor; therefore love is the fulfilling of the law.

St. John Paul II: Encyclical *Evangelium Vitæ*

The Culture of Death

12. …[W]hile the climate of widespread moral uncertainty can in some way be explained by the multiplicity and gravity of today's social problems, and these can sometimes mitigate the subjective responsibility of individuals, it is no less true that we are confronted by an even larger reality, which can be described as a veritable structure of sin. This reality is characterized by the emergence of a culture which denies solidarity and in many cases takes the form of a veritable "culture of death." This culture is actively fostered by powerful cultural, economic and political currents which encourage an idea of society excessively concerned with efficiency. Looking at the situation from this point of view, it is possible to speak in a certain sense of a war of the powerful against the weak: a life which would require greater acceptance, love and care is considered useless, or held to be an intolerable burden, and is therefore rejected in one way or another. A person who, because of illness, handicap or, more simply, just by existing, compromises the well-being or life-style of those who are more favored tends to be looked upon as an enemy to be resisted or eliminated. In this way a kind of "conspiracy against life" is unleashed. This conspiracy involves not only individuals in their personal, family or group relationships, but goes far beyond, to the point of damaging and distorting, at the international level, relations between peoples and States…

20. How is it still possible to speak of the dignity of every human person when the killing of the weakest and most innocent is permitted? In the name of what justice is the most unjust of discriminations practiced: some individuals are held to be deserving of defense and others are denied that dignity? When this happens, the process leading to the breakdown of a genuinely human co-existence and the disintegration of the State itself has already begun.

To claim the right to abortion, infanticide and euthanasia, and to recognize that right in law, means to attribute to human freedom a perverse and evil significance: that of an absolute power over others and against others. This is the death of true freedom: "Truly, truly, I say to you, every one who commits sin is a slave to sin" (Jn 8:34).

VOCABULARY

ADULTERY
Sexual relations between a married person and one to whom he or she is not married. Adultery is opposed to the Sacrament of Matrimony, because it contradicts the equal dignity of man and woman and the unity and exclusivity of married love.

ANARCHY
A state of disorder due to absence of authority; lawlessness.

BEATITUDES
The teachings of Christ in the Sermon on the Mount on the meaning and way to true happiness (see Mt 5:3-12). These are at the heart of Christ's preaching.

CHASTITY
The moral virtue that is directed toward the positive integration of sexuality within a person, moderating the sexual appetite.

COMMANDMENTS
A norm of moral or religious action.

DECALOGUE
From the Greek for "ten words," the Ten Commandments given by God through Moses.

DETRACTION
The action of taking away from a person's merit or reputation by disclosing another's true faults or sins. This is a sin against the Eighth Commandment because each person has a right to his good name.

EUTHANASIA
From the Greek meaning "good death," an action or omission of an action that, by itself or by intention, causes a person's death in order to eliminate suffering. It is a sin against the Fifth Commandment.

FORNICATION
Sexual intercourse between an unmarried man and an unmarried woman; a sin against the Sixth Commandment.

GOSSIP
Idle speech about another person's affairs, especially of an intimate nature. The word can also refer to a person who gossips. Gossip is a sin against the Eighth Commandment.

INFANTICIDE
The act of killing a newly born child, a sin against the Fifth Commandment.

JUST WAR
The principle that war may be legitimately waged, under certain specific conditions, for the protection of a nation's rights.

MASTURBATION
The deliberate stimulation of the genital organs in order to derive sexual pleasure. Masturbation is a sin against the Sixth Commandment.

MODESTY
Reserve or propriety in speech, dress, and behavior. A modest person avoids clothing that is overly revealing or may excite the senses, leading others to sin.

PERJURY
To make a promise without any intention of completing it, or to lie under oath, a sin against the Eighth Commandment.

PORNOGRAPHY
Printed or visual material containing explicit descriptions or displays of sexual organs or activity, intended to cause sexual excitement in the reader or viewer. The use of pornography is a sin against the Sixth Commandment.

VOCABULARY Continued

RAPE
The forcible violation of the sexual intimacy of another person. This act deeply wounds the respect, freedom, and physical and moral integrity to which every person has a right. It is a sin against the Sixth Commandment.

RASH JUDGMENT
The formation of an opinion about someone's character without sufficient evidence. It is a sin against the Eighth Commandment.

SCANDAL
An attitude or behavior that leads another to do evil.

SLANDER
A maliciously false statement or report intended to defame or injure a person. It is a sin against the Eighth Commandment.

SUICIDE
The act of taking one's own life; self-murder. This is forbidden by the Fifth Commandment.

STUDY QUESTIONS

1. Why is sin always a personal act?

2. In what ways can people share responsibility for sin?

3. What are "structures of sin"?

4. In what ways is it legitimate to speak of "social sin"?

5. What authority does an unjust law have?

6. What is the Decalogue?

7. How do the two "tablets" of the Decalogue differ from one another?

8. What does the First Commandment require? State its requirements in positive and negative terms.

9. What does the Second Commandment require? State its requirements in positive and negative terms.

10. What does the Third Commandment require? State its requirements in positive and negative terms.

11. What does the Fourth Commandment require? State its requirements in positive and negative terms.

12. What does the Fifth Commandment require? State its requirements in positive and negative terms.

13. What do the Sixth and Ninth Commandments require? State their requirements in positive and negative terms.

14. What do the Seventh and Tenth Commandments require? State their requirements in positive and negative terms.

15. What does the Eighth Commandment require? State its requirements in positive and negative terms.

16. What are the Beatitudes and how do they relate to the Commandments?

PRACTICAL EXERCISES

1. Choose one Commandment (or set, for those that are paired in the chapter) and its related Beatitude. Explain the virtues and sins related to that Commandment and corresponding Beatitude. Then draw up a detailed, practical plan by which someone could grow in those virtues and avoid those sins over the course of a month.

2. Read the full text of the Decalogue in the Book of Exodus. Compare and contrast the Commandments relating to God to those relating to moral behavior. How do they differ in their presentation? Why do you think they differ in the ways they do?

3. Read St. John Paul II's description of a "conspiracy against life" in the encyclical *Evangelium Vitæ*. Explain in detail how such a conspiracy affects your local community. Show your research.

4. Use the Eighth Commandment and our discussion of it to critique a periodical and a television news program. What do these media do morally well? How could they improve their moral content and approach? How do they differ, in moral quality, from one another?

Christ on the Way to Calvary by Paolo.
"To claim the right to abortion, infanticide and euthanasia, and to recognize that right in law, means to attribute to human freedom a perverse and evil significance: that of an absolute power over others and against others." (*EV* 20)

FROM THE CATECHISM

1716 The Beatitudes are at the heart of Jesus' preaching. They take up the promises made to the chosen people since Abraham. The Beatitudes fulfill the promises by ordering them no longer merely to the possession of a territory, but to the Kingdom of heaven.

1717 The Beatitudes depict the countenance of Jesus Christ and portray his charity. They express the vocation of the faithful associated with the glory of his Passion and Resurrection; they shed light on the actions and attitudes characteristic of the Christian life; they are the paradoxical promises that sustain hope in the midst of tribulations; they proclaim the blessings and rewards already secured, however dimly, for Christ's disciples; they have begun in the lives of the Virgin Mary and all the saints.

1718 The Beatitudes respond to the natural desire for happiness. This desire is of divine origin: God has placed it in the human heart in order to draw man to the One who alone can fulfill it:

> We all want to live happily; in the whole human race there is no one who does not assent to this proposition, even before it is fully articulated.[29]

> How is it, then, that I seek you, Lord? Since in seeking you, my God, I seek a happy life, let me seek you so that my soul may live, for my body draws life from my soul and my soul draws life from you.[30]

> God alone satisfies.[31]

1719 The Beatitudes reveal the goal of human existence, the ultimate end of human acts: God calls us to his own beatitude. This vocation is addressed to each individual personally, but also to the Church as a whole, the new people made up of those who have accepted the promise and live from it in faith.

1724 The Decalogue, the Sermon on the Mount, and the apostolic catechesis describe for us the paths that lead to the Kingdom of heaven. Sustained by the grace of the Holy Spirit, we tread them, step by step, by everyday acts. By the working of the Word of Christ, we slowly bear fruit in the Church to the glory of God.[32]

ENDNOTES – CHAPTER SIX

1. John Paul II, *RP* 16.
2. *RP* 16.
3. *On Free Choice of the Will*, 1.5.
4. Ex 34:28; Dt 4:13, 10:4.
5. Ex 31:18; Dt 5:22.
6. Cf. Dt 31:9, 24.
7. Cf. Ex 20:1-17.
8. Cf. Dt 5:6-22.
9. Cf. for example Hos 4:2; Jer 7:9; Ez 18:5-9.
10. Dt 5:22.
11. Ex 25:16; 31:18 ; 32:15 ; 34:29 ; 40:1-2.
12. Cf. *DH* 1.
13. Cf. *AA* 13 ; Leo XIII, *Immortale Dei* 3, 17; Pius XI, *Quas Primas* 8, 20.
14. Mk 12:29-31; cf. Dt 6:4-5; Lv 19:18; Mt 22:34-40; Lk 10:25-28.
15. Rom 13:8-10.
16. *Letter to Families*, 6.
17. Cf. Gn 4:8-12.
18. Gn 4:10-11.
19. Gn 9:5-6.
20. Cf. Lv 17:14.
21. John Paul II, *Evangelium Vitæ* 56.
22. Cf. Gn 1:26-29.
23. *GS* 69 § 1.
24. Pope Benedict XVI, *Jesus of Nazareth: From the Baptism in the Jordan to the Transfiguration* (New York: Doubleday, 2007), 70.
25. *Sermon* 9.16.
26. The expression from the French writer Elizabeth Leseur, *Journal et Pensees de Chaque Jour* (Paris:1918), 31.
27. Cf. Mt 22:39; Mk 12:31; Lk 10:27f.
28. Cf. Sacred Congregation for the Doctrine of the Faith: Instruction on Certain Aspects of the Theology of Liberation *Libertatis Nuntius*; August 6, 1984 IV, 14-15: ASS 76 (1984), 885f.
29. St. Augustine, *De moribus eccl.* 1, 3, 4: PL 32, 1312.
30. St. Augustine, *Conf.* 10, 20: PL 32, 791.
31. St. Thomas Aquinas, *Expos. in symb. apost.* I.
32. Cf. the Parable of the Sower: Mt 13:3-23.

Social Doctrine of the Catholic Church
CHAPTER 7

Today's Challenges

Peter asked Jesus "Quo vadis?" (Where are you going?) to which Jesus replied, "Romam vado iterum crucifigi." (I am going to Rome to be crucified again). The meeting gave Peter the courage to continue his ministry, and he returned to Rome, eventually to be martyred.

Social Doctrine of the Catholic Church

CHAPTER SEVEN

Today's Challenges

CHRIST WANTS A CIVILIZATION OF LOVE. WE MUST OVERCOME THE OBSTACLES.

For they gave according to their means, as I can testify, and beyond their means, of their own free will, begging us earnestly for the favor of taking part in the relief of the saints—and this, not as we expected, but first they gave themselves to the Lord and to us by the will of God…Now as you excel in everything—in faith, in utterance, in knowledge, in all earnestness, and in your love for us—see that you excel in this gracious work also. I say this not as a command, but to prove by the earnestness of others that your love also is genuine. For you know the grace of our Lord Jesus Christ, that though he was rich, yet for your sake he became poor, so that by his poverty you might become rich…I do not mean that others should be eased and you burdened, but that as a matter of equality your abundance at the present time should supply their want, so that their abundance may supply your want, that there may be equality. As it is written, "He who gathered much had nothing over, and he who gathered little had no lack."

—2 Corinthians 8:3-5, 7-11, 13-15

IN THIS CHAPTER, WE WILL ADDRESS SEVERAL QUESTIONS:

- What are the major obstacles to human fulfillment in Christ?
- What is secularism?
- What is materialism?
- What is individualism?

Christ came to bring a new kind of life to the world (cf. Jn 10:10, 20:31). It is a spiritual life, not material, and so it is hidden from sight, like a mustard seed buried in the earth (cf. Mt 13:31) or yeast mixed into dough (cf. Lk 13:21). The life itself is invisible, and yet its effects are visible everywhere: "Go and tell John what you hear and see: the blind receive their sight and the lame walk, lepers are cleansed and the deaf hear, and the dead are raised up, and the poor have good news preached to them" (Mt 11:4-5). The new life is intensely personal, but it has vast consequences for society.

Christ made clear that people were free to follow him. He wanted each person to cooperate freely in his saving work. Christ gives everyone the right and the power to *refuse* to share his life. For love cannot be coerced; it invites a free response, or it is not truly love.

TODAY'S CHALLENGES

Christ and the Rich Young Ruler by Hofmann.
Christ tells him to obey the Commandments—the necessary minimum for a decent life.

Once a rich young man came up to Christ, knelt, and asked:

> "Good Teacher, what must I do to inherit eternal life?"
>
> And Jesus said to him, "Why do you call me good? No one is good but God alone. You know the commandments: 'Do not kill, Do not commit adultery, Do not steal, Do not bear false witness, Do not defraud, Honor your father and mother.'"
>
> And he said to him, "Teacher, all these I have observed from my youth."
>
> And Jesus looking upon him loved him, and said to him, "You lack one thing; go, sell what you have, and give to the poor, and you will have treasure in heaven; and come, follow me."
>
> At that saying his countenance fell, and he went away sorrowful; for he had great possessions.
>
> And Jesus looked around and said to his disciples, "How hard it will be for those who have riches to enter the kingdom of God!"
>
> And the disciples were amazed at his words. But Jesus said to them again, "Children, how hard it is to enter the kingdom of God! It is easier for a camel to go through the eye of a needle than for a rich man to enter the kingdom of God."
>
> And they were exceedingly astonished, and said to him, "Then who can be saved?"
>
> Jesus looked at them and said, "With men it is impossible, but not with God; for all things are possible with God." (Mk 10:17-27)

So much of Catholic social doctrine is summed up in this brief exchange. The man desires to live in the Kingdom, and he realizes that it will require something of him. He recognizes that he is not there yet. Christ tells him to obey the Commandments—the necessary minimum for a decent life—and the young man tells him that he has always kept the Commandments. "And Jesus looking upon him loved him." Christ himself shows approval to the man! Imagine the power of that moment. Then the Lord calls him

The Widow's Mite by Tissot.
"And a poor widow came, and put in two copper coins, which make a penny. And he called his disciples to him, and said to them, 'Truly, I say to you, this poor widow has put in more than all those who are contributing to the treasury. For they all contributed out of their abundance; but she out of her poverty has put in everything she had, her whole living.'" (Mk 12:42-44)

to something still greater—to give sacrificially, to lay down his life, to take up a cross, to deny himself, to give rather than receive.

Just moments before, the man had arrived—running!—seeking happiness from Christ, and Christ looked on him with love, but the young man went away sad because he had many possessions. He did not exercise dominion over them, and so they exercised dominion over him. They kept him from Christ. They kept him from the Kingdom. If that is how it is for the rich, Christ said, then "how blessed are the poor."

In the encounter between Christ and the rich young man we see:

✣ the necessity of the Commandments;
✣ the proof of the Beatitudes;
✣ the absolute need for God's grace; and
✣ the human freedom to accept or refuse that grace.

We also see the social dimension of human nature. The encounter with Christ was itself a conversation between two men. It was conducted before witnesses. It had a profound effect on those who overheard it. Yet, the young man went away sad, choosing to be alone with his abundant possessions rather than in solidarity with Christ in the society of the Kingdom.

Such encounters still take place today, with the same loving gaze and the same clarification of terms. They take place in every life. They take place, too, in the lives of nations and churches.

In 2008, Pope Benedict XVI made an apostolic journey to the United States. On arriving in the nation's capital, Washington, D.C., he praised the country for its generosity and religious fervor. He cited examples of American aid to countries beset by natural disasters. He commended American creativity and industriousness. He looked upon the country with great love.

But he added that the American people, like all peoples, need to draw closer to Christ. Like the rich young man, they need, he said, to have "an encounter with the living God." They must begin, however, "by clearing away some of the barriers to such an encounter." He did not ask the country to sell all it has and give to the poor. He did, however, ask his listeners to consider *three contemporary obstacles* that fall between human beings and God, especially in countries that are relatively prosperous. Those three obstacles, he said, are *secularism*, *materialism*, and *individualism*.

THE BLESSED VIRGIN MARY: Solidarity with the World

She was a poor woman. In the course of her life she was an immigrant, a refugee, a widow, and pregnant outside wedlock. She lived to see the death of her only child. The country she loved, her ancestral home, was ruled by a foreign superpower that had only minimal respect for the religious traditions of her people.

The Blessed Virgin Mary has always been close to the poor, suffering, oppressed, and needy. We see this even in her earthly life, when she solicited her son Christ's first miracle: He changed water into wine in order to spare newlyweds the embarrassment of a failure in hospitality.

In her heavenly life she remains close to those in need. The native people of modern-day Mexico City suffered conquest first by the Aztecs in the fourteenth century and then by the Spanish conquistadores in the fifteenth and sixteenth centuries. The Aztecs harvested the conquered people as victims for human sacrifice, offered to the snake god Quetzalcoatl. Their lives were burdened with natural and supernatural fears. Yet, they resisted conversion to Christianity. The best efforts of brilliant missionaries proved ineffective.

Then Mary appeared to a peasant man named Juan Diego at Guadalupe and soon the entire continent converted to Catholicism.

Through the centuries, her appearances have followed this pattern. She speaks to the poor—to St. Bernadette at Lourdes in France, to the three children at Fatima in Portugal—to give a consoling message for the whole world.

Working with the Blessed Virgin, people change the world. Humble Juan Diego, an unlikely hero, served as a messenger of Our Lady, through whose maternal intercession, Christ's salvation was brought to millions of people. The seers at Fatima prepared the world for the onslaught of communism and Nazism.

Individuals such as Dorothy Day and Cesar Chavez have known the power of Mary's

On March 16, 2013, just three days after his election, Pope Francis prayed to the Blessed Virgin at the Lourdes Grotto in the Vatican Gardens, a replica of Our Lady of Lourdes grotto in France.

intercession and companionship. In the seventeenth century, the French priest Claude Bernard used the Marian *Memorare* prayer to power his outreach to the poor and his advocacy for prisoners.

Karol Wojtyla went to her often when he was a young man living in a land dominated by one oppressor after another. As Pope he did not hesitate to beseech her to solve the social problems that beset his world (and ours):

> In keeping with Christian piety through the ages, we present to the Blessed Virgin difficult individual situations, so that she may place them before her Son, asking that he alleviate and change them. But we also present to her social situations and the international crisis itself, in their worrying aspects of poverty, unemployment, shortage of food, the arms race, contempt for human rights, and situations or dangers of conflict, partial or total. In a filial spirit we wish to place all this before her "eyes of mercy" (*SRS* 49).

During an Apostolic journey to the United States, Pope Benedict XVI identified three contemporary obstacles that fall between human beings and God. Those three obstacles, he said, are *secularism*, *materialism*, and *individualism*.

SECULARISM

The Holy Father was careful to distinguish unhealthy *secularism* from a healthy *secularity*. It is proper for Catholic lay people to have a secular character. The word "secular" comes from the Latin word meaning "the world" and "the ages." We might say it's the "here and now." It is the business of lay Catholics to transform the world from within. And so they must live in the world with a certain degree of confidence—the confidence of God's children, assured of their heavenly Father's care. The Holy Father spoke of the "just autonomy of the secular order," which nonetheless "cannot be divorced from God the Creator and his saving plan."

There is a tendency for modern people to look at faith as something "spiritual, but not religious." By spiritual, then, they mean subject to opinion and preference, less real than the material world. But that is not how Catholics, as well as many others, view spiritual matters. Biblical Revelation makes it clear that the spiritual dimension of reality is just as real, if not more real, than the material dimension. God is pure spirit and, yet, is the origin and destiny of everything in the material world. Angels, who are spiritual creatures, have been intricately involved in many of the most momentous events in human history. It is absurd to think that spiritual commitments are somehow less binding than material bonds (like citizenship, family membership, and so on). The God of biblical Revelation has established a family bond with his people on earth. This is binding, and "binding" is the root meaning of the word *religion*. Religion is "the ties that bind." A religion that makes no demands on believers is not truly a religion.

Religion entails duty, responsibility, commitment, and identity. It means something to say, "I am Catholic"; and it must be more than a private matter. Christian commitment involves the whole person, body and soul, with everything these entail. To be human is to be social, and so Christian commitment cannot be left in a drawer or a closet when we leave the house to take part in public life. Pope Benedict XVI spoke of Catholics who maintain "external social bonds but without an integral, interior conversion to the law of Christ." Such people, "rather than being transformed and renewed in mind," choose instead "to conform themselves to the spirit of this age." Nowhere is this as evident as in the "scandal given by Catholics who promote an alleged right to abortion."

TODAY'S CHALLENGES

The Pope called for Catholics to grow in their understanding of the Faith and especially of the natural law and then simply to exercise their rights and duties as citizens and as Catholics. Catholics should be well trained in apologetics—the art of explaining and defending the Faith—and should address moral issues in terms of natural law, which is accessible to everyone.

As we saw earlier in the book (Chapter 1), these methods worked to transform the Roman Empire. They can work to change other "secular" regimes.

It is important that we get this right. Catholic social doctrine is not a religious agenda for politics. It is not a party platform. It is not a blueprint for theocracy. It is, rather, the rule by which we, as citizens and as Catholics, can reliably measure all social programs and political proposals, fashioning alternatives as we see fit.

BL. SALVADOR HUERTA GUTIERREZ: Martyr and "Wizard of Cars"

Salvador Huerta Gutierrez was born in 1880 in Magdalena in the Mexican state of Jalisco. He lived during a time of intense persecution of the Church in Mexico. But he and his family, including two brothers who were priests, remained steadfast in the Faith.

Salvador was a devoted husband and father to twelve children. He did what he could to support his family; and whatever he did, he did very well. For a while he worked in the mines and became adept with explosives. But the mines were very dangerous, and he had more than a few brushes with death.

What he did best was repair automobiles. He was the most respected mechanic around. Eventually, he ran his own garage, and his neighbors called him the *El Mago de Coches*, the Wizard of Cars. He earned the respect of his customers and his workers, even though he forbade the use of profanity on his property. The locals said his workshop was a school and a temple.

Salvador went to Mass every day. He made a holy hour before the Blessed Sacrament, and he prayed the Rosary with his family.

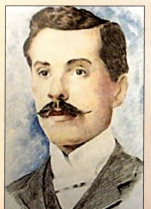

He made no effort to hide his faith, even though the Mexican Constitution of 1917 banned any public display of religion. By 1926, Catholics had organized a resistance movement, known as the *Cristeros*. There were outbreaks of violence, followed by reprisals and assassinations of clergy.

In April 1927, Salvador attended funeral rites for a slain resistance leader. When he went back to his garage, the police were waiting for him. They ordered him to come along "to fix the chief's car." He never returned.

He was tortured, hung by his thumbs. He was interrogated about the whereabouts of his priest-brothers. He said nothing.

The next day, he and his brother Ezequiel were led to their execution. At the cemetery, Salvador asked for a lighted candle and held it in front of his chest. He cried out: "Long live Christ the King and Our Lady of Guadalupe! Shoot me so that I will die for God, because I love him."

He was beatified by Pope Benedict XVI in 2005.

Catholic social doctrine is, moreover, neither "liberal" nor "conservative." It transcends both tendencies and corrects their ideological blind spots. It liberates us, said Pope Benedict XVI, from both the "tyranny of relativism"[1] and the "tyranny of convention."[2]

Relativism holds that there is no absolute truth in morality, and so any kind of behavior must be accepted. The only beliefs that relativism cannot accommodate are those that claim to possess the truth. Relativism inevitably becomes a tyranny, suppressing religious belief. When tolerance is seen as the supreme social virtue, truth is the one thing that cannot be tolerated, because truth must expose error and stand in opposition to it.

"Convention" becomes tyranny when it resists legitimate development, enshrining as traditional what is merely habitual. Even after two thousand years of Christianity, the social order must still be purified. It is helpful to examine social conventions against Christian principles and the natural law, which are universal and transcend custom.

MATERIALISM

Catholic tradition places a premium on reason, and it was this disposition that enabled the empirical sciences to grow and flourish. Nicholas Copernicus, the great astronomer, was a priest. Gregor Mendel, the founder of genetics, was a monk. Nicholas Steno, the founder of geology and paleontology, was a convert to Catholicism and a bishop. Antoine Lavoisier, who founded modern chemistry, was a devout layman, as was the biologist Louis Pasteur and the great mathematician Blaise Pascal.

Catholics value sensory data because they know that God created an ordered universe, and in the order of creation they come to know the mind of the creator.

We are not, however, reductionists. We do not reduce reality to what is merely visible, audible, and measurable. We affirm spiritual realities that cannot be contained or controlled—love, for example, free will, the service of others, and the value of sacrifice. Pope Benedict XVI said: "It is easy to be entranced

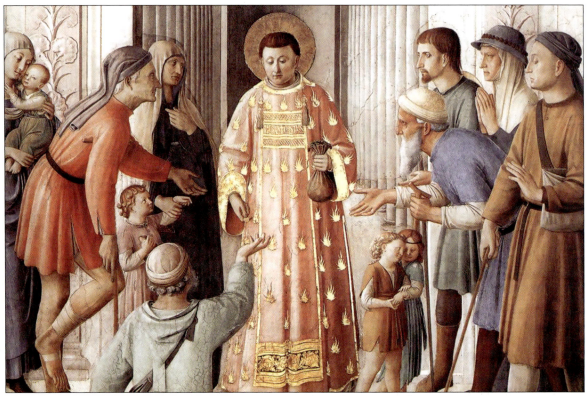

St. Lawrence Distributing Alms (detail) by Fra Angelico.
We are created by God, who is spirit, and we are a unique composite of spirit and matter. It is not enough just to fill our bellies and get enough sleep. If we neglect our spiritual component, we will never be fulfilled.

TODAY'S CHALLENGES

by the almost unlimited possibilities that science and technology place before us; it is easy to make the mistake of thinking we can obtain by our own efforts the fulfillment of our deepest needs. This is an illusion."

A classic definition of the human person is "a creature composed of body and soul, made in the image and likeness of God." We are created by God, who is spirit, and we are a unique composite of spirit and matter. It is not enough just to fill our bellies and get enough sleep. If we neglect our spiritual component, we will never be fulfilled.

Yet, many people do just that. They measure their lives, their personal progress, their success based on how much money they make, what kind of car they drive, and the size of their home.

None of these things, however, bring happiness and fulfillment. They do not satisfy. People who set only material goals never feel that they have acquired enough. In fact, their possessions create new needs that must be fulfilled, and which produce further needs. A person who owns priceless artworks or expensive cars must invest in security systems and worry about thieves.

Poor family in India washing clothes in a roadside ditch.
Unless people acknowledge that human nature is spiritual and created, they are unlikely to recognize the universality of human dignity.

Material wants tend to multiply needs. Possessions come to possess their owners, occupying more and more of their attention. They can never satisfy and never make anyone truly happy in a lasting way. A poor child browsing a gallery can sometimes enjoy far greater freedom to appreciate a particular work of art than can the person who owns the painting!

Poor people can enjoy greater freedom to be satisfied with what they have, even as they strive to improve conditions for their families. However, they, too, can be subject to the miseries of materialism, if they allow their poverty to fill them with envy, resentment, bitterness, or acquisitiveness.

Materialism can have a toxic effect on proposed solutions to social problems. Unless people acknowledge that human nature is spiritual and created, they are unlikely to recognize the universality of human dignity. Finding some other basis for their definition of humanity, they will invariably define some humans outside the limits of the community. Those who judge human beings based on productivity will have little use for people with disabilities. Those who believe sex, apart from marriage, is a basic human right will have little use for the inconvenient lives conceived out of wedlock. Those lives will be defined out of humanity. Similar thinking has been used to discount the dignity of people in comas, people with dementia, people with developmental delays—unproductive lives, when measured by a utilitarian yardstick.

Societies, however, do not run on utility alone. Love, which is the only thing that truly satisfies human beings, serves no apparent material purpose. Yet, money and property will not make up for its absence.

INDIVIDUALISM

At the beginning of the book, we stated that our vocation is to love as God loves. God is eternal, interpersonal love: the Blessed Trinity. We are made to live like God. It is not good for us to be alone (Gn 2:18).

We fulfill our vocation through the loving service of others. Spouses serve one another in love; parents serve their children; friends, their friends. Some professions are service-oriented by nature, for example, medicine, government, or counseling.

To give oneself is to act in a godlike way. For God is not a solitude, but a Trinity of Persons living in a communion of love. To live like God, to share in his nature (2 Pt 1:4), is every Christian's vocation and every human being's fulfillment.

In social life, we experience this in *solidarity* with one another. The antithesis of solidarity is *individualism*, the habit of being self-reliant and self-directed. Individualism is a hallmark of American culture, and Pope Benedict XVI recognizes that it arises from a good impulse—from the belief that human beings should not be constrained by the circumstances of birth or ancestry. Many of the heroes in American literature and history are people who have overcome bad situations through prodigious effort. The guiding myth is that America's independence from Europe's colonial powers brought about every individual's virtual independence from limitations, beginning with situational limitations, but including also the whole complex of culture, customs, and morals.

To succeed in such a world, one must be autonomous—literally, "a law unto oneself," beholden to no other law and no other people. Pope Benedict XVI noted the flaw in this approach to life. Individualism, he said, "obscures the relational dimension of the person and leads him to close himself off in his own little world, to be attentive mostly to his own needs and desires, worrying little about others."

Christ on the Mount of Olives by Overbeck. We should possess ourselves in order to give ourselves away in service.

But that "little world" is not a real world. It is a world of the individual's own making. In focusing on "his own needs and desires," the individualist ensures that he (or she) will never be satisfied—because only love satisfies; and love begins with denial of self for the sake of another. Pope Benedict explained:

> Faith tells us that the human person is a being called to live in relationships; that the "I" can find itself precisely by approaching a "you" who accepts and loves him or her. This "You" is first and foremost God, the only One who can give the human being unconditional acceptance and infinite love; and it is also others, starting with those who are closest. Rediscovering this relational dimension as a constitutive element of one's existence is the first step to bringing a more human society into being. Moreover it is also the task of institutions to foster the growth of the awareness that we are part of one reality in which each one, like the parts of the human body, is important to the whole…[3]

A preoccupation with oneself is frustrating, because it creates a needy self who cannot be fulfilled. The consequences begin with frustration and proceed to loneliness. When many people approach life in this way—when nations become aggregates of individualists—the social consequences are devastating. For individualists do not function well in society's fundamental unit: the family. Individualism leads to a breakdown of the family.

Autonomy and individualism are costly and endlessly demanding. They require easy divorce (to be free from family obligations), contraception (to be free of the demands of children), and euthanasia (to be free of the "burden" of sick family members). Individualism demands that the law accommodate the "necessary" means of removing people who are inconvenient.

Individualism recognizes no duty to the common good, but rather exalts self-interest. When facing any decision, the individualist asks: *What's in it for me? Why shouldn't I look out for myself first? No one else will look out for me.*

In a society of individualists, the "common good" becomes what pleases the most people, or what pleases the mob, no matter the cost in human dignity or minority rights.

The truth is that I am most myself when I forget myself and focus on others. This is what human beings were made to do. The individualist is right about the value of self-discipline and self-possession, but wrong about the reasons and goals. We should possess ourselves in order to give ourselves away in service. Only then can we truly become ourselves, in living like Jesus Christ.

TODAY'S CHALLENGES

ST. GIANNA MOLLA: Medic and Mother

St. Gianna Beretta Molla was a wife, mother, and medical doctor who lived in the mid-twentieth century. She was born in Italy in 1922 in a large, devout Catholic family—the tenth of thirteen children—a family that would also produce two priests and one nun.

Gianna considered entering religious life, but ultimately decided to pursue medicine instead. Although she remained focused on her medical studies, she also devoted much of her free time to charity as a volunteer. She graduated from medical school in 1949 and immediately went to work among the poor and the elderly, opening a clinic near her hometown in 1950. She received an additional degree in children's medicine in 1952 in order to give special attention to the mothers with young children who came to her for help.

This was when Gianna met her future husband, Pietro Molla, an engineer who lived across the street from her clinic. They were married at their local parish in late 1955 in a ceremony presided over by her older brother, Fr. Guiseppe. Little more than a year later, Gianna gave birth to her first child, Pierluigi. Gianna and Pietro welcomed him with great joy, and over the next three years, they celebrated the births of two more children, Mariolina and Laura.

In the fall of 1961, after two miscarriages, Gianna again became pregnant. During the course of this pregnancy, however, Gianna's doctors discovered that she had developed a tumor that was threatening both her life and the life of her unborn child. The doctors recommended that she abort her child and undergo surgery to remove the tumor. But for Gianna, this was unacceptable. In addition, she said, "If you must decide between me and the child, do not hesitate. Choose the child—I insist on it. Save the baby."

St. Gianna Beretta Molla.
Gianna's husband and children were present at her canonization in 2004.

On Good Friday in 1962, after nine months of pregnancy, Gianna checked into the hospital, giving birth the following day to a baby girl, Gianna Emanuela. Although the doctors struggled to save the lives of both mother and child, in the end, the complications of the delivery proved too much for the elder Gianna. She died exactly one week after the birth of her infant daughter, having indeed been called by Christ to lay down her life for the life of another.

At her canonization in 2004—at which Gianna's husband and children were present—Gianna Molla was praised by St. John Paul II for this heroic act of self-giving. Christ, "having loved his own…[,] loved them to the end" (Jn 13:1). Gianna loved her own child even to the point of dying for her. Her feast day is April 28.

A Forgotten Man.
Individualism creates a misshapen society. While appearing to affirm each person's rights, individualism actually knocks out the underpinnings of all human rights.

Living in a self-centered way is one of the effects of Original Sin. God created us to live and act in a way that is centered on him and on others, not ourselves. We imitate God when we care for others for God looks out for every human being. He brings us into being, watches over us in life, and draws us into his Church, his communion of saints. The Church herself gives evidence of his concern, as do the family and the community.

A truly enlightened self-interest should lead us away from the dead end of individualism and toward the love of others. True and lasting fulfillment is never found in money or material possessions. Real happiness can be found only in fulfilling our nature, fulfilling God's plan for us, and responding to our supernatural vocation.

Individualism, the turning in on oneself, has dire social and economic consequences when it becomes habitual and cultural, a widespread attitude and worldview. From such a foundation "structures of sin" arise. Indeed, Pope Benedict XVI traced the worldwide recession, which began in 2007, to the individualistic mindset:

> Are not speculation in leases, the increasingly difficult integration of young people in the labor market, the loneliness of so many of the elderly, the anonymity which often characterizes life in the neighborhoods of the city and the at times superficial view of situations of marginalization and poverty a consequence of this mindset?...
>
> In a society which values personal freedom and autonomy, it is easy to lose sight of our dependence on others as well as the responsibilities that we bear towards them...Yet from the beginning, God saw that "it is not good for man to be alone" (Genesis 2:18). We were created as social beings who find fulfillment only in love—for God and for our neighbor. If we are truly to gaze upon him who is the source of our joy, we need to do so as members of the people of God (cf. Spe Salvi, 14). If this seems counter-cultural, that is simply further evidence of the urgent need for a renewed evangelization of culture.[4]

A Christian belongs to a family—the family of God—and thus cannot be an individualist. The *Catechism* makes clear that an individualist will find it difficult, if not impossible, to pray with sincerity:

> Finally, if we pray the Our Father sincerely, we leave individualism behind, because the love that we receive frees us from it. The "our" at the beginning of the Lord's Prayer, like the "us" of the last four petitions, excludes no one. If we are to say it truthfully, our divisions and oppositions have to be overcome.[5] (CCC 2792)

TODAY'S CHALLENGES

Individualism creates a misshapen society. Since it considers every individual's moral conclusions to be as valid as any other's, all morals must be relative. While appearing to affirm each person's rights, this approach actually knocks out the underpinnings of all human rights. While appearing to affirm the dignity of individual opinion, it renders human dignity vulnerable to opinions that deny it altogether.

Since individualism also destroys solidarity, it leaves people weak before tyranny—whether it is the tyranny of a mob or the tyranny of a despot. Isolated individuals cannot easily withstand such force, especially when they have been conditioned to tolerate every sort of evil as in the name of individual choice.

CONCLUSION

As long as fallen people live in society, there will be social problems and social concerns. It is our nature and our vocation to live together; but our tendency to sin makes it difficult to share a common life. Thus, Christ foretold that we would always have poverty (see Mt 26:11) and always endure scandals (Mt 18:7).

There is a human tendency to seek social solutions to social problems, but Christ offered no political platform, no grand scheme for fixing society. Rather he established a social means for individuals to reform their lives. He established the Church, with her Sacraments, as a means of grace and transformation in the world. Social problems are resolved in the smallest increments, when individuals move toward Christ and lead their friends and family members along by their example.

The Last Judgment (detail) by Van Eyck. Perfect justice will be realized only in eternal life, through the perfect mercy of God.

Christians working within society will transform it from within. Our work can be redemptive when it shares in the life of Christ and cooperates with the work of the Holy Spirit. Grace builds on nature; and, in fact, "the preparation of man for the reception of grace is already a work of grace" (CCC 2001). Yet, God calls us to cooperate with his grace. By work done well and offered to God, they will restore all things in Christ (cf. Eph 1:10) and redeem the time (cf. Eph 5:16). Grace builds on nature, but we must be open to grace. To that end, Pope Benedict XVI counsels lay Catholics to live a sustained and disciplined life of prayer, even as they go about their work, their studies, their family life, and friendships.

"Charity and justice are not only social but also spiritual actions, accomplished in the light of the Holy Spirit," he said. "We must not lose ourselves in pure activism but always let ourselves also be penetrated in our activities by the light of the word of God and thereby learn true charity, true service to others, which does not need many things—it certainly needs the necessary things—but needs above all our heartfelt affection and the light of God."[6] Charity is superior to all other virtues and is the form of the virtues; far from being extra or optional, charity completes justice and perfects it.

In such an integrated life, the works of justice do not exclude the works of charity. Nor is justice opposed to mercy and peace. Charity should complete justice and perfect it; charity is not extra or optional.

Such integrated lives integrate well with other lives and make for a better society—better, not perfect. A perfect world cannot be built by human efforts alone. Perfect justice will be realized only in eternal life, through the perfect mercy of God.

> And I saw the holy city, new Jerusalem, coming down out of heaven from God…and I heard a loud voice from the throne saying, "Behold, the dwelling of God is with men. He will dwell with them, and they shall be his people, and God himself will be with them; he will wipe away every tear from their eyes, and death shall be no more, neither shall there be mourning nor crying nor pain any more, for the former things have passed away." And he who sat upon the throne said, "Behold, I make all things new." (Rev 21:2-5)

The Saints
PILLARS OF THE CHURCH

ST. CLEMENT OF ALEXANDRIA

St. Clement of Alexandria (ca. 150-215) was a Greek convert to the Faith, theologian, and Father of the Church.

St. Clement of Alexandria (ca.150-215)

Who is the Rich Man That Shall Be Saved?

Riches, then, which benefit also our neighbors, are not to be thrown away. For they are possessions, inasmuch as they are possessed; and they are goods, inasmuch as they are useful and provided by God for people's use; and they are available to us, and are placed in our power, as material and instruments that are for good use by those who know how to use the instrument. If you use it skillfully, it is skillful; if you lack skill, it is affected by your lack of skill. The instrument itself bears no blame.

Such an instrument is wealth. Are you able to put it to good use? It is subservient to righteousness. Does one make a wrong use of it? It is, on the other hand, a minister of wrong. For its nature is to be subservient, not to rule. So do not blame something that, of itself, is neither good nor evil, but blameless. Rather, you should blame the person who has the power of using it well or ill, by the power of free choice. I am talking about the mind and judgment of man, which has freedom in itself and self-determination in the treatment of what is assigned to it. So let no man destroy wealth rather than the passions of the soul, which are incompatible with the better use of wealth. So that, becoming virtuous and good, he may be able to make a good use of these riches. The renunciation, then, and selling of all possessions, is to be understood as meaning the passions of the soul…

SUPPLEMENTARY READING

Pope Benedict XVI: Address to the United States Bishops, April 16, 2008

Dear Brother Bishops,

It gives me great joy to greet you today, at the start of my visit to this country…As this year also marks the bicentenary of the elevation of the founding see of Baltimore to an Archdiocese, it gives me an opportunity to recall with admiration and gratitude the life and ministry of John Carroll, the first Bishop of Baltimore—a worthy leader of the Catholic community in your newly independent nation. His tireless efforts to spread the Gospel in the vast territory under his care laid the foundations for the ecclesial life of your country and enabled the Church in America to grow to maturity. Today the Catholic community you serve is one of the largest in the world, and one of the most influential. How important it is, then, to let your light so shine before your fellow citizens and before the world, "that they may see your good works and give glory to your Father who is in heaven" (Mt 5:16).

Many of the people to whom John Carroll and his fellow bishops were ministering two centuries ago had travelled from distant lands. The diversity of their origins is reflected in the rich variety of ecclesial life in present-day America. Brother bishops, I want to encourage you and your communities to continue to welcome the immigrants who join your ranks today, to share their joys and hopes, to support them in their sorrows and trials, and to help them flourish in their new home. This, indeed, is what your fellow countrymen have done for generations. From the beginning, they have opened their doors to the tired, the poor, the "huddled masses yearning to breathe free" (cf. Sonnet inscribed on the Statue of Liberty). These are the people whom America has made her own.

Of those who came to build a new life here, many were able to make good use of the resources and opportunities that they found, and to attain a high level of prosperity. Indeed, the people of this country are known for their great vitality and creativity. They are also known for their generosity. After the attack on the Twin Towers in September 2001, and again after Hurricane Katrina in 2005, Americans displayed their readiness to come to the aid of their brothers and sisters in need. On the international level, the contribution made by the people of America to relief and rescue operations after the tsunami of December 2004 is a further illustration of this compassion. Let me express my particular appreciation for the many forms of humanitarian assistance provided by American Catholics through Catholic Charities and other agencies. Their generosity has borne fruit in the care shown to the poor and needy, and in the energy that has gone into building the nationwide network of Catholic parishes, hospitals, schools, and universities. All of this gives great cause for thanksgiving.

America is also a land of great faith. Your people are remarkable for their religious fervor and they take pride in belonging to a worshipping community. They have confidence in God, and they do not hesitate to bring moral arguments rooted in biblical faith into their public discourse. Respect for freedom of religion is deeply ingrained in the American consciousness—a fact which has contributed to this country's attraction for generations of immigrants, seeking a home where they can worship freely in accordance with their beliefs…

It is in this fertile soil, nourished from so many different sources, that all of you, brother bishops, are called to sow the seeds of the Gospel today. This leads me to ask how, in the twenty-first

Pope Benedict XVI washes the feet of his fellow priests on Holy Thursday.

SUPPLEMENTARY READING continued

century, a bishop can best fulfill the call to "make all things new in Christ, our hope"? How can he lead his people to "an encounter with the living God," the source of that life-transforming hope of which the Gospel speaks (cf. *Spe Salvi*, 4)? Perhaps he needs to begin by clearing away some of the barriers to such an encounter. While it is true that this country is marked by a genuinely religious spirit, the subtle influence of secularism can nevertheless color the way people allow their faith to influence their behavior. Is it consistent to profess our beliefs in church on Sunday, and then during the week to promote business practices or medical procedures contrary to those beliefs? Is it consistent for practicing Catholics to ignore or exploit the poor and the marginalized, to promote sexual behavior contrary to Catholic moral teaching, or to adopt positions that contradict the right to life of every human being from conception to natural death? Any tendency to treat religion as a private matter must be resisted. Only when their faith permeates every aspect of their lives do Christians become truly open to the transforming power of the Gospel.

For an affluent society, a further obstacle to an encounter with the living God lies in the subtle influence of materialism, which can all too easily focus the attention on the hundredfold, which God promises now in this time, at the expense of the eternal life which he promises in the age to come (cf. Mk 10:30). People today need to be reminded of the ultimate purpose of their lives. They need to recognize that implanted within them is a deep thirst for God. They need to be given opportunities to drink from the wells of his infinite love. It is easy to be entranced by the almost unlimited possibilities that science and technology place before us; it is easy to make the mistake of thinking we can obtain by our own efforts the fulfillment of our deepest needs. This is an illusion. Without God, who alone bestows upon us what we by ourselves cannot attain (cf. *Spe Salvi*, 31), our lives are ultimately empty. People need to be constantly reminded to cultivate a relationship with him who came that we might have life in abundance (cf. Jn 10:10). The goal of all our pastoral and catechetical work, the object of our preaching, and the focus of our sacramental ministry should be to help people establish and nurture that living relationship with "Christ Jesus, our hope" (1 Tim 1:1).

In a society which values personal freedom and autonomy, it is easy to lose sight of our dependence on others as well as the responsibilities that we bear towards them. This emphasis on individualism has even affected the Church (cf. *Spe Salvi*, 13-15), giving rise to a form of piety which sometimes emphasizes our private relationship with God at the expense of our calling to be members of a redeemed community. Yet from the beginning, God saw that "it is not good for man to be alone" (Gen 2:18). We were created as social beings who find fulfillment only in love—for God and for our neighbor. If we are truly to gaze upon him who is the source of our joy, we need to do so as members of the people of God (cf. *Spe Salvi*, 14). If this seems counter-cultural, that is simply further evidence of the urgent need for a renewed evangelization of culture.

Here in America, you are blessed with a Catholic laity of considerable cultural diversity, who place their wide-ranging gifts at the service of the Church and of society at large. They look to you to offer them encouragement, leadership and direction. In an age that is saturated with information, the importance of providing sound formation in the faith cannot be overstated. American Catholics have traditionally placed a high value on religious education, both in schools and in the context of adult formation programs. These need to be maintained and expanded. The many generous men and women who devote themselves to charitable activity need to be helped to renew their dedication through a "formation of the heart": an "encounter with God in Christ which awakens their love and opens their spirits to others" (*Deus Caritas Est*, 31). At a time when advances

SUPPLEMENTARY READING Continued

in medical science bring new hope to many, they also give rise to previously unimagined ethical challenges. This makes it more important than ever to offer thorough formation in the Church's moral teaching to Catholics engaged in health care. Wise guidance is needed in all these apostolates, so that they may bear abundant fruit; if they are truly to promote the integral good of the human person, they too need to be made new in Christ our hope.

As preachers of the Gospel and leaders of the Catholic community, you are also called to participate in the exchange of ideas in the public square, helping to shape cultural attitudes. In a context where free speech is valued, and where vigorous and honest debate is encouraged, yours is a respected voice that has much to offer to the discussion of the pressing social and moral questions of the day. By ensuring that the Gospel is clearly heard, you not only form the people of your own community, but in view of the global reach of mass communication, you help to spread the message of Christian hope throughout the world.

Clearly, the Church's influence on public debate takes place on many different levels. In the United States, as elsewhere, there is much current and proposed legislation that gives cause for concern from the point of view of morality, and the Catholic community, under your guidance, needs to offer a clear and united witness on such matters. Even more important, though, is the gradual opening of the minds and hearts of the wider community to moral truth. Here much remains to be done. Crucial in this regard is the role of the lay faithful to act as a "leaven" in society. Yet it cannot be assumed that all Catholic citizens think in harmony with the Church's teaching on today's key ethical questions. Once again, it falls to you to ensure that the moral formation provided at every level of ecclesial life reflects the authentic teaching of the Gospel of life.

In this regard, a matter of deep concern to us all is the state of the family within society.

Indeed, Cardinal [Francis] George [of Chicago] mentioned earlier that you have included the strengthening of marriage and family life among the priorities for your attention over the next few years. In this year's World Day of Peace Message I spoke of the essential contribution that healthy family life makes to peace within and between nations. In the family home we experience "some of the fundamental elements of peace: justice and love between brothers and sisters, the role of authority expressed by parents, loving concern for the members who are weaker because of youth, sickness or old age, mutual help in the necessities of life, readiness to accept others and, if necessary, to forgive them" (no. 3). The family is also the primary place for evangelization, for passing on the Faith, for helping young people to appreciate the importance of religious practice and Sunday observance. How can we not be dismayed as we observe the sharp decline of the family as a basic element of Church and society? Divorce and infidelity have increased, and many young men and women are choosing to postpone marriage or to forego it altogether. To some young Catholics, the sacramental bond of marriage seems scarcely distinguishable from a civil bond, or even a purely informal and open-ended arrangement to live with another person. Hence we have an alarming decrease in the number of Catholic marriages in the United States together with an increase in cohabitation, in which the Christ-like mutual self-giving of spouses, sealed by a public promise to live out the demands of an indissoluble lifelong commitment, is simply absent. In such circumstances, children are denied the secure environment that they need in order truly to flourish as human beings, and society is denied the stable building blocks which it requires if the cohesion and moral focus of the community are to be maintained.

As my predecessor, Pope John Paul II, taught, "The person principally responsible in the Diocese for the pastoral care of the family is the bishop…he must devote to it personal interest, care, time, personnel and resources, but above

SUPPLEMENTARY READING continued

all personal support for the families and for all those who…assist him in the pastoral care of the family" (*Familiaris Consortio*, 73). It is your task to proclaim boldly the arguments from faith and reason in favor of the institution of marriage, understood as a lifelong commitment between a man and a woman, open to the transmission of life. This message should resonate with people today, because it is essentially an unconditional and unreserved "yes" to life, a "yes" to love, and a "yes" to the aspirations at the heart of our common humanity, as we strive to fulfill our deep yearning for intimacy with others and with the Lord…

As I conclude my words to you this evening, I commend the Church in your country most particularly to the maternal care and intercession of Mary Immaculate, Patroness of the United States. May she who carried within her womb the hope of all the nations intercede for the people of this country, so that all may be made new in Jesus Christ her Son. My dear brother bishops, I assure each of you here present of my deep friendship and my participation in your pastoral concerns. To all of you, and to your clergy, religious and lay faithful, I cordially impart my Apostolic Blessing as a pledge of joy and peace in the Risen Lord.

Pope Benedict XVI: In Conversation with the United States Bishops, April 16, 2008

After the Holy Father's address (excerpted above), he was asked to give his assessment of the challenge of increasing secularism in public life and relativism in intellectual life, and his advice on how to confront these challenges pastorally and evangelize more effectively.

I touched upon this theme briefly in my address. It strikes me as significant that here in America, unlike many places in Europe, the secular mentality has not been intrinsically opposed to religion. Within the context of the separation of Church and State, American society has always been marked by a fundamental respect for religion and its public role, and, if polls are to be believed, the American people are deeply religious. But it is not enough to count on this traditional religiosity and go about business as usual, even as its foundations are being slowly undermined. A serious commitment to evangelization cannot prescind from a profound diagnosis of the real challenges the Gospel encounters in contemporary American culture.

Of course, what is essential is a correct understanding of the just autonomy of the secular order, an autonomy which cannot be divorced from God the Creator and his saving plan (cf. *Gaudium et Spes*, 36). Perhaps America's brand of secularism poses a particular problem: It allows for professing belief in God, and respects the public role of religion and the Churches, but at the same time it can subtly reduce religious belief to a lowest common denominator. Faith becomes a passive acceptance that certain things "out there" are true, but without practical relevance for everyday life. The result is a growing separation of faith from life: living "as if God did not exist." This is aggravated by an individualistic and eclectic approach to faith and religion: Far from a Catholic approach to "thinking with the Church," each person believes he or she has a right to pick and choose, maintaining external social bonds but without an integral, interior conversion to the law of Christ. Consequently, rather than being transformed and renewed in mind, Christians are easily tempted to conform themselves to the spirit of this age (cf. Rom 12:3). We have seen this emerge in an acute way in the scandal given by Catholics who promote an alleged right to abortion.

On a deeper level, secularism challenges the Church to reaffirm and to pursue more actively her mission in and to the world. As the Council made clear, the lay faithful have a particular responsibility in this regard. What is needed, I am convinced, is a greater sense of the intrinsic relationship between the Gospel and the natural law on the one hand, and, on the other, the pursuit of authentic human good, as embodied in civil law and in personal moral decisions. In a society that rightly values personal liberty, the Church needs to promote at every level of her teaching—in catechesis, preaching, seminary and university instruction—an apologetics

SUPPLEMENTARY READING (Continued)

aimed at affirming the truth of Christian revelation, the harmony of faith and reason, and a sound understanding of freedom, seen in positive terms as a liberation both from the limitations of sin and for an authentic and fulfilling life. In a word, the Gospel has to be preached and taught as an integral way of life, offering an attractive and true answer, intellectually and practically, to real human problems. The "dictatorship of relativism," in the end, is nothing less than a threat to genuine human freedom, which only matures in generosity and fidelity to the truth.

Much more, of course, could be said on this subject: Let me conclude, though, by saying that I believe that the Church in America, at this point in her history, is faced with the challenge of recapturing the Catholic vision of reality and presenting it, in an engaging and imaginative way, to a society which markets any number of recipes for human fulfillment. I think in particular of our need to speak to the hearts of young people, who, despite their constant exposure to messages contrary to the Gospel, continue to thirst for authenticity, goodness, and truth. Much remains to be done, particularly on the level of preaching and catechesis in parishes and schools, if the new evangelization is to bear fruit for the renewal of ecclesial life in America.

St. John Paul II: Apostolic Exhortation *Ecclesia in America* (*The Church in America*), 1999

"Repent therefore and be converted" (Acts 3:19)

The Urgency of the Call to Conversion

26. "The time is fulfilled and the kingdom of God is close at hand: repent and believe the Good News" (Mk 1:15). These words with which Jesus began his Galilean ministry still echo in the ears of bishops, priests, deacons, consecrated men and women and the lay faithful throughout America. Both the recent celebration of the fifth centenary of the first evangelization of America and the commemoration of the two-thousandth anniversary of the birth of Jesus, the Great Jubilee we are preparing to celebrate, summon everyone alike to a deeper sense of our Christian vocation. The greatness of the Incarnation and gratitude for the gift of the first proclamation of the Gospel in America are an invitation to respond readily to Christ with a more decisive personal conversion and a stimulus to ever more generous fidelity to the Gospel. Christ's call to conversion finds an echo in the words of the Apostle: "It is time now to wake from sleep, because our salvation is closer than when we first became believers" (Rom 13:11). The encounter with the living Jesus impels us to conversion.

In speaking of conversion, the New Testament uses the word *metanoia*, which means a change of mentality. It is not simply a matter of thinking differently in an intellectual sense, but of revising the reasons behind one's actions in the light of the Gospel. In this regard, Saint Paul speaks of "faith working through love" (Gal 5:6). This means that true conversion needs to be prepared and nurtured through the prayerful reading of Sacred Scripture and the practice of the Sacraments of Reconciliation and the Eucharist. Conversion leads to fraternal communion, because it enables us to understand

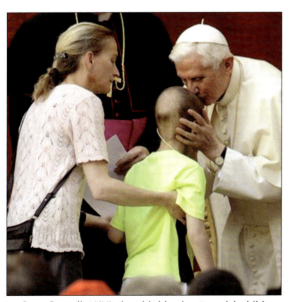

Pope Benedict XVI gives his blessing to a sick child. "I think in particular of our need to speak to the hearts of young people, who, despite their constant exposure to messages contrary to the Gospel, continue to thirst for authenticity, goodness, and truth."

SUPPLEMENTARY READING Continued

that Christ is the head of the Church, his Mystical Body; it urges solidarity, because it makes us aware that whatever we do for others, especially for the poorest, we do for Christ himself. Conversion, therefore, fosters a new life, in which there is no separation between faith and works in our daily response to the universal call to holiness. In order to speak of conversion, the gap between faith and life must be bridged. Where this gap exists, Christians are such only in name. To be true disciples of the Lord, believers must bear witness to their faith, and "witnesses testify not only with words, but also with their lives."[7] We must keep in mind the words of Jesus: "Not every one who says to me, 'Lord, Lord!' shall enter the kingdom of heaven, but he who does the will of my Father who is in heaven" (Mt 7:21). Openness to the Father's will supposes a total self-giving, including even the gift of one's life: "The greatest witness is martyrdom."[8]

The Social Dimension of Conversion

27. Yet conversion is incomplete if we are not aware of the demands of the Christian life and if we do not strive to meet them. In this regard, the Synod Fathers noted that unfortunately "at both the personal and communal level there are great shortcomings in relation to a more profound conversion and with regard to relationships between sectors, institutions and groups within the Church."[9] "He who does not love his brother whom he has seen, cannot love God whom he has not seen" (1 Jn 4:20).

Fraternal charity means attending to all the needs of our neighbor. "If any one has the world's goods and sees his brother in need, yet closes his heart against him, how does God's love abide in him?" (1 Jn 3:17). Hence, for the Christian people of America conversion to the Gospel means to revise "all the different areas and aspects of life, especially those related to the social order and the pursuit of the common good."[10] It will be especially necessary "to nurture the growing awareness in society of the dignity of every person and, therefore, to promote in the community a sense of the duty to participate in political life in harmony with the Gospel."[11] Involvement in the political field is clearly part of the vocation and activity of the lay faithful.[12]

In this regard, however, it is most important, especially in a pluralistic society, to understand correctly the relationship between the political community and the Church, and to distinguish clearly between what individual believers or groups of believers undertake in their own name as citizens guided by Christian conscience and what they do in the name of the Church in communion with their Pastors. The Church which, in virtue of her office and competence, can in no way be confused with the political community nor be tied to any political system, is both a sign and safeguard of the transcendent character of the human person....[13]

Solidarity, the Fruit of Communion

52. "Truly, I say to you, as you did it to one of the least of these my brethren, you did it to me" (Mt 25:40; cf. 25:45). The awareness of communion with Christ and with our brothers and sisters, for its part the fruit of conversion, leads to the service of our neighbors in all their needs, material and spiritual, since the face of Christ shines forth in every human being. "Solidarity is thus the fruit of the communion which is grounded in the mystery of the triune God, and in the Son of God who took flesh and died for all. It is expressed in Christian love which seeks the good of others, especially of those most in need."[14]

For the particular Churches of the American continent, this is the source of a commitment to reciprocal solidarity and the sharing of the spiritual gifts and material goods with which God has blessed them, fostering in individuals a readiness to work where they are needed. Taking the Gospel as its starting-point, a culture of solidarity needs to be promoted, capable of inspiring timely initiatives in support of the poor and the outcast, especially refugees forced to leave their villages and lands in order to flee violence. The Church in America must encourage the international agencies of the continent to establish an economic order dominated not only by the profit motive but also by the pursuit of the

SUPPLEMENTARY READING (Continued)

common good of nations and of the international community, the equitable distribution of goods and the integral development of peoples.[15]

The Church's Teaching, a Statement of the Demands of Conversion

53. At a time when in the sphere of morality there is a disturbing spread of relativism and subjectivism, the Church in America is called to proclaim with renewed vigor that conversion consists in commitment to the Person of Jesus Christ, with all the theological and moral implications taught by the Magisterium of the Church. There is a need to recognize "the role played by theologians, catechists and religion teachers who, by setting forth the Church's teaching in fidelity to the Magisterium, cooperate directly in the correct formation of the consciences of the faithful."[16] If we believe that Jesus is the Truth (cf. Jn 14:6), we cannot fail to desire ardently to be his witnesses in order to bring our brothers and sisters closer to the full truth that dwells in the Son of God made man, who died and rose from the dead for the salvation of the human race. "In this way we will be able to be, in this world, living beacons of faith, hope, and charity."[17]

The Church's Social Doctrine

54. Faced with the grave social problems which, with different characteristics, are present throughout America, Catholics know that they can find in the Church's social doctrine an answer which serves as a starting-point in the search for practical solutions. Spreading this doctrine is an authentic pastoral priority. It is therefore important "that in America the agents of evangelization (bishops, priests, teachers, pastoral workers, etc.) make their own this treasure which is the Church's social teaching and, inspired by it, become capable of interpreting the present situation and determine the actions to take."[18] In this regard, special care must be taken to train lay persons capable of working, on the basis of their faith in Christ, to transform earthly realities. In addition, it will help to promote and support the study of this doctrine in every area of the life of the particular Churches in America, especially in the universities, so that it may be more deeply known and applied to American society. The complex social reality of the continent is a fruitful field for the analysis and application of the universal principles contained in this doctrine.

To this end, it would be very useful to have a compendium or approved synthesis of Catholic social doctrine, including a "Catechism," which would show the connection between it and the new evangelization. The part which the *Catechism of the Catholic Church* devotes to this material, in its treatment of the seventh commandment of the Decalogue, could serve as the starting-point for such a "Catechism of Catholic Social Doctrine." Naturally, as in the case of the *Catechism of the Catholic Church*, such a synthesis would only formulate general principles, leaving their application to further treatment of the specific issues bound up with the different local situations.[19]

An important place in the Church's social doctrine belongs to the right to dignified labor. Consequently, given the high rates of unemployment found in numerous countries in America and the harsh conditions in which many industrial and rural workers find themselves, "it is necessary to value work as a factor of the fulfillment and dignity of the human person. It is the ethical responsibility of an organized society to promote and support a culture of work."[20]

The Globalization of Solidarity

55. As I mentioned earlier, the complex phenomenon of globalization is one of the features of the contemporary world particularly visible in America. An important part of this many-faceted reality is the economic aspect. By her social doctrine the Church makes an effective contribution to the issues presented by the current globalized economy. Her moral vision in this area "rests on the threefold cornerstone of human dignity, solidarity and subsidiarity."[21] The globalized economy must be analyzed in the light of the principles of social justice, respecting the preferential option for the poor who must be allowed to take their place in

SUPPLEMENTARY READING Continued

such an economy, and the requirements of the international common good. For "the Church's social doctrine is a moral vision which aims to encourage governments, institutions and private organizations to shape a future consonant with the dignity of every person. Within this perspective it is possible to examine questions of external debt, internal political corruption and discrimination both within and between nations."[22]

The Church in America is called not only to promote greater integration between nations, thus helping to create an authentic globalized culture of solidarity,[23] but also to cooperate with every legitimate means in reducing the negative effects of globalization, such as the domination of the powerful over the weak, especially in the economic sphere, and the loss of the values of local cultures in favor of a misconstrued homogenization.

Social Sins which Cry to Heaven

56. The Church's social doctrine also makes possible a clearer appreciation of the gravity of the "social sins which cry to heaven because they generate violence, disrupt peace and harmony between communities within single nations, between nations and between the different regions of the continent."[24] Among these must be mentioned: "the drug trade, the recycling of illicit funds, corruption at every level, the terror of violence, the arms race, racial discrimination, inequality between social groups and the irrational destruction of nature."[25] These sins are the sign of a deep crisis caused by the loss of a sense of God and the absence of those moral principles which should guide the life of every person. In the absence of moral points of reference, an unbridled greed for wealth and power takes over, obscuring any Gospel-based vision of social reality.

Not infrequently, this leads some public institutions to ignore the actual social climate. More and more, in many countries of America, a system known as "neoliberalism" prevails; based on a purely economic conception of man, this system considers profit and the law

St. John Paul II.
"There is no authentic and stable democracy without social justice."

of the market as its only parameters, to the detriment of the dignity of and the respect due to individuals and peoples. At times this system has become the ideological justification for certain attitudes and behavior in the social and political spheres leading to the neglect of the weaker members of society. Indeed, the poor are becoming ever more numerous, victims of specific policies and structures which are often unjust.[26]

On the basis of the Gospel, the best response to this tragic situation is the promotion of solidarity and peace, with a view to achieving real justice. For this to happen, encouragement and support must be given to all those who are examples of honesty in the administration of public finances and of justice. So, too, there is a need to support the process of democratization presently taking place in America,[27] since a democratic system provides greater control over potential abuses.

SUPPLEMENTARY READING Continued

"The rule of law is the necessary condition for the establishment of an authentic democracy."[28] For democracy to develop, there is a need for civic education and the promotion of public order and peace. In effect, "there is no authentic and stable democracy without social justice. Thus the Church needs to pay greater attention to the formation of consciences, which will prepare the leaders of society for public life at all levels, promote civic education, respect for law and for human rights, and inspire greater efforts in the ethical training of political leaders."[29]

The Ultimate Foundation of Human Rights

57. It is appropriate to recall that the foundation on which all human rights rest is the dignity of the person. "God's masterpiece, man, is made in the divine image and likeness. Jesus took on our human nature, except for sin; he advanced and defended the dignity of every human person, without exception; he died that all might be free. The Gospel shows us how Christ insisted on the centrality of the human person in the natural order (cf. Lk 12:22-29) and in the social and religious orders, even against the claims of the Law (cf. Mk 2:27): defending men, women (cf. Jn 8:11) and even children (cf. Mt 19:13-15), who in his time and culture occupied an inferior place in society. The human being's dignity as a child of God is the source of human rights and of corresponding duties."[30] For this reason, "every offense against the dignity of man is an offense against God himself, in whose image man is made."[31] This dignity is common to all, without exception, since all have been created in the image of God (cf. Gen 1:26). Jesus' answer to the question "Who is my neighbor?" (Lk 10:29) demands of each individual an attitude of respect for the dignity of others and of real concern for them, even if they are strangers or enemies (cf. Lk 10:30-37). In all parts of America the awareness that human rights must be respected has increased in recent times, yet much still remains to be done, if we consider the violations of the rights of persons and groups still taking place on the continent.

Preferential Love for the Poor and the Outcast

58. "The Church in America must incarnate in her pastoral initiatives the solidarity of the universal Church towards the poor and the outcast of every kind. Her attitude needs to be one of assistance, promotion, liberation and fraternal openness. The goal of the Church is to ensure that no one is marginalized."[32] The memory of the dark chapters of America's history, involving the practice of slavery and other situations of social discrimination, must awaken a sincere desire for conversion leading to reconciliation and communion.

Concern for those most in need springs from a decision to love the poor in a special manner. This is a love which is not exclusive and thus cannot be interpreted as a sign of partiality or sectarianism;[33] in loving the poor the Christian imitates the attitude of the Lord, who during his earthly life devoted himself with special compassion to all those in spiritual and material need.

The Church's work on behalf of the poor in every part of America is important; yet efforts are still needed to make this line of pastoral activity increasingly directed to an encounter with Christ who, though rich, made himself poor for our sakes, that he might enrich us by his poverty (cf. 2 Cor 8:9). There is a need to intensify and broaden what is already being done in this area, with the goal of reaching as many of the poor as possible. Sacred Scripture reminds us that God hears the cry of the poor (cf. Ps 34:7) and the Church must heed the cry of those most in need. Hearing their voice, "she must live with the poor and share their distress. By her lifestyle, her priorities, her words, and her actions, she must testify that she is in communion and solidarity with them."[34]

VOCABULARY

INDIVIDUALISM
Belief in the primary importance of the individual and in the values of personal independence and self-reliance.

MATERIALISM
The belief that nothing exists except physical matter; also, a tendency to value possessions and physical comfort above spiritual life.

RELATIVISM
The belief that knowledge and morality do not correspond to any absolute truth, but are rather conditioned by individual experience or cultural context.

SECULARISM
The doctrinaire exclusion of religion from public life.

SECULARITY
The special character of the laity, at work and living in the world (see *LG* 31).

STUDY QUESTIONS

1. What three currents in thought did Pope Benedict XVI identify as obstacles to human fulfillment?

2. Why is the Blessed Virgin Mary an especially appropriate intercessor for social causes?

3. What is the difference between secularity and secularism?

4. What is secularism? How does it foster materialism?

5. What is materialism? How does it affect one's approach to life?

6. Is Christianity incompatible with the empirical sciences?

7. What is individualism?

8. How does individualism lead to moral relativism?

9. Why is prayer an important component in works of justice and charity?

PRACTICAL EXERCISES

1. Study the platform of a major political party in your country. Analyze its points in terms of how well they confront, overcome, or avoid the problems of secularism, materialism, and individualism. Does the party seem particularly beset by one of these obstacles? If so, why?

2. Read the document *Christifideles Laici* by St. John Paul II, along with Chapter 31 of *Lumen Gentium*, from the Second Vatican Council. Write an essay explaining the difference between the "secular character," which is proper to the laity, and "secularism."

3. Explain why seemingly benign outlooks, like relativism and traditionalism, can become "tyrannies." Give examples, from recent history, of both the "tyranny of relativism" and the "tyranny of convention."

4. Compare and contrast "secularism" and "secularity." What do they have in common? How do they differ?

FROM THE CATECHISM

2453 The seventh commandment forbids theft. Theft is the usurpation of another's goods against the reasonable will of the owner.

2454 Every manner of taking and using another's property unjustly is contrary to the seventh commandment. The injustice committed requires reparation. Commutative justice requires the restitution of stolen goods.

2455 The moral law forbids acts which, for commercial or totalitarian purposes, lead to the enslavement of human beings, or to their being bought, sold, or exchanged like merchandise.

2456 The dominion granted by the Creator over the mineral, vegetable, and animal resources of the universe cannot be separated from respect for moral obligations, including those toward generations to come.

2457 Animals are entrusted to man's stewardship; he must show them kindness. They may be used to serve the just satisfaction of man's needs.

2458 The Church makes a judgment about economic and social matters when the fundamental rights of the person or the salvation of souls requires it. She is concerned with the temporal common good of men because they are ordered to the sovereign Good, their ultimate end.

2459 Man is himself the author, center, and goal of all economic and social life. The decisive point of the social question is that goods created by God for everyone should in fact reach everyone in accordance with justice and with the help of charity.

2460 The primordial value of labor stems from man himself, its author and beneficiary. By means of his labor man participates in the work of creation. Work united to Christ can be redemptive.

2461 True development concerns the whole man. It is concerned with increasing each person's ability to respond to his vocation and hence to God's call (cf. *CA* 29).

2462 Giving alms to the poor is a witness to fraternal charity: it is also a work of justice pleasing to God.

2463 How can we not recognize Lazarus, the hungry beggar in the parable (cf. Lk 17:19-31), in the multitude of human beings without bread, a roof or a place to stay? How can we fail to hear Jesus: "As you did it not to one of the least of these, you did it not to me" (Mt 25:45)?

Christ and the Adulteress by Polidoro da Lanciano.

In Pope Francis' first Angelus Address on March 17, 2013 given to 150,000 people gathered in St. Peter's Square, he spoke of Jesus and the adulterous woman: "In this Fifth Sunday of Lent, the Gospel presents us with the story of the adulterous woman whom Jesus saves from being condemned to death. It captures Jesus' attitude: we do not hear words of contempt, we do not hear words of condemnation, but only words of love, of mercy, that invite us to conversion. 'Neither do I condemn you. Go and sin no more!' Well, brothers and sisters! God's face is that of a merciful father who is always patient. Have you thought about God's patience, the patience that He has with each of us? That is His mercy. He always has patience, is always patient with us, understanding us, awaiting us, never tiring of forgiving us if we know how to return to him with a contrite heart. 'Great is the Lord's mercy', says the Psalm."

ENDNOTES – CHAPTER SEVEN

1. Pope Benedict has used this phrase often, from the beginning of his pontificate. See, for example, his General Audience of August 5, 2009, and his address to the diplomatic corps accredited to the Holy See on January 8, 2007.
2. See Pope Benedict XVI, *Jesus of Nazareth: From the Baptism in the Jordan to the Transfiguration* (New York: Doubleday, 2007), 91.
3. Address to the Regional Board of Lazio and the Municipal Council of Rome, January 12, 2012.
4. Ibid.
5. Cf. Mt 5:23-24, 6:14-15.
6. General Audience, April 25, 2012.
7. Synod of Bishops, Second Extraordinary General Assembly, Final Summary *Ecclesia sub Verbo Dei Mysteria Christi Celebrans pro Salute Mundi* (December 7, 1985), II, B, a, 2: Enchiridion Vaticanum 9, 1795.
8. *Propositio* 30.
9. *Propositio* 34.
10. Ibid.
11. Ibid.
12. Cf. *LG* 31.
13. Cf. *GS* 76; *CL* 42.
14. *Propositio* 67.
15. Cf. ibid.
16. *Propositio* 68.
17. Ibid.
18. *Propositio* 69.
19. Cf. Synod of Bishops, Second Extraordinary General Assembly, Final Report *Ecclesia sub Verbo Dei Mysteria Christi Celebrans pro Salute Mundi* (December 7, 1985), II, B, a, 4: Enchiridion Vaticanum 9, 1797; John Paul II, Apostolic Constitution *Fidei Depositum* (October 11, 1992): AAS 86 (1994), 117; CCC 24.
20. *Propositio* 69.
21. *Propositio* 74.
22. Ibid.
23. Cf. *Propositio* 67.
24. *Propositio* 70.
25. Ibid.
26. Cf. *Propositio* 73.
27. Cf. *Propositio* 70.
28. *Propositio* 72.
29. Ibid.
30. Ibid.
31. Third General Conference of the Latin American Bishops, Puebla 1979, Message to the Peoples of Latin America, 306.
32. *Propositio* 73.
33. Cf. Congregation for the Doctrine of the Faith, Instruction *Libertatis Conscientia* (March 22, 1986), 68: AAS 79 (1987), 583-584.
34. *Propositio* 73.

ART AND PHOTO CREDITS

Cover
Return of the Prodigal Son (detail), Bartolome Esteban Murillo; National Gallery of Art, Washington, D.C.

Front Pages
- iii See Cover Credit
- iv *Healing of the Cripple and Raising of Tabatha* (detail of left view), Masolino; Cappella Brancacci, Santa Maria del Carmine, Florence, Italy
- vii *The Good Shepherd*, Bernhard Plockhorst; Public Domain
- ix *Come Unto Me*, Carl H. Bloch; Frederiksborg Palace Chapel, Denmark
- x *The Eleusa* or *Virgin of Tenderness*, Icon, 17th century, Historic Museum, Sanok, Poland

Introduction
- 1 *Sermon on the Mount*, Carl H. Bloch; Frederiksborg Palace Chapel, Denmark
- 3 *St. Peter's Square*, ©L'Osservatore Romano
- 4 *John Paul II*; *John Paul II: A Light for the World*; ©L'Osservatore Romano
- 5 *The Expulsion from the Garden of Eden* (detail), Masaccio; Cappella Brancacci, Santa Maria del Carmine, Florence, Italy
- 6 *The Fall of Man* (detail), Hendrik Goltzius; National Gallery of Art, Washington, D.C.
- 7 *Noah Sacrificing after the Deluge*, Benjamin West; The San Antonio Museum Association, Texas
- 8 *Poverty in Mexico*; Luke Mata, Photographer; MTF Archives
- 9 *Pentecost* (detail), Francisco Zurbaran; Cadiz Museum, Cadiz, Spain; Archivo Oronoz
- 10 *Baptism of Christ*, Juan Fernandez de Navarrete; Museo del Prado, Madrid, Spain
- 12 *Ministry of the Apostles*, Russian Icon, Fyodor Zubov; Yaroslavl Museum–Preserve, Yaroslavl, Russia
- 15 *Prophet Jeremiah* (detail), Michelangelo; Sistine Chapel, Vatican
- 17 *St. Dominic in Prayer* (detail), El Greco; Private Collection
- 18 *The Charity of St. Elizabeth of Hungary* (detail), Edmund Blair Leighton; Private Collection,

Chapter 1
- 19 *Disputation on the Trinity*, Andrea Del Sarto; Galleria Palatina (Palazzo Pitti), Florence, Italy
- 21 *Christ Healing by the Well of Bethesda*, Carl H. Bloch; Frederiksborg Palace Chapel, Denmark
- 22 *The Good Samaritan* (detail), Pelegrin Clave y Roque; Royal Catalan Academy of Fine Arts of St. George, Barcelona, Spain
- 23 *Bl. Teresa of Calcutta*, MTF Archives
- 24 *The Holy Trinity*, Antonio de Pereda; Museum of Fine Arts, Budapest, Hungary
- 25 *Circle of Friendship*; ©Crestock Corporation
- 26 *The Holy Trinity*, Andrea Previtali; Accademia Carrara, Bergamo, Italy
- 27 *Father Damien as a Seminarian*, ca. 1863; Sacred Hearts Archives, Hawaii
- 28 *Pentecost* (detail), Adriaen Van Der Werff; Staatsgalerie, Schleissheim Palace, Oberschleissheim, Germany
- 29 *The Ointment of the Magdalene*, James Tissot; Brooklyn Museum, New York
- 30 *Pope Paul VI Meets with Patriarch Athenagoras I*; Archivo Oronoz
- 31 *Bl. Teresa of Calcutta*, MTF Archives
- 32 *Let the Children Come to Me*, Carl Christian Vogel von Vogelstein; Public Domain
- 33 *John Paul II*; ©L'Osservatore Romano
- 34 *John Paul II, World Youth Day in Denver, CO* 1993; *John Paul II: A Light for the World*; ©L'Osservatore Romano
- 39 *Father Damien with the Kalawao Girls Choir*, ca. 1870; Hawaii State Archives
- 40 *Men's Ward at Kalighat, Home of the Pure Heart (Nirmal Hriday)*, Calcutta, India; Mark Makowiecki, Photographer
- 42 *Sermon on the Mount*, Altarpiece, Henrik Olrik; Sankt Matthæus Kirke, Copenhagen, Denmark

Chapter 2
- 43 *The Tribute Money*, Sir Anthony Van Dyck; Palazzo Rosso, Genoa, Italy
- 45 *Curses Against the Pharisees* (detail), James Tissot; Brooklyn Museum, New York
- 46 *Homer and His Guide* (detail), William Bouguereau; Milwaukee Art Museum, Milwaukee, Wisconsin
- 47 *John Howard Griffin*; Don Rutledge, Photographer
- 48 *Martin Luther King*; AP/Wide World Photos
- 49 *Lincoln Memorial*; Washington, D.C.; Public Domain

ART AND PHOTO CREDITS

50 *Declaration of Independence*, John Trumbull; United States Capitol Rotunda, Washington, D.C.
51 *Fetus in Bubbly Surroundings*; Blend Images Stock Photos
52 *Jacques Maritain*; Public Domain
53 *Prophet Amos*, Russian Icon, Eighteenth Century; Iconostasis of Kizhi Monastery, Russia
54 *Prophet Isaiah*, Michelangelo; Sistine Chapel, Vatican
55 *Moses Receiving the Tables of the Law* (detail), Tintoretto; Madonna dell'Orto, Venice, Italy
57 *Triumph of St. Thomas Aquinas* (detail), Benozzo Gozzoli; Musee du Louvre, Paris, France
61 *Pope Leo XIII*, Official Portrait, Vatican Album of the Ecumenical Council; U.S. Library of Congress Prints and Photographs
63 *Christ and the Children* (detail), Carl H. Bloch; Frederiksborg Palace Chapel, Denmark
64 *Parable of the Man Who Hoards*, James Tissot; Brooklyn Museum, New York
66 *Pope John Paul II*; AP/Wide World Photos

Chapter 3

67 *Mass of St. Basil*, Pierre Subleyras; The Hermitage, St. Petersburg, Russia
69 *He Did No Miracles but He Healed Them* (detail), James Tissot; Brooklyn Museum, New York
70 *Christ in Majesty*, Illumination; Codex Bruchsal 1, Bl. 1v, Badische Landesbibliothek, Karlsruhe, Germany
71 *Coalbrookdale by Night*, Philip James de Loutherbourg; Science Museum/Science & Society Picture Library, London, England
72 *A Little Spinner in the Mollohan Mills, Newberry, SC*, 1908; Sara R. Hine, Photographer; U.S. Library of Congress Prints and Photographs
73 *Pope Leo XIII*; Archivo Oronoz
75 *Cesar Chavez Day Poster* (detail); United States Department of Labor
76 *Pope Pius XI*; Vatican Embassy, Madrid, Spain; Archivo Oronoz
77 *John XXIII*; Venice, Italy; Archivo Oronoz
78 top: *John XXIII Signing "Pacem in Terris"*; Public Domain
   bottom: *Pope Paul VI*; Archivo Oronoz
79 *John Paul II*; ©L'Osservatore Romano
80 *John Paul II*; ©L'Osservatore Romano
81 *John Paul II*; ©L'Osservatore Romano
82 *Pope Benedict XVI*; ©L'Osservatore Romano
83 *Dorothy Day and Mother Teresa*, 1979; Bill Barrett, Photographer; Marquette University Archives
84 *Famine*; AP/Wide World Photos
85 *Second Vatican Council*; St. Peter's Basilica, Vatican; Archivo Oronoz
86 *Ellis Island*, 1902; U.S. Library of Congress Prints and Photographs
87 *St. Clement Striking the Rock below the Holy Lamb*, Bernardino Fungai; Public Domain
91 *The "Baker" Explosion*, Operation Crossroads; Nuclear Weapon Test by the U.S. at Bikini Atoll, Micronesia, July 25, 1946; U.S. Department of Defense
94 *Poverty in Serbia* (Gypsy Camp); Public Domain
96 *Poverty in Soweto, South Africa*; Public Domain

Chapter 4

97 *The Prodigal's Return*, Sir Edward John Poynter; Forbes Magazine Collection
99 *Sermon on the Mount*, Cosimo Rosselli; Sistine Chapel, Vatican
100 *The Poor Lazarus at the Rich Man's Door*, James Tissot; Brooklyn Museum, New York
101 *Destitute Woman at San Miguel Allende*, Guanajuato, Mexico (detail); Tomas Castelazo, Photographer
102 *Sacred Heart of Jesus*, Charles Bosseron Chambers; restoredtraditions.com
103 *Ecce Homo*, Mihaly Munkacsy; Deri Museum, Debrecen, Hungary
104 *Berlin Wall Victims Memorial*; Magnus Manske, Photographer
105 *John Paul II Meets with Lech Walesa*, January 1981; Public Domain

ART AND PHOTO CREDITS

106 *Lech Walesa*, Public Domain
107 *Girl Begging in India*; Steve Evans, Photographer
108 *Shahbaz Bhatti*; Public Domain
109 *John Paul II and Bl. Teresa of Calcutta at Nirmal Hriday*, Calcutta, India, 1986; ©L'Osservatore Romano
110 *Juana Maria Condesa Lluch*; Public Domain
116 *Homeless Man Begging on Sidewalk*; ©Crestock Corporation

Chapter 5
117 *Christ Carrying the Cross*, Titian; Museo del Prado, Madrid, Spain
119 *Creation of Adam*, Michelangelo; Sistine Chapel, Vatican
120 *Allegory of Freewill and Sin*, Francois Maitre; Illustration for *City of God* by St. Augustine (ca. 1475-80); Museum Meermanno Westreenianum, The Hague, Netherlands
121 *Christ on the Cross*, El Greco, Oil on Copper, 1570; Private Collection
122 *Holy Family*, Claudio Coello; Museum of Fine Arts, Budapest, Hungary
123 *Extended Hispanic Family*; Blend Images, Stock Photography
124 *Pope Benedict XVI Administered Baptism to Fourteen Babies*, January 10, 2010, Feast of the Baptism of the Lord, Vatican
125 *Jesus Before Pilate, Second Interview* (detail), James Tissot; Brooklyn Museum, New York
126 *Lazarus at the Rich Man's Gate*, Fyodor Bronnikov; Radishchev State Art Museum, Saratov, Russia
127 *Parable of Lazarus and Dives* (detail), Illumination from Codex Aureus of Echternach; German National Museum, Nuremberg, Germany
128 *Poverty in Mexico* (flipped); Luke Mata, Photographer; MTF Archives
129 *St. Gregory of Nazianzus*, Icon; Public Domain
130 *Poverty in the Philippines*; Flat Earth Stock Photography
131 *Adam and Eve's Life of Toil*, (detail from the Grabow Altarpiece), Master Bertram; Kunsthalle, Hamburg, Germany
132 *Jesus Grew Strong in Spirit and Wisdom*, Unknown Master; Private Collection
133 *European Union Flag Logo*; Public Domain
134 *Dorothy Day's Last Arrest*, 1973; Bob Fitch, Photographer; Jim Forest Collection
135 *Homeless Children in Bangladesh*; Md. Saiful Aziz Shamseer, Photographer
136 *The Miracle of the Loaves and Fishes*, Lambert Lombard; Rockox House, Antwerp, Belgium
137 *St. Luigi Guanella*; Private Collection
138 Digital Stock, Stock Photography
139 *Children Celebrating the Beauty of Nature*; ©Crestock Corporation
140 *Legend of St. Francis: 2. St. Francis Giving his Mantle to a Poor Man*, Giotto; Upper Church, San Francesco, Assisi, Italy
141 *St. John Chrysostom*, Byzantine Mosaic; Cathedral of Hagia Sophia, Istanbul, Turkey
145 *Becoming Family*, Fall 2001: 39; Jim Summaria, Photographer; MTF Archives
147 *Presentation in the Temple* (detail), Philippe de Champaigne; Musees Royaux des Beaux-Arts, Brussels, Belgium

Chapter 6
149 *The Worship of the Golden Calf*, W.C. Simmonds (after C.F. Vos, *The Child's Story Bible*); Private Collection
151 *Christ Walking on the Waters*, Julius Sergius von Klever; Private Collection
152 *Portrait of Dred Scott*, Louis Schultze; Missouri Historical Society, St. Louis, Missouri
153 *Pilate Washing His Hands* (detail) by Duccio; Museo dell'Opera del Duomo, Siena, Italy
154 *Tables of the Law with the Golden Calf* (detail) by Cosimo Rosselli; Sistine Chapel, Vatican
155 *Moses and the Burning Bush*, Andreas Brugger; Salem Minster, Baden-Wuerttemberg, Germany
156 *The Adoration of the Golden Calf*, Nicolas Poussin; National Gallery, London, England
157 *The Child Jesus Going down with His Parents to Nazareth*, William Charles Dobson; Tate Collection, UK
158 *The Rest on the Return from Egypt*, Federico Fiori Barocci; Pinacoteca, Vatican
159 *Rest on the Flight to Egypt* (detail), Caravaggio; Galleria Doria Pamphilj, Rome, Italy
160 *Queen Fabiola and King Baudouin of Belgium* (detail); Royal House of Belgium Official Portrait
161 *Christ Carrying the Cross*, Titian; Museo del Prado, Madrid, Spain

ART AND PHOTO CREDITS

162 *Christ Taken Prisoner*, Giuseppe Cesari; Staatliche Museen, Kassel, Germany
163 *St. Paul's Cathedral after the London Blitz*, 1940; Public Domain
164 *The Wedding*; Stockbyte, Stock Photography
165 *Bl. Franz Jagerstatter*; Public Domain
168 *Polluted Waters in Galicia, Spain*; Luis Miguel Bugallo Sanchez, Photographer
169 *What Is Truth?* (detail), Nikolai Nikolaevich Ge (Gay); Tretyakov Gallery, Moscow, Russia
170 *Giorgio La Pira*; Public Domain
171 *Giorgio La Pira*; Public Domain
172 *No. 28 Scenes from the Life of Christ: 12. Judas' Betrayal* (detail), Giotto; Cappella Scrovegni (Arena Chapel), Padua, Italy
173 *Mount of Beatitudes and Chapel of the Beatitudes*; Pictorial Library of Bible Lands; Todd Bolen, Photographer
174 *Jesus Preaching on the Mount* (detail), Gustave Dore; Private Collection
177 *Jesus Washing Peter's Feet*, Ford Madox Brown; Tate Collection, UK
179 *Christ Discovered in the Temple*, Simone Martini, 1342; Walker Art Gallery, Liverpool, England
183 *Christ on the Way to Calvary*, Giovanni di Paolo; The Walters Art Museum, Baltimore, Maryland

Chapter 7
185 *Domine quo vadis?*, Annibale Carracci; National Gallery, London, England
187 *Christ and the Rich Young Ruler*, Heinrich Hofmann; Riverside Church, New York, New York
188 *The Widow's Mite*, James Tissot; Brooklyn Museum, New York
189 *Pope Francis Prays at the Lourdes Grotto, Vatican Gardens*; ©L'Osservatore Romano
190 *Pope Benedict XVI, Apostolic Visit to the United States*; ©L'Osservatore Romano
191 *Bl. Salvador Huerta Gutierrez*; Public Domain
192 *St. Lawrence Distributing Alms* (detail), Fra Angelico; Cappella Niccolina, Palazzi Pontifici, Vatican
193 *Women washing clothes in a ditch in Mumbai, India*; Antonio Milena, Photographer/Agencia Brasil
194 *Christ on the Mount of Olives*, Johann Friedrich Overbeck; Hamburger Kunsthalle, Hamburg, Germany
195 *St. Gianna Beretta Molla*; Public Domain
196 *Forgotten Man in India*; ©Crestock Corporation
197 *Crucifixion and Last Judgment*, Diptych, (detail), Jan Van Eyck; Metropolitan Museum of Art, New York
198 *St. Clement of Alexandria*, 1584 Book Illustration; Andre Thevet, Author; Public Domain
199 *Pope Benedict Washing the Feet of Fellow Priests*; ©L'Osservatore Romano
203 *Pope Benedict XVI Blessing a Sick Child*; ©L'Osservatore Romano
206 *John Paul II in Prayer*; ©L'Osservatore Romano
210 *Christ and the Adulteress*, Polidoro da Lanciano; Museum of Fine Arts, Budapest, Hungary

Altar Cross by Gian Lorenzo Bernini,
Treasury of the Vatican

INDEX

A

Abortifacient. *See* Contraception
Abortion, "right" to, 51, 53
Abortion, business of, 51
Adultery, 11, 46, 122-123, 152, 155, 157, 164, 166, 168, 174, 187. *See also* Marriage
Anarchy, 72, 83, 158
Apostles
    community of, 9
    Teaching of the Twelve. *See Didache*
Aquinas, St. Thomas. *See* Thomas Aquinas
Aristocracy, 71-72, 119
Assisted suicide, 81, 161. *See also* Suicide
Athenagoras I, 30
Augustine of Hippo, St., 20, 25, 32, 45, 56-57, 82, 102, 123, 152, 175-176

B

Baptism
    child of God, 10, 28
    new life in Christ, 10
Basil of Caesarea, St., 69-71, 120
Baudouin, king, 153, 160
Beatitudes, 54, 99, 150, 172-175, 188
    and the Decalogue. *See* Decalogue, and the Beatitudes
Benedict XVI, Pope, 2, 73-74, 82, 84, 104-105, 118, 122, 128, 133, 138-139, 171, 173, 188, 190, 192, 194, 196, 197
    Caritas in Veritate, 2, 74, 84, 104-105
    Deus Caritas Est, 2, 73-74, 82
Bernard Nathanson, Dr., 51
Bhatti, Shahbaz. *See* Shahbaz Bhatti
Blessed Trinity. *See* Trinity
Body. *See also* Christ, Mystical Body of
Brothers and Sisters to Us. *See* USCCB
Burial, 21, 175

C

Capital punishment, 159, 162. *See also* Death penalty
Capitalism, *Laissez-faire*, 73, 76-77, 79, 81, 131, 133
Cardinal Virtue, 45. *See also* Fortitude; Justice; Prudence; Temperance
Caritas in Veritate. *See* Benedict XVI
Catholic Worker. *See* Dorothy Day
Centesimus Annus. *See* John Paul II
Cesar Chavez, 75, 153, 189
Charity (love), 109. *See also* Commandment, New Commandment of Love
    and justice. *See* Justice, and charity
    comes from God, 31
    God is, 23, 25
    martyr of. *See* Damien of Molokai
Chavez, Cesar. *See* Cesar Chavez
Christ
    Anointed One. *See* Christ, Messiah
    Incarnation, 9
    Messiah, 9
    Mystical Body of, 9, 28-29
    Redeemer, 7
Chrysostom. *See* John Chrysostom
Church
    as communion. *See* Communion, in the Church
    Magisterium of. *See* Magisterium
    Mystical Body of Christ. *See* Christ, Mystical Body of
    teaching authority of. *See* Magisterium
Civil authority, 78, 85, 158. *See also* Government
Class struggle, 68, 76, 78, 105, 131, 134. *See also* Karl Marx, Marxism
Clement
    of Alexandria, St., 198
    St. Clement I, 87
Cold War. *See* War, Cold
Commandment
    Greatest, 31
    New Commandment of Love, 22
    Ten. *See* Decalogue
Common good, 49, 53, 78, 85, 98-99, 101-103, 106-107, 123, 126, 130-131, 133, 135-136, 138, 158, 162, 168-169, 171, 194
Communion
    in the Church, 32
    of Christ and Christians, 26
    of Saints, 10
    of the Trinity, 25
Communism, 72-73, 75-77, 79, 81, 104-105, 133, 189. *See also* Karl Marx, Marxism
Compendium of the Social Doctrine of the Church. *See* Pontifical Council for Justice and Peace
Condesa Lluch, Bl. Juana Maria. *See* Juana Maria Condesa Lluch
Conscience, social, 69
Contraception, 81, 194
Criminal
    activity, 75, 163
    defense of, 46, 81, 100. *See also* Death penalty
Culture of death, 81, 159, 189
Culture of Life and the Penalty of Death, A. *See* USCCB

D

Damien of Molokai, St., 27, 31
Day of the Lord. *See* Judgment, General
Day, Dorothy. *See* Dorothy Day
De Veuster, Damien. *See* Damien of Molokai
Death penalty, 81, 103, 162. *See also* USCCB, *A Good Friday Appeal to End the Death Penalty*
Decalogue
    and the Beatitudes, 172-173, 150, 154-156, 164, 175-176, 188
Defamation, 52
Defense. *See* Right, to self-defense
Democracy, 72, 105-106
Deus Caritas Est. *See* Benedict XVI
Development
    of doctrine, 74, 99
    societal, 49, 78-81, 85-86, 98, 123, 131, 135-136, 192
Didache, 11-12
Disability
    developmental, 121, 137
    physical, 47, 159, 193
Divine nature, human person partakes in 26
Divine Person, of the Trinity, 25. *See also* Father; Son; Holy Spirit
Divorce, 122-123, 170, 194. *See also* Marriage
Dorothy Day, 83, 189
Drugs, 163

E

Economic Justice for All: A Pastoral Letter on Catholic Social Teaching and the U.S. Economy. *See* USCCB
Economics, 75, 84, 100, 104, 109
Ecumenism: 30
Elderly, 21, 128, 195-196
Eminent domain. *See* Private property, limit of

INDEX

Emmanuel Mounier, 133
Euthanasia, 81, 159, 161, 194
Evangelium Vitæ. See John Paul II

F

Family
    beginning of social order, 157-158
    call to, 122-124
    fundamental building block of society, 3
    Holy, 132, 157
    human, 78, 80, 131
    of God, 196
Fortitude, 45, 103
Franz Jagerstatter, Bl., 165-166
Freedom. *See* Presidential Medal of Freedom

G

Gianna Beretta Molla, St., 195
Giorgio la Pira, 169
"God is love." *See* Charity, God is
Good Friday Appeal to End the Death Penalty, A. See USCCB
Goods, 167-169. *See also* Universal destination of goods
Government, role of, 48, 50, 52, 84, 102, 104, 107, 121, 153, 158, 193. *See also* Civil authority
Griffin, John Howard. *See* John Howard Griffin
Guanella, St. Luigi. *See* Luigi Guanella

H

Handicap, 160-161
Holy Spirit, 26, 28
    Pentecost, 28, 32
    works through the Sacraments, 28
Homeless, sheltering the, 69, 72, 175
Homelessness, 8, 23, 83, 128
Huerta Gutierrez, Bl. Salvador. *See* Salvador Huerta Gutierrez
Human life
    end is God, 78
    preferential option for, 159
    sacredness of, 159
    sin against. *See* Abortion; Assisted suicide; Contraception; Euthanasia; Infanticide; Murder; Suicide
Human nature
    created by God, 3, 5
    fallen, 3, 6

Human person
    and creation, 5
    dignity of, 44, 98-99, 121, 162
    fulfillment of, 5
    social nature of, 3-4
Humani Generis. See Pius XII
Hunger, 8, 84, 126
    and thirst for righteousness, 172, 174-175

I

Illness, 47, 54, 69, 75, 128, 161, 175, 194
    mental, 47, 128
Imprisonment. *See* Prison
Individualism, 49, 105, 188, 193-194, 196-197
Industry, 71-72, 84, 104, 131. *See also* Revolution, Industrial
    pornographic, 52, 166. *See also* Pornography
    private ownership of, 76
Infanticide, 159. *See also* Murder

J

Jacques Maritain, 52, 133
Jagerstatter, Bl. Franz. *See* Franz Jagerstatter
John Chrysostom, St., 70, 141
John Donne, 3
John Howard Griffin, 47, 153
John Paul II, Bl., 20, 33-34, 50, 52, 68, 79-81, 86, 105-106, 123-126, 128, 130-132, 134-135, 138, 150, 152, 157, 171, 195
    Centesimus Annus, 20, 68, 74, 81, 125, 128
    Evangelium Vitæ, 74, 81, 122
    Laborem Exercens, 74, 79-80
    Letter to Families, 31, 124
    Sollicitudo Rei Socialis, 4, 74, 80-81, 86, 128
John XXIII, Bl., 74, 77, 81, 126
    Mater et Magistra, 74, 77
    Pacem in Terris, 74, 77-78, 126
Joseph Pieper, 46
Joseph the Worker, St., 134
Juana Maria Condesa Lluch, Bl., 110
Judgment
    General, 54
    justice and, 54
Just War. *See* War, just

Justice, 45, 56-57
    and charity, 46
    and goodness, 46
    commutative, 49
    directed toward others, 45
    distributive, 49
    follows rights. *See* Right, precedes justice
    in Scripture, 53-54
    in the Old Testament, 45
    Judgment and. *See* Judgment, justice and
    legal, 49
    social, 46, 49
Justin Martyr, St., 21

K

Karl Marx, 72
Marxism, 81, 104-105, 131, 134. *See also* Communism
Kindness, 20-21, 32, 45, 47, 129-130

L

La Pira, Giorgio. *See* Giorgio la Pira
Laborem Exercens. See John Paul II
Laissez-faire capitalism. *See* Capitalism, *Laissez-faire*
Law
    divine. *See* Decalogue
    moral. *See* Moral law
    natural. *See* Natural law
Leo XIII, Pope, 73, 76, 81
    Rerum Novarum, 73-77, 79, 81, 86, 104, 133
Letter to Families. See John Paul II
Libel, 52
Luigi Guanella, St., 137
Lust, 12, 164, 174

M

Magisterium, 70-71
Maritain, Jacques. *See* Jacques Maritain
Marriage
    created by God, 5
    sin against, 46
Martyr
    of charity. *See* Damien of Molokai
    St. Justin. *See* Justin Martyr
Marx, Karl. *See* Karl Marx
Mary, Blessed Virgin
    in the *Protoevangelium*, 7
    Our Lady of Guadalupe, 75, 191
    solidarity with us, 189

INDEX

Mater et Magistra. See John XXIII
Materialism, 103, 168, 174, 188, 192-193
Medicine, 47, 128, 193, 195
    medical care, 75, 128
Mit Brennender Sorge. See Pius XI
Molla, St. Gianna Beretta. *See* Gianna Beretta Molla
Monarchy, 71-72, 125
Moral law, 4, 8, 85, 154-155
Moses, 8
Mother Teresa. *See* Teresa of Calcutta
Mounier, Emmanuel. *See* Emmanuel Mounier
Murder, 8, 11-12, 44, 48, 125, 152-153, 155, 159, 161, 174
Mystical Body of Christ. *See* Christ, Mystical Body of

N

Nathanson, Dr. Bernard. *See* Bernard Nathanson
National Catholic War Council. *See* War, National Catholic War Council
Natural disaster, 69, 188
Natural law, 52
Natural right. *See* Right, natural
Needy, responsibility for, 53, 69-70, 108, 128-129, 137, 189
Noah, 8
Nobel Peace Prize, 23, 106

O

Octogesima Adveniens. See Paul VI
Old age. *See* Elderly
Original holiness and justice, 6
Original Sin, 5. *See also* Original holiness and justice
    effects of, 5-6, 8. *See also* Human nature, fallen
    God's response to, 7

P

Pacem in Terris. See John XXIII
Participation, 5, 101, 105, 107, 124, 155
Paul VI, Pope, 30, 74, 78, 80-81, 84
    Octogesima Adveniens, 74
    Populorum Progressio, 74, 78, 80, 84

Peace, 4, 7, 9, 11, 21-23, 30-31, 49, 77-78, 80-81, 84-85, 99, 101-102, 123, 133, 135, 138, 150, 158-159, 163, 170-171, 197. *See also* Nobel Peace Prize; Peacemaker; Pontifical Council for Justice and Peace; World Day of Peace
    false understanding of, 22, 53
Peacemaker, 173-174
Pentecost. *See* Holy Spirit
Person
    divine. *See* Divine person
    human. *See* Human person
Pieper, Joseph. *See* Joseph Pieper
Pius XI, Pope, 73-74, 76, 81, 104
    Mit Brennender Sorge, 74, 122
    Quadragesimo Anno, 74, 76, 104
Pius XII, *Humani Generis*, 122
Politics, 6, 84, 100, 133, 170-171, 191
Polygamy, 122. *See also* Marriage
Polytheism, 20
Pontifical Council for Justice and Peace, 86
    Compendium of the Social Doctrine of the Church, 86, 98, 103
Poor
    individual. *See* Poverty
    in spirit, 172, 174
    nation, 78
    preferential option for, 126-128, 131
Populorum Progressio. See Paul VI
Pornography, 52, 166-167. *See also* Industry, pornographic
Poverty
    monetary, 4, 8, 23, 68-69, 73, 80, 101, 118, 128, 130, 137, 167, 169, 189, 196
    of Christ, 186
    of spirit. *See* Poor, in spirit
Presidential Medal of Freedom, 23, 75
Prison, 3, 21, 48, 54, 75, 162, 166, 175, 189
Private property
    limit of, 107, 128-131, 139, 168
    right to, 73, 76, 107, 125, 128-131, 168
Progress. *See* Development, societal; Paul VI, *Populorum Progressio*
Prophet, 8
Prosperity. *See* Development, societal

Protestant Reformation. *See* Reformation
Protoevangelium. See Mary; Christ, Redeemer
Prudence, 45, 102-103
Purity, 150, 164, 166-167, 175

Q

Quadragesimo Anno. See Pius XI

R

Reformation, 71
Relativism, 192. *See also* Truth, relativism and
Republic, 125
Rerum Novarum. See Leo XIII
Responsibility, 2, 49, 80, 103, 107, 123-126, 135, 138-140, 151, 161-162, 164, 190, 196. *See also* Right
Revolution
    American, 72
    French, 72
    Industrial, 4, 71, 73, 110, 132
    response to, 72-73
    social, 72, 125
Riches. *See* Wealth
Right, 46. *See also* Responsibility
    in *Declaration of Independence*, 50, 52
    in U.S. Constitution, 50
    in *Universal Declaration of Human Rights*, 52
    natural, 48
    precedes justice, 46, 53
    source of, 50, 52
    to abortion. *See* Abortion, "right" to
    to bodily integrity, 48
    to life, 48, 51
    to personal and vocational freedom, 48
    to self-defense, 48
    to hold property, 48

S

Sacrament. *See* Divine nature, human person partakes in, 26
Salvador Huerta Gutierrez, Bl., 191
Secularism, 72, 188, 190-191
Security
    individual, 2, 85, 101, 130, 136, 167-169, 193
    societal, 53, 102

INDEX

Self-defense. *See* Right, to self-defense
Shahbaz Bhatti, 108
Sickness. *See* Illness
Sin
   against Marriage. *See* Marriage, sin against
   personal, 6, 151-153
   social, 151-153
Slander, 52
Socialism, 72-73, 76, 104
Sociology, 84, 104
Solidarity, 68, 81, 98-99, 105-108, 129-131, 133-136, 138-139, 152, 158, 167, 169, 189, 194, 197
   labor movement, 106
   with Christ, 188
Sollicitudo Rei Socialis. *See* John Paul II
Sowing Weapons of War. *See* USCCB
Sterilization, 48, 81, 121, 123
Stewardship, 123, 128, 135, 138-140, 167, 169
Strike (refusal to work), 75, 106
Subsidiarity, 98-99, 104-105, 107, 109, 124, 133, 158, 169
Suicide, 159, 161. *See also* Assisted suicide

T

Temperance, 45
Ten Commandments. *See* Decalogue
Teresa of Calcutta, Bl., 23, 31
Tertullian, 20-22
The Challenge of Peace: God's Promise and Our Response. *See* USCCB
Theft, 12, 44, 46, 49, 125, 152, 155, 168-169, 174, 176
Thirst, 54, 175
   and hunger for righteousness. *See* Hunger, and thirst for righteousness
Thomas Aquinas, St., 45-46, 56-57, 101-102, 162-163, 176
Tolerance, 192
Treason, 52, 156
Trinity, 25
   central mystery of the Faith, 26
Trust, 118, 169, 172
   goods held in. *See* Goods
   in God, 165
Truth, 77, 81, 85, 98, 107, 169, 172
   moral, 155
   relativism and, 192. *See also* Relativism
Tyranny, 68, 104, 158, 197

U

Universal destination of goods, 107, 128, 130, 138-139, 168
USCCB (United States Conference of Catholic Bishops)
   Brothers and Sisters to Us, 86
   A Culture of Life and the Penalty of Death, 86
   A Good Friday Appeal to End the Death Penalty, 86
   Economic Justice for All: A Pastoral Letter on Catholic Social Teaching and the U.S. Economy, 86
   Sowing Weapons of War, 86
   The Challenge of Peace: God's Promise and Our Response, 86

V

Virtue, 45-46, 49, 53, 56, 81, 135, 173. *See also* Justice; Fortitude; Prudence; Solidarity; Temperance
Von Ketteler, Wilhelm Emmanuel. *See* Wilhelm Emmanuel von Ketteler

W

War, 4, 8, 72, 83, 103, 166
   Cold, 77, 80
   just, 48, 163-164
   National Catholic War Council, 85-86
   World War I, 68, 74, 85, 165
   World War II, 47, 68, 75, 77, 133, 160, 165-166, 170
Wealth, 136, 169, 176, 187, 198
   individual, 70, 78, 110, 127, 141
   national, 135
Weapon. *See also* USCCB, *Sowing Weapons of War*
   nuclear (atomic), 77
   of mass destruction, 77
   proliferation of, 118
Wilhelm Emmanuel von Ketteler, bishop, 72-73
Work, 79-80, 131-132. *See also* Strike
   dignity of, 131-132, 134
Worker, 53, 72-77, 79, 83, 106, 110, 131-132, 134. *See also* Joseph the Worker
   Christ as, 79
   working class, 73, 170
World Day of Peace, 138
World War. *See* War, World War I; War, World War II